082
In4o

72732

| DATE DUE | | | |
|---|---|---|---|
| | | | |
| | | | |
| | | | |
| | | | |
| | | | |
| | | | |
| | | | |
| | | | |
| | | | |
| | | | |
| | | | |
| | | | |
| | | | |

GAYLORD M-2  PRINTED IN U.S.A.

# OUTSPOKEN ESSAYS

# OUTSPOKEN ESSAYS

BY

## WILLIAM RALPH INGE, C.V.O., D.D.

DEAN OF ST. PAUL'S

## LONGMANS, GREEN, AND CO.

### 39 PATERNOSTER ROW, LONDON

FOURTH AVENUE & 30TH STREET, NEW YORK
BOMBAY, CALCUTTA, AND MADRAS

1919

# PREFACE

ALL the Essays in this volume, except the first, have appeared in the *Edinburgh Review*, the *Quarterly Review*, or the *Hibbert Journal*. I have to thank the Publishers and Editors of those Reviews for their courtesy in permitting me to reprint them. The articles on *The Birth-Rate, The Future of the English Race, Bishop Gore and the Church of England,* and *Cardinal Newman* are from the *Edinburgh Review*; those on *Patriotism, Catholic Modernism, St. Paul,* and *The Indictment against Christianity* are from the *Quarterly Review*; those on *Institutionalism and Mysticism* and *Survival and Immortality* from the *Hibbert Journal.* I have not attempted to remove all traces of overlapping, which I hope may be pardoned in essays written independently of each other; but a few repetitions have been excised.

15074 RCS Aug 8......

*Originally published in 1919 by and reprinted*

*with the permission of Longmans, Green Co., Ltd.*

082
In 40
72732
Jan., 1971

First Greenwood reprinting, 1968


LIBRARY OF CONGRESS catalogue card number: LC 68-8739

# CONTENTS

Πότερα θέλεις σοι μαλθακὰ ψευδῆ λέγω,
ἢ σκλῆρ' ἀληθῆ; φράζε, σὴ γὰρ ἡ κρίσις.

*Euripides.*

The case of historical writers is hard ; for if they tell the truth they provoke man, and if they write what is false they offend God.—*Matthew Paris.*

Quattuor sunt maxime comprehendendae veritatis offendicula ; videlicet, fragilis et indignae auctoritatis exemplum, consuetudinis diuturnitas, vulgi sensus imperiti, et propriae ignorantiae occultatio cum ostentatione sapientiae superioris.—*Roger Bacon.*

Iudicio perpende ; et si tibi vera videntur,
Dede manus ; aut si falsum est, accingere contra.

*Lucretius.*

Eventu rerum stolidi didicere magistro.

*Claudian.*

'Αλλ' ἦ τοι μὲν ταῦτα θεῶν ἐν γούνασι κεῖται.

*Homer.*

# OUTSPOKEN ESSAYS

## I

## OUR PRESENT DISCONTENTS

### (August, 1919)

The Essays in this volume were written at various times before and during the Great War. In reading them through for republication, I have to ask myself whether my opinions on social science and on the state of religion, the two subjects which are mainly dealt with in this collection, have been modified by the greatest calamity which has ever befallen the civilised world, or by the issue of the struggle. I find very little that I should now wish to alter. The war has caused events to move faster, but in the same direction as before. The social revolution has been hurried on ; the inevitable counter-revolution has equally been brought nearer. For if there is one safe generalisation in human affairs, it is that revolutions always destroy themselves. How often have fanatics proclaimed ' the year one ' ! But no revolutionary era has yet reached ' year twenty-five.' As regards the national character, there is no sign, I fear, that much wisdom has been learnt. We are more wasteful and reckless than ever. The doctrinaire democrat still vapours about democracy, though representative government has obviously lost both its power and its prestige. The labour party still hugs its comprehensive assortment of economic heresies. Organised religion remains as impotent as it was before the war. But one fact has emerged with startling clearness. Human nature has not been changed by civilisation. It has neither been levelled up nor levelled down to an average mediocrity. Beneath the dingy uniformity of international fashions in dress, man remains what he has always been— a splendid fighting animal, a self-sacrificing hero, and a bloodthirsty savage. Human nature is at once sublime and horrible, holy and satanic. Apart from the accumulation of knowledge and experience, which are external and precarious acquisitions, there is no proof that we have changed much since the first stone age.

The war itself, as we shall soon be compelled to recognise, had its roots deep in the political and social structure of Europe. The growth of wealth and population, and the law of diminishing returns, led to a scramble for unappropriated lands producing the raw materials of industry. It was, in a sense, a war of capital ; but capitalism is no accretion upon the body politic ; it is the creator of the modern world and an essential part of a living organism. The Germans unquestionably made a deep-laid plot to capture all markets and cripple or ruin all competitors. Their aims and methods were very like those of the Standard Oil Trust on a still larger scale. The other nations had not followed the logic of competition in the same ruthless manner ; there were several things which they were not willing to do. But war to the knife cannot be confined to one of the combatants ; the alternative, *Weltmacht oder Niedergang*, was thrust by Germany upon the Allies when she chose that motto for herself. If the modern man were as much dominated by economic motives as is sometimes supposed, the suicidal results of such a conflict would have been apparent to all ; but the poetry and idealism of human nature, no longer centred, as formerly, in religion, had gathered round a romantic patriotism, for which the belligerents were willing to sacrifice their all without counting the cost. Like other idealisms, patriotism varies from a noble devotion to a moral lunacy.

But there was another cause which led to the war. Germany was a curious combination of seventeenth century theory and very modern practice. An Emperor ruling by divine right was the head of the most scientific state that the world has seen. In many ways Germany, with an intelligent, economical, and uncorrupt Government, was a model to the rest of the world. But the whole structure was menaced by that form of individualistic materialism which calls itself social democracy, and which in practice is at once the copy of organic materialism and the reaction against it. The motives for drilling a whole nation in the pursuit of purely national and purely material- istic aims are not strong enough to prevent disintegra- tion. The German *Kriegsstaat* was falling to pieces through internal fissures. A successful war might give the empire a new lease of life ; otherwise, the rising tide of revolution was certain to sweep it away. As Sir Charles Walston has shown, it was for some years doubtful whether the democratic movement would obtain control before the bureaucracy and army chiefs succeeded in precipitating a war. There was a kind of race between the two forces. This was the situation which Lord Haldane found still existing in his famous visit to Germany. In the event, the conservative powers were able to strike and to rush public opinion. Perhaps the bureaucracy was carried along by its own momentum. Two or three years before the war a German publicist, replying to an eminent English- man, who asked him who really directed the policy of Germany, answered : ' It is a difficult question. Nominally, of course, the Emperor is responsible ; but he is a man of moods, not a strong man. In reality, the machine runs itself. Whither it is carrying us we none of us know ; I fear towards some great disaster.' This seems to be the truth of the matter. No doubt, a romantic imperialism, with dreams of restoring the empire of Charlemagne, was a factor in the criminal enterprise. No doubt the natural ambitions of officers, and the greed of contractors and speculators, played their part in promoting it. But when we consider that Germany held all the winning cards in a game of peaceful penetration and economic competition, we should attribute to the Imperial Government a strange recklessness if we did not conclude that the political condition of Germany itself, and the automatic working of the machine, were the main causes why the attack was made. There is, in fact, abundant evidence that it was so. The scheme failed only because Germany was foolish enough to threaten England before settling accounts with Russia. But this, again, was the result of internal pressure. Hamburg, and all the interests which the name stands for, cared less for expansion in the East than for the capture of markets overseas. For this important section of conservative Germany, England was the enemy. So the gauntlet was thrown down to the whole civilised world at once, and the odds against Germany were too great.

For the time being, the world has no example of a strong monarchy. The three great European empires are, at the time of writing, in a state of septic dissolution. The victors have sprung to the welcome conclusion that democracy is everywhere triumphant, and that before long no other type of civilised state will exist. The amazing provincialism of American political thought accepts this conclusion without demur ; and our public men, some of whom doubtless know better, have served the needs of the moment by effusions of political nonsense which almost surpass the orations delivered every year on the Fourth of July. But no historian can suppose that one of the most widespread and successful forms of human association has been permanently extinguished because the Central Empires were not quite strong enough to conquer Europe, an attempt which has always failed, and probably will always fail. The issue is not fully decided, even for our own generation. The ascendancy will belong to that nation which is the best organised, the most strenuous, the most intelligent, the most united. Before the war none would have hesitated to name Germany as holding this position ; and until the downfall of the Empire the nation seemed to possess those qualities unimpaired. The three Empires collapsed in hideous chaos as soon as they deposed their monarchs. In the case of Russia, it is difficult to imagine any recovery until the monarchy is restored ; and Germany would probably be well-advised to choose some member of the imperial family as a constitutional sovereign. A monarch frequently

represents his subjects better than an elected assembly ;
and if he is a good judge of character he is likely to have
more capable and loyal advisers. President Wilson's
declaration that ' a steadfast concert for peace can never
be maintained except by a partnership of democratic
nations ; for no autocratic government could ever be
trusted to keep faith within it,' is one of the most childish
exhibitions of doctrinaire *naïveté* which ever proceeded
from the mouth of a public man. History gives no countenance to the theory that popular governments are either
more moral or more pacific than strong monarchies. The
late Lord Salisbury, in one of his articles in the *Quarterly
Review*, spoke the truth on this subject. ' Moderation,
especially in the matter of territory, has never been a
characteristic of democracy. Wherever it has had free
play, in the ancient world or the modern, in the old
hemisphere or the new, a thirst for empire and a readiness
for aggressive war has always marked it. Though governments may have an appearance and even a reality of pacific
intent, their action is always liable to be superseded by
the violent and vehement operations of mere ignorance.'
The United States are no exception to this rule. They
have extended their dominion by much the same means
as the empire of the Tsars or our own. Texas and Upper
California, the Philippines and Porto Rico, were annexed
forcibly ; New Mexico, Alaska, and Louisiana were bought ;
Florida was acquired by treaty ; Maine filched from Canada.
In no case were the wishes of the inhabitants consulted.
Our own experience of republicanism is the same. It was
during the short period when Great Britain had no king that
Cromwell's court-poet, Andrew Marvell, urged him to com-
plete his glorious career by demolishing our present allies :

> A Cæsar he, ere long, to Gaul,
> To Italy an Hannibal.

On the other hand, none of the ' autocrats ' wanted
this war. The Kaiser was certainly pushed into it.

Democracy is a form of government which may be
rationally defended, not as being good, but as being less
bad than any other. Its strongest merits seem to be :

first, that the citizens of a democracy have a sense of proprietorship and responsibility in public affairs, which in times of crisis may add to their tenacity and endurance. The determination of the Federals in the American Civil War, and of the French and British in the four years' struggle against Germany, may be legitimately adduced as arguments for democracy. When De Tocqueville says that 'it is hard for a democracy to begin or to end a war,' the second is truer than the first. And, secondly, the educational value of democracy is so great that it may be held to counterbalance many defects. Mill decides in favour of democracy mainly on the ground that 'it promotes a better and higher form of national character than any other polity,' since government by authority stunts the intellect, narrows the sympathies, and destroys the power of initiative. 'The perfect commonwealth,' says Mr. Zimmern, 'is a society of free men and women, each at once ruling and being ruled.' It is also fair to argue that monarchies do not escape the worst evils of democracies. An autocracy is often obliged to oppress the educated classes and to propitiate the mob. Domitian massacred senators with impunity, and only fell ' *postquam cerdonibus esse timendus coeperat.*' If an autocracy does not rest on the army, which leads to the chaos of praetorianism, it must rely on ' *panem et circenses.*' Hence it has some of the worst faults of democracy, without its advantages. As Mr. Graham Wallas says : ' When a Tsar or a bureaucracy finds itself forced to govern in opposition to a vague national feeling which may at any moment create an overwhelming national purpose, the autocrat becomes the most unscrupulous of demagogues, and stirs up racial or religious or social hatred, or the lust for foreign war, with less scruple than a newspaper proprietor under a democracy.' The autocrat, in fact, is often a slave, as the demagogue is often a tyrant. Lastly, the democrat may urge that one of the commonest accusations against democracy—that the populace chooses its rulers badly—is not true in times of great national danger. On the contrary, it often shows a sound instinct in finding the strongest man to carry it through a crisis. At such times the parrots and monkeys are discarded, and a Napoleon or a Kitchener is given a free hand, though he may have despised all the demagogic arts. In other words, a democracy sometimes knows when to abdicate. The excesses of revolutionists are not an argument against democracy, since revolutions are anything rather than democratic.

Nevertheless, the indictment against democracy is a very heavy one, and it is worth while to state the main items in the charge.

1. Whatever may be truly said about the good sense of a democracy during a great crisis, at ordinary times it does not bring the best men to the top. Professor Hearnshaw, in his admirable ' Democracy at the Crossroads,' collects a number of weighty opinions confirming this judgment. Carlyle, who proclaimed the merits of silence in some thirty volumes, blames democracy for ignoring the ' noble, silent men ' who could serve it best, and placing power in the hands of windbags. Ruskin, Matthew Arnold, Sir James Stephen, Sir Henry Maine, and Lecky, all agree that ' the people have for the most part neither the will nor the power to find out the best men to lead them.' In France the denunciations of democratic politicians are so general that it would be tedious to enumerate the writers who have uttered them. One example will suffice ; the words are the words of Anatole Beaulieu in 1885 :

The wider the circle from which politicians and state-functionaries are recruited, the lower seems their intellectual level to have sunk. This deterioration in the personnel of government has been yet more striking from the moral point of view. Politics have tended to become more corrupt, more debased, and to soil the hands of those who take part in them and the men who get their living by them. Political battles have become too bitter and too vulgar not to have inspired aversion in the noblest and most upright natures by their violence and their intrigues. The élite of the nation in more than one country are showing a tendency to have nothing to do with them. Politics is an industry in which a man, to prosper, requires less intelligence and knowledge than boldness and capacity for intrigue. It has already become in some states the most ignominious of careers. Parties are syndicates for exploitation, and its forms become ever more shameless.

A later account of French politics, drawn from inside knowledge and experience, is the remarkable novel, ' Les Morts qui parlent,' by the Vicomte Le Vogüé. Readers of this book will not forget the description of the *bain de haine* in which a new deputy at once finds himself plunged, and the canker of corruption which eats into the whole system. It is no wonder that the majority of Frenchmen do not care to record their votes. In 1906, 5,209,606 votes were given, 6,383,852 electors did not go to the poll. The record of democracy in the new countries is no better. We must regretfully admit that Louis Simond was right when he said, ' Few people take the trouble to persuade the people, except those who see their interest in deceiving them.'

2. The democracy is a ready victim to shibboleths and catchwords, as all demagogues know too well. ' The abstract idea,' as Schérer says, ' is the national aliment of popular rhetoric, the fatal form of thought which, for want of solid knowledge, operates in a vacuum.' The politician has only to find a fascinating formula ; facts and arguments are powerless against it. The art of the demagogue is the art of the parrot ; he must utter some senseless catchword again and again, working on the suggestibility of the crowd. Archbishop Trench, ' On the Study of Words,' notices this fact of psychology and the use which is commonly made of it.

If I wanted any further evidence of the moral atmosphere which words diffuse, I would ask you to observe how the first thing men do, when engaged in controversy with others, is ever to assume some honourable name to themselves, such as, if possible, shall beg the whole subject in dispute, and at the same time to affix on their adversaries a name which shall place them in a ridiculous or contemptible or odious light. A deep instinct, deeper perhaps than men give any account of to themselves, tells them how far this will go ; that multitudes, utterly unable to weigh the arguments on one side or the other, will yet be receptive of the influences which these words are evermore, however imperceptibly, diffusing. By argument they might hope to gain over the reason of a few, but by help of these nicknames the prejudices and passions of the many.

The chief instrument of this base art is no longer the public speech but the newspaper.

The psychology of the crowd has been much studied lately, by Le Bon and other writers in France, by Mr. Graham Wallas in England. I think that Le Bon is in danger of making The Crowd a mystical, superhuman entity. Of course, a crowd is made up of individuals, who remain individuals still. We must not accept the stuffed idol of Rousseau and the socialists, ' The General Will,' and turn it into an evil spirit. There is no General Will. All we have a right to say is that individuals are occasionally guided by reason, crowds never.

3. Several critics of democracy have accused it not only of rash iconoclasm, but of obstinate conservatism and obstructiveness. It seems unreasonable to charge the same persons with two opposite faults ; but it is true that where the popular emotions are not touched, the masses will cling to old abuses from mere force of habit. As Maine says, universal suffrage would have prohibited the spinning-jenny and the power-loom, the threshing-machine and the Gregorian calendar ; and it would have restored the Stuarts. The theory of democracy—*vox populi vox dei*—is a pure superstition, a belief in a divine or natural sanction which does not exist. And superstition is usually obstructive. ' We erect the temporary watchwords of evanescent politics into eternal truths ; and having accepted as platitudes the paradoxes of our fathers, we perpetuate them as obstacles to the progress of our children.' [1]

4. A more serious danger is that of vexatious and inquisitive tyranny. This is exercised partly through public opinion, a vulgar, impertinent, anonymous tyrant who deliberately makes life unpleasant for anyone who is not content to be the average man. But partly it is seen in constant interference with the legislature and the executive. No one can govern who cannot afford to be unpopular, and no democratic official can afford to be un-popular. Sometimes he has to wink at flagrant injustice and oppression ; at other times a fanatical agitation compels

[1] *Times Literary Supplement*, July 18, 1918.

him to pass laws which forbid the citizen to indulge perfectly harmless tastes, or tax him to contribute to the pleasures of the majority. In many ways a Russian under the Tsars was far less interfered with than an Englishman or American or Australian.

5. But the two diseases which are likely to be fatal to democracy are anarchy and corruption. A democratic government is almost necessarily weak and timid. A democracy cannot tolerate a strong executive for fear of seeing the control pass out of the hands of the mob. The executive must be unarmed and defenceless. The result is that it is at the mercy of any violent and anti-social faction. No civilised government has ever given a more ludicrous and humiliating object-lesson than the Cabinet and House of Commons in the years before the war, in face of the outrages committed by a small gang of female anarchists. The legalisation of terrorism by the trade-unions was too tragic a surrender to be ludicrous, but it was even more disgraceful. None could be surprised when, during the war, the Government shrank from dealing with treasonable conspiracy in the same quarter.

The *Times* for May 24, 1917, contained a noteworthy example of justice influenced by pressure, and therefore applied with flagrant inequality. In parallel columns appeared reports of ' sugar-sellers fined ' and ' strike leaders released.' The former paid the full penalty of their misdeeds because no body of outside opinion maintained them. The latter, who were stated to have committed offences for which the maximum penalty was penal servitude for life, got off scot-free because they were members of a powerful organisation which was able to bring immense weight to bear on the Government.[1]

The ' immense weight ' was, of course, the threat of virtually betraying the country to the Germans. The country is at this moment at the mercy of any lawless faction which may choose either to hold the community to ransom by paralysing our trade and channels of supply, or by organised violence against life and property. Democracy is powerless against sectional anarchism ;

[1] Hearnshaw, *Democracy at the Crossroads*, p. 63.

and when such movements break out there is no remedy
except by substituting for democracy a government of a
very different type.

Democracy is, in fact, a disintegrating force. It
is strong in destruction, and tends to fall to pieces when
the work of demolition (which may of course be a necessary
task) is over. Democracy dissolves communities into
individuals and collects them again into mobs. It pulls
up by the roots the social order which civilisation has
gradually evolved, and leaves men *déracinés*, as Bourget
says in one of his best novels, homeless and friendless,
with no place ready for them to fill. It is the opposite
extreme to the caste system of India, which, with all its
faults, does not seem to breed the European type of *enragé*,
the enemy of society as such.

6. The corruption of democracies proceeds directly
from the fact that one class imposes the taxes and another
class pays them. The constitutional principle, ' No
taxation without representation,' is utterly set at nought
under a system which leaves certain classes without any
effective representation at all. At the present time it
is said that one-tenth of the population pays five-sixths
of the taxes. The class which imposes the taxes has refused
to touch the burden of the war with one of its fingers ;
and every month new doles at the public expense are
distributed under the camouflage of ' social reform.'
At every election the worldly goods of the minority are
put up to auction. This is far more immoral than the
old-fashioned election bribery, which was a comparatively
honest deal between two persons ; and in its effects it
is far more ruinous. Democracy is likely to perish,
like the monarchy of Louis XVI, through national
bankruptcy.

Besides these defects, the democracy has ethical
standards of its own, which differ widely from those of
the educated classes. Among the poor, ' generosity
ranks far before justice, sympathy before truth, love
before chastity, a pliant and obliging disposition before
a rigidly honest one. In brief, the less admixture of intellect required for the practice of any virtue, the higher it

stands in popular estimation.' [1] In this country, at any
rate, democracy means a victory of sentiment over reason.
Some may prefer the softer type of character, and may
hope that it will make civilisation more humane and
compassionate than it has been in the past. Unfortunately,
experience shows that none is so cruel as the disillusioned
sentimentalist. He thinks that he can break or ignore
nature's laws with impunity ; and then, when he finds
that nature has no sentiment, he rages like a mad dog,
and combines with his theoretical objection to capital
punishment a lust to murder all who disagree with him.
This is the genesis of Jacobinism and Bolshevism.

But whether we think that the bad in democracy
predominates over the good, or the good over the bad, a
question which I shall not attempt to decide, the popular
balderdash about it corresponds to no real conviction.
The upper class has never believed in it ; the middle class
has the strongest reasons to hate and fear it. But how
about the lower class, in whose interests the whole machine
is supposed to have been set going ? The working man
has no respect for either democracy or liberty. His whole
interest is in transferring the wealth of the minority to
his own pocket. There was a time when he thought that
universal suffrage would get for him what he desires ;
but he has lost all faith in constitutional methods. To
levy blackmail on the community, under threats of civil
war, seems to him a more expeditious way of gaining his
object. Monopolies are to be established by pitiless
coercion of those who wish to keep their freedom. The
trade unions are large capitalists ; they are well able to
start factories for themselves and work them for their own
exclusive profit. But they find it more profitable to hold
the nation to ransom by blockading the supply of the
necessaries of life. The new labourer despises productivity
for the same reason that the old robber barons did : it is
less trouble to take money than to make it. The most
outspoken popular leaders no longer conceal their contempt
for and rejection of democracy. The socialists perceive the

---

[1] Miss M. Loane. Mr. Stephen Reynolds has said the same.

irreconcilable contradiction between the two ideas,[1] and they are right. Democracy postulates community of interest or loyal patriotism. When these are absent it cannot long exist. Syndicalism, which seems to be growing, is the antipodes of socialism, but, like socialism, it can make no terms with democracy. 'If syndicalism triumphs,' says its chief prophet Sorel, 'the parliamentary régime, so dear to the intellectuals, will be at an end.' 'The syndicalist has a contempt for the vulgar idea of democracy ; the vast unconscious mass is not to be taken into account when the minority wishes to act so as to benefit it.'[2] 'The effect of political majorities,' says Mr. Levine, ' is to hinder advance.' Accordingly, political methods are rejected with contempt. The anarchists go one step further. Bakunin proclaims that 'we reject all legislation, all authority, and all influence, even when it has proceeded from universal suffrage.' These powerful movements, opposed as they are to each other, agree in spurning the very idea of democracy, which Lord Morley defines as government by public opinion, and which may be defined with more precision as direct government by the votes of the majority among the adult members of a nation. Even a political philosopher like Mr. Lowes Dickinson says, ' For my part, I am no democrat.'

Who then are the friends of this *curieux fétiche*, as Quinet called democracy ? It appears to have none, though it has been the subject of fatuous laudation ever since the time of Rousseau. The Americans burn incense before it, but they are themselves ruled by the Boss and the Trust.

The attempt to justify the labour movement as a legitimate development of the old democratic Liberalism

---

[1] Professor Hearnshaw quotes : ' Il y a opposition évidente et irréductible entre les principes socialistes et les principes démocratiques. Il n'y a pas de conceptions politiques qui soient séparées par des abîmes plus profonds que la démocratie et le socialisme ' (Le Bon). ' Socialism must be built on ideas and institutions totally different from the ideas and institutions of democracy ' (Levine). ' La démocratie tend à la conciliation des classes, tandis que le socialisme organise la lutte de classe ' (Lagardelle).

[2] A. D. Lewis, *Syndicalism and the General Strike.*

is futile. Freedom to form combinations is no doubt
a logical application of *laisser faire*; and the anarchic
possibilities latent in *laisser faire* have been made plain in
the anti-democratic movements of labour. But Liberalism
rested on a too favourable estimate of human nature
and on a belief in the law of progress. As there is no
law of progress, and as civilised society is being destroyed
by the evil passions of men, Liberalism is, for the time,
quite discredited. It would also be true to say that there
is a fundamental contradiction between the two dogmas
of Liberalism. These were, that unlimited competition
is stimulating to the competitors and good for the country,
and that every individual is an end, not a means. Both
are anarchical; but the first logically issues in individualistic anarchy, the last in communistic anarchy. The
economic and the ethical theory of Liberalism cannot be
harmonised. The result—cruel competition tempered by
an artificial process of counter-selection in favour of the
unfittest—was by no means satisfactory. But it was
better than what we are now threatened with.

That the labour movement is economically rotten it
is easy to prove. In the words of Professor Hearnshaw,
' the government has ceased to govern in the world of
labour, and has been compelled, instead of governing, to
bribe, to cajole, to beg, to grovel. It has purchased brief
truces at the cost of increasing levies of Danegeld drawn
from the diminishing resources of the patient community.
It has embarked on a course of payment of blackmail
which must end either in national bankruptcy or in the
social revolution which the anarchists seek.' The powerful
trade-unions are now plundering both the owners of their
' plant,' and the general public. It is easy to show that
their members already get much more than their share of
the national wealth. Professor Bowley [1] has estimated
that an equal division of the national income would give
about £160 a year to each family, free of taxes. But even
this estimate, discouraging as it is, seems not to allow
sufficiently for the fact that under the present system

---

[1] *The Division of the Product of Industry.*

much of the income of the richer classes is counted twice or three times over. Abolish large incomes, and jewels, pictures, wines, furs, special and rare skill like that of the operating surgeon and fashionable portrait painter, lose all or most of their money value. All the large professional incomes, except those of the low comedian and his like, are made out of the rich, and are counted at least twice for income-tax. It is certain that a large part of the national income could not be ' redistributed,' and that in the attempt to do so credit would be destroyed and wealth would melt like a snow man. The miners, therefore, are not seeking justice ; they are blackmailing rich and poor alike by their monopoly of one of the necessaries of life. And now they strike against paying income-tax !

It is not necessary or just to bring railing accusations against any class as a body. Power is always abused, and in this case there is much honest ignorance, stimulated by agitators who are seldom honest. In a recent number of the *Edinburgh Review* Sir Lynden Macassey speaks of the widespread, almost universal, fallacies to which the hand-worker has fallen a victim. They believe that all their aspirations can be satisfied out of present-day profits and production. They believe that in restricting output they are performing a moral duty to their class. They do not believe that the prosperity of the country depends upon its production, and are opposed to all labour-saving devices. They refuse co-operation because they desire the continuance of the class-war. Such perversity would seem hardly credible if it were not attested by overwhelming evidence. The Government remedy is first to create unemployment and then to endow it—the shortest and maddest road to ruin since the downfall of the Roman Empire.

We may have a faint hope that some of these fallacies will be abandoned by the workmen when their destructive results can no longer be concealed. But sentimentalism seems to be incurable. It erects irrationality into an act of religious faith, gives free rein to the emotion of pity, and thinks that it is imitating the Good Samaritan by robbing the Priest and Levite for the benefit of the man by the road-side. The sentimentalist shows a bitter hatred against those who wish to cure an evil by removing its causes. A good example is the language of writers like Mr. Chesterton about eugenics and population. If social maladies were treated scientifically, the trade of the emotional rhetorician would be gone.

We have seen that democracy—the rule of majorities—has been discredited and abandoned in action, though officially we all bow down before it. Another popular delusion is that the chief change in the last fifty years has been a conversion of the world from individualism to socialism. In the language of the Christian socialists, who wish to combine the militant spirit and organisation of medieval Catholicism with a bid for the popular vote, we have ' rediscovered the Corporate Idea.' But if we take socialism, not in the narrower sense of collectivism, which would be an economic experiment, but in the wider sense of a keen consciousness of the solidarity of the community as an organic whole, there is very little truth in the commonly held notion that we have become more socialistic. It is easy to see how the idea has arisen. It became necessary to find some theoretical justification for raising taxes, no longer for national needs, but for the benefit of the class which imposed them ; and this justification was found in the theory that all wealth belongs to ' the State,' and may be justly divided up as ' the State '—that is to say, the majority of the voters—may determine. Whenever the question arises of voting new doles to the dominant section of the people at the expense of the minority, our new political philosophers profess themselves fervent socialists. But true socialism, which is almost synonymous with patriotism, is as conspicuously absent in those who call themselves socialists as it is strong in those who repudiate the title. This paradox can be easily proved. The most socialistic enterprise in which a nation ever engages is a great war. A nation at war is conscious of its corporate unity and its common interests, as it is at no other time. The nation then calls upon every citizen to surrender all his personal rights and to offer his life and limbs in the service of the community. And what

has been the record of the ' socialists ' in the struggle
for national existence in which we have been engaged ?
In the years preceding the war they ridiculed the idea that
the country was in danger of being attacked, and used
all their power to prevent us from preparing against attack.
They steadily opposed the teaching of patriotism in the
schools. When the war began, they prevented the Government from introducing compulsory service until our
French Allies, who were left to bear the brunt, were on
the point of collapse ; they, in very many cases, refused
to serve themselves, thereby avowing that, as far as they
were concerned, they were willing to see their country
conquered by a horde of cruel barbarians ; and they nearly
handed over our armies to destruction by fomenting
strikes at the most critical periods of the war. This attitude
cannot be accounted for by any conscientious objection
to violence, which is in fact their favourite weapon, except
against the enemies of their country. Their socialism is,
in truth, individualism run mad ; it is the very antithesis
to the consciousness of organic unity in a nation, which
is the spiritual basis of socialism. In this sense, the
nation as a whole has shown a fine socialistic temper ;
but the disgraceful exception has been the socialist party.
The intense and perverted individualism of the so-called
socialist is shown in another way. Whatever liberties
a State may permit to its citizens, it is certain that no
nation can be in a healthy condition unless the government keeps in its own hands the keys of birth and of
death. The State has the right of the farmer to decide
how many cows should be allowed to graze upon ten acres
of grass ; the right of the forester to decide how many
square feet are required for each tree in a wood. It has
also the right and the duty of the gardener to pull up
noxious weeds in his flower-beds. But the socialist
vehemently repudiates both these rights. Being an ultra-
individualist, he is in favour of *laisser faire,* where *laisser
faire* is most indefensible and most disastrous.

It would be easy to maintain that the organic idea was
more potent, both under medieval feudalism and under
nineteenth-century industrialism, than it is now. In

C

former days, economic and social equality were not even
aimed at, because it was thought inevitable that in a social
organism there must be subordination and a hierarchy of
functions. Essentially, and in the sight of God, all are
equal, or, rather, the essential differences between man
and man are absolutely independent of social status.
In a few years Lazarus may be in heaven and Dives in
hell. Beside this equality of moral opportunity and
tremendous inequality in self-chosen destiny, the status
of master and servant seemed of small importance ; it
was a temporary and trivial accident. Accordingly, in
feudal times, as to-day in really Catholic communities,
feelings of injustice and social bitterness were seldom
aroused and class differences take on a more genial colour.
In spite of the lawlessness and brutality of the Middle
Ages it is probable that men were happier then than they
are now.

The French Revolution, which was a disintegrating sol-
vent, pulverised society, and was impotent to reconstruct
it. Yet under the industrial régime which followed in
this country, the nation was conscious of its unity.
The system was the best that could have been devised
for increasing the population and aggregate wealth of the
country ; and even those who suffered most under it were
not without pride in its results. The ill-paid workman
of the last century would have thought it a poor thing
to do a deliberately bad day's work.

I am not praising either the age of feudalism or the
' hungry forties ' of the nineteenth century. In the latter
case especially the sacrifice exacted from the poor was
too great for the rather vulgar success of which it was
the condition. But to call that age the period of individualism, and our own generation the period of socialism,
is in my opinion a profound mistake. In Germany, too,
the real socialists are not the ' Spartacist ' scoundrels
who have betrayed and ruined their country, but the
bureaucracy with their *Deutschland über Alles*. If I
were a little more of a socialist, I could almost admire
them, in spite of all their crimes.

The landed gentry (and in honesty I must add the

endowed clergy) are a survival of feudalism, as the capitalist is a survival of industrialism. Both have to a large extent survived their functions. The mailclad baron, round whose fortified castle the peasants and others gathered for protection, has become the country gentleman, against whom the indictment is not so much that his only pursuit is pleasure, as that his only pleasure is pursuit. 'The rich man in his castle, the poor man at his gate' were intelligible while the rich man protected the poor man from being plundered and killed by marauders; but in our times nobody wants a castle or to live under the shadow of a castle. The clerical profession was a necessity when most people could neither read nor write. But to-day our best prophets and preachers are laymen. As at ancient Athens, in the time of Aristophanes, 'the young learn from the schoolmaster, the mature from the poets.' Similarly, the captain of industry cannot hold the same autocratic position as formerly, in view of the growing intelligence and capacity of the workmen; and the capitalist who is not a captain of industry is a debtor to the community to an extent which he does not always realise. This class is becoming painfully conscious of its vulnerability.

There are, therefore, irrational survivals in our social order; and though it may be proved that they are not a severe burden on the community, it is natural that popular bitterness and discontent should fasten upon them and exaggerate their evil results. It cannot be disputed that this bitterness and discontent were becoming very acute in the years before the war. An increasing number of persons saw no meaning and no value in our civilisation. This feeling was common in all classes, including the so-called leisured class; and was so strong that many welcomed with joy the clear call to a plain duty, though it was the duty of facing all the horrors of war. What is the cause of this discontent? There are few more important questions for us to answer.

Those who find the cause in the existence of the survivals which we have mentioned are certainly mistaken. It is no new thing that there should be a small class more or less parasitic on the community. The whole number of persons who pay income-tax on £5000 a year and upwards is only 13,000 out of 46 millions, and their wealth, if it could be divided up, would make no appreciable difference to the working man. The wage-earners are better off than they have ever been before in our history, and the danger of revolution comes not from the poor, but from the privileged artisans who already have incomes above the family average. We must look elsewhere for an explanation of social unrest. If we consider what are the chief centres of discontent throughout the civilised world, we shall find that they are the great aggregations of population in wealthy industrial countries. Social unrest is a disease of town-life. Wherever the conditions which create the great modern city exist, we find revolutionary agitation. It has spread to Barcelona, to Buenos Ayres, and to Osaka, in the wake of the factory. The inhabitants of the large town do not envy the countryman and would not change with him. But, unknown to themselves, they are leading an unnatural life, cut off from the kindly and wholesome influences of nature, surrounded by vulgarity and ugliness, with no traditions, no loyalties, no culture, and no religion. We seldom reflect on the strangeness of the fact that the modern working-man has few or no superstitions. At other times the masses have evolved for themselves some picturesque nature-religion, some pious ancestor-worship, some cult of saints or heroes, some stories of fairies, ghosts, or demons, and a mass of quaint superstitions, genial or frightening. The modern town-dweller has no God and no Devil ; he lives without awe, without admiration, without fear. Whatever we may think about these beliefs, it is not natural for men and women to be without them. The life of the town artisan who works in a factory is a life to which the human organism has not adapted itself ; it is an unwholesome and unnatural condition. Hence, probably, comes the *malaise* which makes him think that any radical change must be for the better.

Whatever the cause of the disease may be (and I do not pretend that the conditions of urban life are an adequate explanation) the malady is there, and will probably prove fatal to our civilisation. I have given my views on this subject in the essay called *The Future of the English Race.* And yet there is a remedy within the reach of all if we would only try it.

The essence of the Christian revelation is the proclamation of a standard of absolute values, which contradicts at every point the estimates of good and evil current in ' the world.' It is not necessary, in such an essay as this, to write out the Beatitudes, or the very numerous passages in the Gospels and Epistles in which the same lessons are enforced. It is not necessary to remind the reader that in Christianity all the paraphernalia of life are valued very lightly ; that all the good and all the evil which exalt or defile a man have their seat within him, in his own character ; that we are sent into the world to suffer and to conquer suffering ; that it is more blessed to give than to receive ; that love is the great revealer of the mysteries of life ; that we have here no continuing city, and must therefore set our affections and lay up our treasures in heaven ; that the things that are seen are temporal, and the things that are not seen are eternal. This is the Christian religion. It is a form of idealism ; and idealism means a belief in absolute or spiritual values.

When applied to human life, it introduces, as it were, a new currency, which demonetises the old ; or gives us a new scale of prices, in which the cheapest things are the dearest, and the dearest the cheapest. The world's standards are quantitative ; those of Christianity are qualitative. And being qualitative, spiritual goods are unlimited in amount ; they are increased by being shared ; and we rob nobody by taking them.

Secularists ask impatiently what Christianity has done or proposes to do to make mankind happier, by which they mean more comfortable. The answer is (to put it in a form intelligible to the questioner) that Christianity increases the wealth of the world by creating new values. Wealth depends on human valuation. For example, if women were sufficiently well educated not to care about diamonds, the Kimberley mines would pay no dividends, and the rents in Park Lane would go down. The prices of paintings by old masters would decline if millionaires preferred to collect another kind of scalps to decorate their wigwams. Bookmakers and company-promoters live on the widespread passion for acquiring money without working for it. It is hardly possible to estimate the increase of real wealth, and the stoppage of waste, which would result from the adoption of a rational, still more of a Christian, valuation of the good things of life. I have dealt with this subject in the essay on *The Indictment against Christianity*, and have emphasised the importance of taking into consideration, in all economic questions, the *human costs* of production, the factors which make work pleasant or irksome, and especially the moral condition of the worker. Good-will diminishes the toll which labour takes of the labourer; envy and hatred vastly increase it while they diminish its product. It is, of course, impossible that the worker should not resent having to devote his life to making what is useless or mischievous, and to ministering to the irrational wastefulness of luxury. Christianity, in condemning the selfish and irresponsible use of money, seeks to remove one of the chief causes of social bitterness. Senseless extravagance is the best friend of revolution.

The abuse poured upon ‘ the old political economy,’ as it is called, is only half deserved. As compared with the insane doctrines now in favour with the working-man, the old political economy was sound and sensible. Hard work, thrift, and economy in production are, in truth, as we used to be told, the only ways to increase the national wealth, and the contrary practices can only lead to economic ruin. There is not much fault to find with the old economists so long as they recognised that their science was an abstract science, which for its own purposes dealt with an unreal abstraction—the ‘ economic man.’ Every science is obliged to isolate one aspect of reality in this way. But when political economy was treated as a philosophy of life it began to be mischievous. A book on ‘ the science of the stomach,’ without knowledge of physiology or the working of other organs, would not be of much use. Man has never been a merely acquisitive being; for example, he is also a fighting and a praying being. If our dominant motives were changed, the whole conditions dealt with by political economy would change with them. There have been civilisations in which the passion for accumulation was comparatively weak; and notoriously there are many persons in whom it is wholly absent. Devotion to art, to scientific investigation, and to religion is strong enough, where it exists, to kill 'the economic man' in human nature. A civilised nation honours its idealists, and recognises the immense benefit which they confer on the community by creating or re-vealing new and inexhaustible values; in an uncivilised country they can hardly live. Ruskin and William Morris saw, and doubtless exaggerated, the danger to which spiritual values were exposed at the hands of the dominant economism. Our danger now is that neglect of the simplest economic laws may plunge the nation into such misery that the people will no longer be willing to support art, science, learning, and philosophy. A large section of the labour party has the same standard of values as the hated 'capitalist,' and detests those whom it calls intellectuals and sky-pilots because they depreciate the currency which their class, no less than the capitalist, believes to be the only sound money.

It may be asked whether there is any reason to think that there is now less regard for the higher, the qualitative values of life, than at other periods. My opinion is that ever since the time of Rousseau and his contemporaries, we have been led astray by a will-of-the-wisp akin to the apocalyptic dreams of the Jews in the last two centuries before Christ, dreams which also filled the minds of the first generation of Christians. The Greeks never made the mistake of throwing their ideals into the future, a practice which, as Dr. Bosanquet has said, 'is the death of all sane idealism.' The belief in 'a good time coming' is a Jewish delusion. It nourished the Jews in their amazing obstinacy, and led to the annihilation of their State which, to the very end, they saw in their dreams bruising all other nations with a rod of iron, and break-ing them in pieces like a potter's vessel. But, as any idealism is better than none, the Hebrew race has won remarkable triumphs, though of a kind which it never desired.

The myth of progress is our form of apocalyptism. In France it began with sentimentalism, developing normally into homicidal mania. In England it took the form of a kind of Deuteronomic religion. As a reward for our national virtues, our population expanded, our exports and imports went up by leaps and bounds, and our empire received additions every decade. It was plain that when Christ said ' Blessed are the meek, for they shall inherit the earth,' He was thinking of the British Empire. The whole structure of our social order encouraged the measurement of everything by quantitative standards. Everyone could understand that a generation which travels sixty miles an hour must be five times as civilised as one which only travelled twelve. Thus the beneficent ' law of progress ' was exemplified in that nation which had best deserved to be its exponent. The myth in question is that there is a natural law of improvement, manifested by greater complexity of structure, by increase of wants and the means to satisfy them. A nation advances in civilisation by increasing in wealth and population, and by multiplying the accessories and paraphernalia of life.

Belief in this alleged law has vitiated our natural science, our political science, our history, our philosophy, and even our religion. Science declared that ' the survival of the fittest ' was a law of nature, though nature has condemned to extinction the majestic animals of the saurian era, and has carefully preserved the bug, the louse, and the spirochaeta pallida.

> We dined as a rule on each other ;
> What matter ? the toughest survived,

is a fair parody of this doctrine. In political science, by a portentous snobbery, the actual evolution of European government was assumed to be in the line of upward progress. Our histories contrasted the benighted condition of past ages with the high morality and general enlightenment of the present. In philosophy, the problem of evil was met by the theory that though the Deity is not omnipotent yet, He is on His way to become so. He means well, and if we give Him time, He will make a real success of His creation. Human beings, too, commonly make a very poor thing of their lives here. But continue their training after they are dead and they will all come to perfection. We have been living on this secularised idealism for a hundred and fifty years. It has driven out the true idealism, of which it is a caricature, and has made the deeper and higher kind of religious faith abnormally difficult. Even the hope of immortality has degenerated into a belief in apparitions and voices from the dead.

Nature knows nothing of this precious law. Her figure is not the vertical line, nor even the spiral, but the circle—the vicious circle, according to Samuel Butler. 'Men eat birds, birds eat worms, worms eat men again.' Some stars are getting hotter, others cooler. Life appears at a certain temperature and is extinguished at another temperature. Evolution and involution balance each other and go on concurrently. The normal condition of every species on this planet is not progress but stationariness. 'Progress,' so-called, is an incident of adaptation to new conditions. Bees and ants must have spent millennia in perfecting their organisation ; now that they have reached a stable equilibrium, no more changes are perceptible. The 'progress' of humanity has consisted almost entirely in the transformation of the wild man of the woods, not into *homo sapiens* but into *homo faber,* man the tool-maker, a process of which nature expresses her partial disapproval by plaguing us with diverse diseases and taking away our teeth and claws. It is not certain that there has been much change in our intellectual and moral endowments since pithecanthropus dropped the first half of his name. I should be sorry to have to maintain that the Germans of to-day are morally superior to the army which defeated Quintilius Varus, or that the modern Turks are more humane than the hordes of Timour the Tartar. If there is to be any improvement in human nature itself we must look to the infant science of eugenics to help us.

It is not easy to say how this myth of progress came to take hold of the imagination, in the teeth of science and experience. Quinet speaks of the ' fatalistic optimism ' of historians, of which there have certainly been some strange examples. We can only say that secularism, like other religions, needs an eschatology, and has produced one. A more energetic generation than ours looked forward to a gradual extension of busy industrialism over the whole planet ; the present ideal of the masses seems to be the greatest idleness of the greatest number, or a Fabian farm-yard of tame fowls, or (in America) an ice-water-drinking gynæcocracy. But the superstition cannot flourish much longer. The period of expansion is over, and we must adjust our view of earthly providence to a state of decline. For no nation can flourish when it is the ambition of the large majority to put in fourpence and take out ninepence. The middle-class will be the first victims ; then the privileged aristocracy of labour will exploit the poor. But trade will take wings and migrate to some other country where labour is good and comparatively cheap.

The dethronement of a fetish may give a sounder faith its chance. In the time of decay and disintegration which lies before us, more persons will seek consolation where it can be found. ' Happiness and unhappiness,' says Spinoza, ' depend on the nature of the object which we love. When a thing is not loved, no quarrels will arise concerning it, no sadness will be felt if it perishes, no envy if it is possessed by another ; no fear, no hatred, no disturbance of the mind. All these things arise from the love of the perishable. But love for a thing eternal and infinite feeds the mind wholly with joy, and is itself untainted with any sadness ; wherefore it is greatly to be desired and sought for with our whole strength.' It is well known that these noble words were not only sincere, but the expression of the working faith of the philosopher ; and we may hope that many who are doomed to suffer hardship and spoliation in the evil days that are coming will find the same path to a happiness which cannot be taken from them. Spinoza's words, of course, do not point only to religious exercises and meditation. The spiritual world includes art and science in all their branches, when these are studied with a genuine devotion to the Good, the True, and the Beautiful for their own sakes. We shall need ' a remnant ' to save Europe from relapsing into barbarism ; for the new forces are almost wholly cut off from the precious traditions which link our civilisation with the great eras of the past. The possibility of another dark age is not remote ; but there must be enough who value our best traditions to preserve them till the next spring-time of civilisation. We must take long views, and think of our great-grandchildren.

It is tempting to dream of a new Renaissance, under which the life of reason will at last be the life of mankind. Though there is little sign of improvement in human nature, a favourable conjunction of circumstances may bring about a civilisation very much better than ours to-day. For a time, at any rate, war may be practically abolished, and the military qualities may find another and a less pernicious outlet. ' Sport,' as Santayana says, ' is a liberal form of war stripped of its compulsions and malignity ; a rational art and the expression of a civilised instinct.' The art of living may be taken in hand seriously. Some of the ingenuity which has lately been lavished on engines of destruction may be devoted to improvements in our houses, which should be easily and cheaply put together and able to be carried about in sections ; on labour-saving devices which would make servants unnecessary ; and on international campaigns against diseases, some of the worst of which could be extinguished for ever by twenty years of concerted effort. A scientific civilisation is not impossible, though we are not likely to live to see it. And, if science and humanism can work together, it will be a great age for mankind. Such hopes as these must be allowed to float before our minds : they are not unreasonable, and they will help us to get through the twentieth century, which is not likely to be a pleasant time to live in.

Some writers, like Mr. H. G. Wells, recognising the danger which threatens civilisation, have suggested the formation of a society for mutual encouragement in the higher life. Mr. Wells developed this idea in his ' Modern

Utopia.' He contemplated a brotherhood, like the Japanese Samurai, living by a Rule, a kind of lay monastic order, who should endeavour to live in a perfectly rational and wholesome manner, so as to be the nucleus of whatever was best in the society of the time. The scheme is interesting to a Platonist, because of its resemblance to the Order of Guardians in the 'Republic.' A very good case may be made out for having an ascetic Order of moral and physical aristocrats, and entrusting them with the government of the country. Plato forbade his guardians to own wealth, and thus secured an uncorrupt administration, one of the rarest and best of virtues in a government. But political- events are not moving in this direction at present ; and the question for us is whether those who believe in science and humanism should attempt to form a society, not to rule the country, but to protect themselves and the ideas which they wish to preserve. But I agree with Mr. Wells' second thoughts, that the time is not ripe for such a scheme.[1] Christianity, ' the greatest new beginning in the world's history,' appeared, as he says, in an age of disintegration, and ' we are in a synthetic rather than a disintegrating phase. . . . *Only a very vast and terrible war-explosion can, I think, change this state of affairs.*' The vast explosion has occurred, and the stage of disintegration, which Mr. Wells ought perhaps to have seen approaching even eleven years ago, has clearly begun. But it will have to go further before the need of such a society is felt. The time may come when the educated classes, and those who desire freedom to live as they think right, will find themselves oppressed, not only in their home-life by the tyranny of the trade-unions, but in their souls by the pulpy and mawkish emotionalism of herd-morality. Then a league for mutual protection may be formed. If such a society ever comes into being, the following principles are, I think, necessary for its success. First, it must be on a religious basis, since religion has a cohesive force greater than any other bond. The religious basis will be a blend of Christian Platonism and Christian

---

[1] *First and Last Things* (pp. 148-9. Published in 1908).

Stoicism, since it must be founded on that faith in absolute spiritual values which is common to Christianity and Platonism, with that sturdy defiance of tyranny and popular folly which was the [strength of Stoicism. Next, it must not be affiliated to any religious organisation; otherwise it will certainly be exploited in denominational interests. Thirdly, it must include some purely disciplinary asceticism, such as abstinence from alcohol and tobacco for men, and from costly dresses and jewellery for women. This is necessary, because it is more important to keep out the half-hearted than to increase the number of members. Fourthly, it must prescribe a simple life of duty and discipline, since frugality will be a condition of enjoying self-respect and freedom. Fifthly, it will enjoin the choice of an open-air life in the country, where possible. A whole group of French writers, such as Proudhon, Delacroix, Leconte de Lisle, Flaubert, Leblond, and Faguet agree in attributing our social *malaise* to life in great towns. The lower death-rates of country districts are a hint from nature that they are right. Sixthly, every member must pledge himself to give his best work. As Dr. Jacks says, ' Producers of good articles respect each other ; producers of bad despise each other and hate their work.' It may be necessary for those who recognise the right of the labourer to preserve his self-respect, to combine in order to satisfy each other's needs in resistance to the trade-unions. Seventhly, there must be provision for community-life, like that of the old monasteries, for both sexes. The members of the society should be encouraged to spend some part of their lives in these institutions, without retiring from the world altogether. Temporary ' retreats ' might be of great value. Intellectual work, including scientific research, could be carried on under very favourable conditions in these lay monasteries and convents, which should contain good libraries and laboratories. Lastly, a distinctive dress, not merely a badge, would probably be essential for members of both sexes.

This last provision tempts me to add that the Government would do well to appoint at once a Royal

Commission, or, rather, two Commissions, to decide on a compulsory national uniform for both sexes. Experts should recommend the most comfortable, becoming, and economical dress that could be devised, with considerable variety for the different trades and professions. Such a law would do more for social equality than any readjustment of taxation. It has been often noticed that every man looks a gentleman in khaki ; and it is to be feared that many war brides have suffered a painful surprise on seeing their husbands for the first time in civilian garb. There need be no suggestion of militarism about the new costume ; but a man's calling might be recorded, like the name of his regiment, on his shoulder-straps, and the absence of such a badge would be regarded as a disgrace, whether the subject was a tramp or one of the idle rich. This suggestion may seem trivial, or even ludicrous ; and I may be reminded of my dislike of meddling legislation ; but the importance of the philosophy of clothes has not diminished since 'Sartor Resartus.' Clerical dignitaries might be trusted to vote for this mitigation of their lot.

Some may wonder why I have not expressed a hope that the guardianship of our intellectual and spiritual birthright may pass into the hands of the National Church. I heartily wish that I could cherish this hope. But organised religion has been a failure ever since the first concordat between Church and State under Constantine the Great. The Church of England in its corporate capacity has never seemed to respect anything but organised force. In the sixteenth century it proclaimed Henry VIII the Supreme Head of the Church ; in the seventeenth century it passionately upheld the 'right divine of kings to govern wrong ' ; in the eighteenth and nineteenth it was the obsequious supporter of the squirearchy and plutocracy ; and now it grovels before the working-man, and supports every scheme of plundering the minority. In fact, we must distinguish sharply between ecclesiasticism, theology, and religion. The future of ecclesiasticism is a political question. In the opinion of some good judges, the acute nationalism now dominant in Europe will quickly pass away, and a duel will supervene between the ' Black

International ' and the ' Red.' Catholicism, it is supposed, will shelter all who dread revolution and all who value traditional civilisation ; its unrivalled organisation will make it the one possible centre of resistance to anarchy and barbarism, and the conflict will go on till one side or the other is overthrown. This prediction, which opens a truly appalling prospect for civilisation, might be less terrible if the Church were to open its arms to a new Renaissance, and become once more, as in the beginning of the modern period, the home of learning and the patroness of the arts. But we must not overlook the new and growing power of science ; and science can no more make terms with Catholic ecclesiasticism than with the Revolution. The Jacobins guillotined Lavoisier, ' having no need of chemists ' ; but the Church burnt Bruno and imprisoned Galileo. Science, too strong to be victimised again, may come between the two enemies of civilisation, the Bolshevik and the Ultramontane ; it is, I think, our best hope.

I am conscious that I have spoken with too little sympathy in one or two of these essays about the Ritualist party. I was more afraid of it a few years ago than I am now. The Oxford movement began as a late wave of the Romantic movement, with wistful eyes bent upon the past. But Romanticism, which dotes on ruins, shrinks from real restoration. Medievalism is attractive only when seen from a short distance. So the movement is ceasing to be either medieval or Catholic or Anglican ; it is becoming definitely Latin. But a Latin Church in England which disowns the Pope is an absurdity. Many of the shrewder High Churchmen are, as I have said in this volume, throwing themselves into political agitation and intrigue, for which Catholics always have a great aptitude ; but this involves them in another inconsistency. For Catholicism is essentially hierarchical and undemocratic, though it keeps a ' career open to the talents.' The spirit of Catholicism breathes in the Third Canto of the ' Paradiso,' where Dante asks the soul of a friend whom he finds in the lowest circle of Paradise, whether he does not desire to go higher. The friend replies : ' Brother, the force of charity quiets our will, making us wish only for what we have and thirst for nothing more. If we desired to be in a sublimer sphere, our desires would be discordant with the will of Him who here allots us our diverse stations. . . . The manner in which we are ranged from step to step in this kingdom pleases the whole kingdom, as it does the King who gives us the power to will as He wills.' Accordingly, these ecclesiastical votaries of democracy cut a strange figure when they seek to legislate for the Church. The High Church scheme (defeated the other day by a small majority) for drawing up a constitution for the Church, consisted in disfranchising the large majority of the electorate and reserving the initiative and veto for the House of Lords (the Bishops). In fact, the constitution which our Catholic democrats would like best for the Church closely resembles that of Great Britain before the first Reform Bill. In the same way the ritualistic clergy, while professing a superstitious reverence for the episcopal office, make a point of flouting the authority of their own bishop. The movement, in my opinion, is beginning to break up, and Rome will be the chief gainer. But many of its leaders have been among the glories of the Church of England, and I could never speak of them with disrespect.

Catholicism, whether Roman or Anglican, stands to lose heavily by the decay of institutionalism as an article of faith. It is becoming impossible for those who mix at all with their fellow-men to believe that the grace of God is distributed denominationally. The Christian virtues, so far as we can see, flower impartially in the souls of Catholic and Protestant, of Churchman and Schismatic, of Orthodox and Heretic. And the test, ' by their fruits ye shall know them,' cannot be openly rejected by any Christian. But fanatical institutionalism has been the driving force of Catholicism as a power in the world, from the very first. The Church has lived by its monopolies and conquered by its intolerance. The war has given a further impetus to the fall of this belief, which, with its dogma, *Extra ecclesiam nulla salus*, was tottering before the crisis came.

The prospects of Christian theology are very difficult to estimate ; and I am so convinced myself of the superiority of the Catholic theology based on Neoplatonism, that I cannot view the matter with impartial detachment. We all tend to predict the triumph of our own opinions. But miracles must, I am convinced, be relegated to the sphere of pious opinion. It is not likely, perhaps, that the progress of science will increase the difficulty of believing them; but it can never again be possible to make the truths of religion depend on physical portents having taken place as recorded. The Christian revelation can stand without them, and the rulers of the Church will soon have to recognise that in very many minds it does stand without them.

I have already indicated what I believe to be the essential parts of that revelation. Whether it will be believed by a larger number of persons a hundred years hence than to-day depends, I suppose, on whether the nation will be in a more healthy condition than it is now. The chief rival to Christianity is secularism; and this creed has some bitter disappointments in store for its worshippers. I cannot help hoping that the human race, having taken in succession every path except the right one, may pay more attention to the narrow way that leadeth unto life. In morals, the Church will undoubtedly have a hard battle to fight. The younger generation has discarded all *tabus*, and in matters of sex we must be prepared for a period of unbridled license. But such lawlessness brings about its own cure by arousing disgust and shame; and the institution of marriage is far too deeply rooted to be in any danger from the revolution.

I have, I suppose, made it clear that I do not consider myself specially fortunate in having been born in 1860, and that I look forward with great anxiety to the journey through life which my children will have to make. But, after all, we judge our generation mainly by its surface currents. There may be in progress a storage of beneficent forces which we cannot see. There are ages of sowing and ages of reaping: the brilliant epochs may be those in which spiritual wealth is squandered, the epochs of apparent decline may be those in which the race is recuperating after an exhausting effort. To all appearance, man has

D

still a great part of his long lease before him, and there is no reason to suppose that the future will be less productive of moral and spiritual triumphs than the past. The source of all good is like an inexhaustible river; the Creator pours forth new treasures of goodness, truth, and beauty for all who will love them and take them. ' Nothing that truly *is* can ever perish,' as Plotinus says; whatever has value in God's sight is safe for evermore. Our half-real world is the factory of souls, in which we are tried, as in a furnace. We are not to set our hopes upon it, but to learn such wisdom as it can teach us while we pass through it. I will therefore end these thoughts on our present discontents with two messages of courage and confidence, one from Chaucer, the other from Blake.

> That thee is sent, receyve in buxomnesse,
> The wrastling for this worlde axeth a fall.
> Her is non hoom, her nis but wildernesse:
> Forth, pilgrim, forth! Forth, beste, out of thy stall!
> Know thy contree, look up, thank God of all:
> Weyve thy lust, and let thy gost thee lede;
> And trouthe shall delivere, it is no drede.

And this:—

> Joy and woe are woven fine,
> A clothing for the soul divine;
> Under every grief and pine
> Runs a joy with silken twine.
> It is right it should be so;
> Man was made for joy and woe;
> And when this we rightly know
> Safely through the world we go.

# PATRIOTISM

## (1915)

THE sentiment of patriotism has seemed to many to mark an arrest of development in the psychical expansion of the individual, a half-way house between mere self-centredness and full human sympathy. Some moralists have condemned it as pure egoism, magnified and disguised. 'Patriotism,' says Ruskin, 'is an absurd prejudice founded on an extended selfishness.' Mr. Grant Allen calls it 'a vulgar vice—the national or collective form of the monopolist instinct.' Mr. Havelock Ellis allows it to be 'a virtue—among barbarians.' For Herbert Spencer it is 'reflex egoism—extended selfishness.' These critics have made the very common mistake of judging human emotions and sentiments by their roots instead of by their fruits. They have forgotten the Aristotelian canon that the 'nature' of anything is its completed development (ἡ φύσις τέλος ἐστιν). The human self, as we know it, is a transitional form. It had a humble origin, and is capable of indefinite enhancement. Ultimately, we are what we love and care for, and no limit has been set to what we may become without ceasing to be ourselves. The case is the same with our love of country. No limit has been set to what our country may come to mean for us, without ceasing to be our country. Marcus Aurelius exhorted himself—'The poet says, Dear city of Cecrops; shall not I say, Dear city of God?' But the city of God in which he wished to be was a city in which he would still live as 'a Roman and an Antonine.' The citizen of heaven knew that it was his duty to 'hunt Sarmatians' on earth, though he was not obliged to imbrue his hands with 'Cæsarism.'

Patriotism has two roots, the love of clan and the love of home. In migratory tribes the former alone counts; in settled communities diversities of origin are often forgotten. But the love of home, as we know it, is a gentler and more spiritual bond than clanship. The word home is associated with all that makes life beautiful and sacred, with tender memories of joy and sorrow, and especially with the first eager outlook of the young mind upon a wonderful world. A man does not as a rule feel much sentiment about his London house, still less about his office or factory. It is for the home of his childhood, or of his ancestors, that a man will fight most readily, because he is bound to it by a spiritual and poetic tie. Expanding from this centre, the sentiment of patriotism embraces one's country as a whole.

Both forms of patriotism—the local and the racial, are frequently alloyed with absurd, unworthy or barbarous motives. The local patriot thinks that Peebles, and not Paris, is the place for pleasure, or asks whether any good thing can come out of Nazareth. To the Chinaman all aliens are 'outer barbarians' or 'foreign devils.' Admiration for ourselves and our institutions is too often measured by our contempt and dislike for foreigners. Our own nation has a peculiarly bad record in this respect. In the reign of James I the Spanish ambassador was frequently insulted by the London crowd, as was the Russian ambassador in 1662; not, apparently, because we had a burning grievance against either of those nations, but because Spaniards and Russians are very unlike Englishmen. That at least is the opinion of the sagacious Pepys on the later of these incidents. 'Lord! to see the absurd nature of Englishmen, that cannot forbear laughing and jeering at anything that looks strange.' Defoe says that the English are ' the most churlish people alive ' to foreigners, with the result that ' all men think an Englishman the devil.' In the 17th and 18th centuries Scotland seems to have ranked as a foreign country, and the presence of Scots in London was much resented. Cleveland thought it witty to write :—

> Had Cain been Scot, God would have changed his doom ;
> Not forced him wander, but confined him home.

And we all remember Dr. Johnson's gibes.

British patriotic arrogance culminated in the 18th and in the first half of the 19th century ; in Lord Palmerston it found a champion at the head of the government. Goldsmith describes the bearing of the Englishman of his day :—

> Pride in their port, defiance in their eye,
> I see the lords of human kind pass by.

Michelet found in England 'human pride personified in a people,' at a time when the characteristic of Germany was 'a profound impersonality.' It may be doubted whether even the arrogant brutality of the modern Prussian is more offensive to foreigners than was the calm and haughty assumption of superiority by our countrymen at this time. Our grandfathers and great-grandfathers were quite of Milton's opinion, that, when the Almighty wishes something unusually great and difficult to be done, He entrusts it to His Englishmen. This unamiable characteristic was probably much more the result of insular ignorance than of a deep-seated pride. 'A generation or two ago,' said Mr. Asquith lately, 'patriotism was largely fed and fostered upon reciprocal ignorance and contempt.' The Englishman seriously believed that the French subsisted mainly upon frogs, while the Frenchman was equally convinced that the sale of wives at Smithfield was one of our national institutions. This fruitful source of international misunderstanding has become less dangerous since the facilities of foreign travel have been increased. But in the relations of Europe with alien and independent civilisations, such as that of China, we still see brutal arrogance and vulgar ignorance producing their natural results.

Another cause of perverted patriotism is the inborn pugnacity of the *bête humaine.* Our species is the most cruel and destructive of all that inhabit this planet. If the lower animals, as we call them, were able to formulate a religion, they might differ greatly as to the shape of the beneficent Creator, but they would nearly all agree that the devil must be very like a big white man.  Mr. McDougall [1] has lately raised the question whether civilised man is less pugnacious than the savage ; and he answers it in the negative.  The Europeans, he thinks, are among the most combative of the human race.  We are not allowed to knock each other on the head during peace ; but our civilisation is based on cut-throat competition ; our favourite games are mimic battles, which I suppose effect for us a ' purgation of the emotions ' similar to that which Aristotle attributed to witnessing the performance of a tragedy : and, when the fit seizes us, we are ready to engage in wars which cannot fail to be disastrous to both combatants. Mr. McDougall does not regret this disposition, irrational though it is.  He thinks that it tends to the survival of the fittest, and that, if we substitute emulation for pugnacity, which on other grounds might seem an unmixed advantage, we shall have to call in the science of eugenics to save us from becoming as sheeplike as the Chinese.  There is, however, another side to this question, as we shall see presently.

Another instinct which has supplied fuel to patriotism of the baser sort is that of acquisitiveness.  This tendency, without which even the most rudimentary civilisation would be impossible, began when the female of the species, instead of carrying her baby on her back and following the male to his hunting-grounds, made some sort of a lair for herself and her family, where primitive implements and stores of food could be kept.  There are still tribes in Brazil which have not reached this first step towards humanisation.  But the instinct of hoarding, like all other instincts, tends to become hypertrophied and perverted ; and with the institution of private property comes another institution—that of plunder and brigandage.  In private life, no motive of action is at present so powerful and so persistent as acquisitiveness, which, unlike most other desires, knows no satiety.  The average man is rich

[1] In his *Introduction to Social Psychology.*

enough when he has a little more than he has got, and not till then. The acquisition and possession of land satisfies this desire in a high degree, since land is a visible and indestructible form of property. Consequently, as soon as the instincts of the individual are transferred to the group, territorial aggrandisement becomes a main pre-occupation of the state. This desire was the chief cause of wars, while kings and nobles regarded the territories over which they ruled as their private estates. Wherever despotic or feudal conditions survive, such ideas are likely still to be found, and to cause dangers to other states. The greatest ambition of a modern emperor is still to be com-memorated as a 'Mehrer des Reichs.'

Capitalism, by separating the idea of property from any necessary connection with landed estate, and democracy, by denying the whole theory on which dynastic wars of conquest are based, have both contributed to check this, perhaps the worst kind of war. It would, however, be a great error to suppose that the instinct of acquisitiveness, in its old and barbarous form, has lost its hold upon even the most civilised nations. When an old-fashioned brigand appears, and puts himself at the head of his nation, he be-comes at once a popular hero. By any rational standard of morality, few greater scoundrels have lived than Frederick the Great and Napoleon I. But they are still names to conjure with. Both were men of singularly lucid intel-lect and entirely medieval ambitions. Their great achievement was to show how under modern conditions aggressive war may be carried on without much loss (except in human life) to the aggressor. They tore up all the conventions which regulated the conduct of warfare, and reduced it to sheer brigandage and terrorism. And now, after a hundred years, we see these methods deliberately revived by the greatest military power in the world, and applied with the same ruthlessness and with an added pedantry which makes them more inhuman. The per-petrators of the crime calculated quite correctly that they need fear no reluctance on the part of the nation, no qualms of conscience, no compassionate shrinking, no remorse. It must, indeed, be a bad cause that cannot count on the

support of the large majority of the people at the *beginning*
of a war. Pugnacity, greed, mere excitement, the con-
tagion of a crowd, will fill the streets of almost any capital
with a shouting and jubilant mob on the day after a war
has been declared.

And yet the motives which we have enumerated are
plainly atavistic and pathological. They belong to a
mental condition which would conduct an individual to
the prison or the gallows. We do not argue seriously
whether the career of the highwayman or burglar is
legitimate and desirable ; and it is impossible to maintain that what is disgraceful for the individual is
creditable for the state. And apart from the consideration that predatory patriotism deforms its own idol and
makes it hateful in the eyes of the world, subsequent history
has fully confirmed the moral instinct of the ancient Greeks,
that national insolence or injustice (ὕβρις) brings its own
severe punishment. The imaginary dialogue which Thucydides puts into the mouth of the Athenian and Melian envoys,
and the debate in the Athenian Assembly about the punishment of revolted Mitylene, are intended to prepare the
reader for the tragic fate of the Sicilian expedition. The
same writer describes the break-up of all social morality
during the civil war in words which seem to herald the
destruction not only of Athens but of Greek freedom.
Machiavelli's ' Prince ' shows how history can repeat itself,
reiterating its lesson that a nation which gives itself
to immoral aggrandisement is far on the road to disintegration. Seneca's rebuke to his slave-holding countrymen, ' Can you complain that you have been robbed of
the liberty which you have yourselves abolished in your
own homes ? ' applies equally to nations which have enslaved or exploited the inhabitants of subject lands. If
the Roman Empire had a long and glorious life, it was
because its methods were liberal, by the standard of ancient
times. In so far as Rome abused her power, she suffered
the doom of all tyrants.

The illusions of imperialism have been made clearer
than ever by the course of modern history. Attempts to
destroy a nationality by overthrowing its government,

proscribing its language, and maltreating its citizens, are never successful. The experiment has been tried with great thoroughness in Poland ; and the Poles are now more of a nation than they were under the oppressive feudal system which existed before the partitions. Our own empire would be a ludicrous failure if it were any part of our ambition to Anglicise other races. The only English parts of the empire were waste lands which we have peopled with our own emigrants. We hauled down the French flag in Canada, with the result that Eastern Canada is now the only flourishing French colony, and the only part of the world where the French race increases rapidly. We have helped the Dutch to multiply with almost equal rapidity in South Africa. We have added several millions to the native population of Egypt, and over a hundred millions to the population of India. Similarly, the Americans have made Cuba for the first time a really Spanish island, by driving out its incompetent Spanish governors and so attracting immigrants from Spain. On the whole, in imperialism nothing fails like success. If the conqueror oppresses his subjects, they will become fanatical patriots, and sooner or later have their revenge ; if he treats them well, and ' governs them for their good,' they will multiply faster than their rulers, till they claim their independence. The Englishman now says, ' I am quite content to have it so ' ; but that is not the old imperialism.

The notion that frequent war is a healthy tonic for a nation is scarcely tenable. Its dysgenic effect, by eliminating the strongest and healthiest of the population, while leaving the weaklings at home to be the fathers of the next generation, is no new discovery. It has been supported by a succession of men, such as Tenon, Dufau, Foissac, de Lapouge, and Richet in France ; Tiedemann and Seeck in Germany ; Guerrini in Italy ; Kellogg and Starr Jordan in America. The case is indeed overwhelming. The lives destroyed in war are nearly all males, thus disturbing the sex equilibrium of the population ; they are in the prime of life, at the age of greatest fecundity ; and they are picked from a list out of which from 20 to

30 per cent. have been rejected for physical unfitness. It seems to be proved that the children born in France during the Napoleonic wars were poor and undersized—30 millimetres below the normal height. War combined with religious celibacy to ruin Spain. ' Castile makes men and wastes them,' said a Spanish writer. ' This sublime and terrible phrase sums up the whole of Spanish history.' Schiller was right ; ' Immer der Krieg verschlingt die besten.' We in England have suffered from this drain in the past ; we shall suffer much more in the next generation.

> We have fed our sea for a thousand years,
>   And she calls us, still unfed,
> Though there's never a wave of all her waves
>   But marks our English dead.

> We have strawed our best to the weed's unrest,
>   To the shark and the sheering gull,
> If blood be the price of admiralty,
>   Lord God, we ha' paid in full.

Aggressive patriotism is thus condemned by common sense and the verdict of history no less than by morality. We are entitled to say to the militarists what Socrates said to Polus :

This doctrine of yours has now been examined and found wanting. And this doctrine alone has stood the test—that we ought to be more afraid of doing than of suffering wrong ; and that the prime business of every man [and nation] is not to seem good, but to be good, in all private and public dealings.

If the nations would render something more than lip-service to this principle, the abolition of war would be within sight ; for, as Ruskin says, echoing the judgment of the Epistle of St. James, ' The first reason for all wars, and for the necessity of national defences, is that the majority of persons, high and low, in all European countries, are thieves.' But it must be remembered that, in spite of the proverb, it takes in reality only one to make a quarrel. It is useless for the sheep to pass resolutions in

favour of vegetarianism, while the wolf remains of a different
opinion.

Our own conversion to pacificism, though sincere, is
somewhat recent. Our literature does not reflect it.
Bacon is frankly militarist :

Above all, for empire and greatness, it importeth most, that
a nation do profess arms, as their principal honour, study, and
occupation. For the things which we formerly have spoken
of are but habilitations towards arms ; and what is habilitation
without intention and act ? . . . It is so plain that a man
profiteth in that he most intendeth, that it needeth not to be
stood upon. It is enough to point at it ; that no nation, which
doth not directly profess arms, may look to have greatness fall
into their mouths.

A state, therefore, ' ought to have those laws or customs,
which may reach forth unto them just occasions of war.'
Shakespeare's ' Henry V ' has been not unreasonably
recommended by the Germans as ' good war-reading.'
It would be easy to compile a *catena* of bellicose maxims
from our literature, reaching down to the end of the 19th
century. The change is perhaps due less to progress in
morality than to that political good sense which has again
and again steered our ship through dangerous rocks. But
there has been some real advance, in all civilised countries.
We do not find that men talked about the ' bankruptcy
of Christianity ' during the Napoleonic campaigns. Even
the Germans think it necessary to tell each other that it
was Belgium who began this war.

But, though pugnacity and acquisitiveness have been
the real foundation of much miscalled patriotism, better
motives are generally mingled with these primitive
instincts. It is the subtle blend of noble and ignoble
sentiment which makes patriotism such a difficult problem
for the moralist. The patriot nearly always believes, or
thinks he believes, that he desires the greatness of his
country because his country stands for something intrin-
sically great and valuable. Where this conviction is absent
we cannot speak of patriotism, but only of the cohesion
of a wolf-pack. The Greeks, who at last perished because
they could not combine, had nevertheless a consciousness

that they were the trustees of civilisation against barbarism ; and in their day of triumph over the Persians they were filled, for a time, with an almost Jewish awe in presence of the righteous judgment of God. The ' Persæ ' of Æschylus is one of the noblest of patriotic poems. The Romans, a harder and coarser race, had their ideal of *virtus* and *gravitas*, which included simplicity of life, dignity and self-restraint, honesty and industry, and devotion to the state. They rightly felt that these qualities constituted a vocation to empire. There was much harshness and injustice in Roman imperialism ; but what nobler epitaph could even the British empire desire than the tribute of Claudian, when the weary Titan was at last stricken and dying :

> Hæc est, in gremium victos quæ sola recepit,
> humanumque genus communi nomine fovit
> matris non dominæ ritu, civesque vocavit
> quos domuit, nexuque pio longinqua revinxit ?

Jewish patriotism was of a different kind. A federation of fierce Bedouin tribes, encamped amid hostile populations, and set in the cockpit of rival empires against which it was impossible to stand, the Israelites were hammered by misfortune into the most indestructible of all organisms, a theocracy. Their religion was to them what, in a minor degree, Roman Catholicism has been to Ireland and Poland, a consecration of patriotic faith and hope. Westphal says the Jews failed because they hated foreigners more than they loved God. They have had good reason to hate foreigners. But undoubtedly the effect of their hatred has been that the great gifts which their nation had to give to humanity have come through other hands, and so have evoked no gratitude. In the first century of our era they were called to an almost superhuman abnegation of their inveterate nationalism, and they could not rise to it. As almost every other nation would have done, they chose the lower patriotism instead of the higher ; and it was against their will that the religion of civilised humanity grew out of Hebrew soil. But they gained this by their choice, tragic though it was, that they have stood by the graves of all the empires that oppressed them, and have preserved their racial integrity and traditions in the most adverse circumstances. The history of the Jews also shows that oppression and persecution are far more efficacious in binding a nation together than community of interest and national prosperity. Increase of wealth divides rather than unites a people ; but suffering shared in common binds it together with hoops of steel.

The Jews were the only race whose spiritual independence was not crushed by the Roman steam-roller. It would be unfair to say that Rome destroyed nations ; for her subjects in the West were barbarous tribes, and in the East she displaced monarchies no less alien to their subjects than her own rule. But she prevented the growth of nationalities, as it is to be feared we have done in India ; and the absence of sturdy independence in the countries round the Mediterranean, especially in the Greek-speaking provinces, made the final downfall inevitable; The lesson has its warning for modern theorists who wish to obliterate the sentiment of nationality, the revival of which, after a long eclipse, has been one of the achievements of modern civilisation. For it was not till long after the destruction of the Western Roman Empire that nationality began to assume its present importance in Europe.

The transition from medieval to modern history is most strongly marked by the emergence of this principle, with all that it involves. At the end of the Middle Ages Europe was at last compelled to admit that the grand idea of an universal state and an universal church had definitely broken down. Hitherto it had been assumed that behind all national disputes lay a *ius gentium* by which all were bound, and that behind all religious questions lay the authority of the Roman Catholic Church, from which there was no appeal. The modern period which certainly does not represent the last word of civilisation, has witnessed the abandonment of these ideas. The change took place gradually. France became a nation when the English raids ceased in the middle of the 15th century. Spain achieved unity a generation later by the union of Castile and Aragon and the expulsion of the Moors from the peninsula. Holland found herself in the heroic struggle against Spain in the 16th century. But the practice of conducting wars by hiring foreign mercenaries, a sure sign that the nationalist spirit is weak, continued till much later. And the dynastic principle, which is the very negation of nationalism, actually culminated in the 18th century; and this is the true explanation of the feeble resistance which Europe offered to the French revolutionary armies, until Napoleon stirred up the dormant spirit of nationalism in the peoples whom he plundered. 'In the old European system,' says Lord Acton, 'the rights of nationalities were neither recognised by governments nor asserted by the people. The interests of the reigning families, not those of the nations, regulated the frontiers; and the administration was conducted generally without any reference to popular desires.' Marriage or conquest might unite the most diverse nations under one sovereign, such as Charles V.

While such ideas prevailed, the suppression of a nation did not seem hateful; the partition of Poland evoked few protests at the time, though perhaps few acts of injustice have recoiled with greater force on the heads of their perpetrators than this is likely to do. Poles have been and are among the bitterest enemies of autocracy, and the strongest advocates of republicanism and racialism, in all parts of the world. The French Revolution opened a new era for nationalism, both directly and indirectly. The deposition of the Bourbons was a national act which might be a precedent for other oppressed peoples. And when the Revolution itself began to trample on the rights of other nations, an uprising took place, first in Spain and then in Prussia, which proved too strong for the tyrant. The apostasy of France from her own ideals of liberty proved the futility of mere doctrines, like those of Rousseau, and compelled the peoples to arm themselves and win their freedom by the sword. The national militarism of Prussia was the direct consequence of her humiliation at Jena and Auerstädt, and of the harsh terms imposed upon her at Tilsit. It is true that the Congress of Vienna attempted to revive the old dynastic system. But for the steady opposition of England, the clique of despots might have reimposed the old yoke upon their subjects. The settlement of 1815 also left the entire centre of Europe in a state of chaos ; and it was only by slow degrees that Italy and Germany attained national unity. Poland, the Austrian Empire, and the Balkan States still remain in a condition to trouble the peace of the world. In Austria-Hungary the clash of the dynastic and the nationalist ideas is strident ; and every citizen of that empire has to choose between a wider and a narrower allegiance.

Europeans are, in fact, far from having made up their minds as to what is the organic whole towards which patriotic sentiment ought to be directed. Socialism agrees with despotism in saying, ' It is the political aggregate, the state,' however much they may differ as to how the state should be administered. For this reason militarism and state-socialism might at any time come to terms. They are at one in exaggerating the ' organic ' unity of a political or geographical *enclave ;* and they are at one in depreciating the value of individual liberty. Loyalty to ' the state ' instead of to ' king and country ' is not an easy or a natural emotion. The state is a bloodless abstraction, which as a rule only materialises as a drill-sergeant or a tax-collector. Enthusiasm for it, and not only for what can be got out of it, does not extend much beyond the Fabian Society. Cæsarism has the great advantage of a visible head, as well as of its appeal to very old and strong thought-habits ; and accordingly, in any national crisis, loyalty to the War-lord is likely to show unexpected strength, and doctrinaire socialism unexpected weakness.

But devotion to the head of the state in his representative capacity is a different thing from the old feudal loyalty. It is far more impersonal ; the ruler, whether an individual or a council, is reverenced as a non-human and non-moral embodiment of the national power, a sort of Platonic idea of coercive authority. This kind of loyalty may very easily be carried too far. In reality, we are members of a great many ' social organisms,' each of which has indefeasible claims upon us. Our family, our circle of acquaintance, our business or profession, our church, our country, the comity of civilised nations, humanity at large, are all social organisms ; and some of the chief problems of ethics are concerned with the adjustment of their conflicting claims. To make any one of these absolute is destructive of morality. But militarism and socialism deliberately make the state absolute. In internal affairs this may lead to the ruthless oppression of individuals or whole classes ; in external relations it produces wars waged with ' methods of barbarism.' The whole idea of the state as an organism, which has been emphasised by social reformers as a theoretical refutation of selfish individualism, rests on the abuse of a metaphor. The bond between the dwellers in the same political area is far less close than that between the organs of a living body. Every man has a life of his own, and some purely personal rights ; he has, moreover, moral links with other human associations, outside his own country, and important moral duties towards them. No one who reflects on the solidarity of interests among capitalists, among hand-workers, or, in a different way, among scholars and artists, all over the world, can fail to see that the apotheosis of the state, whether in the interest of war or of revolution, is an anachronism and an absurdity.

A very different basis for patriotic sentiment is furnished by the scientific or pseudo-scientific theories about race, which have become very popular in our time. When the history of ideas in the 20th century comes to be written, it is certain that among the causes of this great war will be named the belief of the Germans in the superiority of their own race, based on certain historical and ethnological theories which have acted like a heady wine in stimulating the spirit of aggression among them. The theory, stated briefly, is that the shores of the Baltic are the home of the finest human type that has yet existed, a type distinguished by blond hair, great physical strength, unequalled mental vigour and ability, superior morality, and an innate aptitude for governing and improving inferior races. Unfortunately for the world, this noble stock cannot flouri h for very long in climates unlike its own ; but from

the earliest historical times it has ' swarmed ' periodically,
subjugating the feebler peoples of the south, and elevating
them for a time above the level which they were naturally
fitted to reach.  Wherever we find marked energy and
nobleness of character, we may suspect Aryan blood ; and
history will usually support our surmise.  Among the
great men who were certainly or probably Germans were
Agamemnon, Julius Cæsar, the Founder of Christianity,
Dante, and Shakespeare.  The blond Nordic giant is ful-
filling his mission by conquering and imposing his culture
upon other races.  They ought to be grateful to him for
the service, especially as it has a sacrificial aspect, the
lower types having, at least in their own climates, greater
power of survival.

This fantastic theory has been defended in a large
number of German books, of which the ' Foundations of
the Nineteenth Century,' by the renegade Englishman
Houston Chamberlain, is the most widely known.  The
objections to it are numerous.  It is notorious that until
the invention of gunpowder the settled and civilised peoples
of Europe were in frequent danger from bands of hardier
mountaineers, forest-dwellers, or pastoral nomads, who
generally came from the north.  But the formidable fighting powers of these marauders were no proof of intrinsic
superiority.  In fact, the most successful of these con-
querors, if success is measured by the amount of territory
overrun and subdued, were not the ' great blond beasts '
of Nietszche, but yellow monsters with black hair, the Huns
and Tartars.[1]  The causes of Tartar ascendancy had not
the remotest connection with any moral or intellectual
qualities which we can be expected to admire.  Nor can
the Nordic race, well endowed by nature as it undoubtedly
is, prove such a superiority as this theory claims for it.
Some of the largest brains yet measured have been those
of Japanese ; and the Jews have probably a higher average
of ability than the Teutons.  Again, the Germans are not

---

[1] The reasons of their irresistible strength have been explained
in a most brilliant manner by Dr. Peisker in the first volume of the
' Cambridge Medieval History.'

descended from a pure Nordic stock. The Northern type
can be best studied in Scandinavia, where the people share
with the Irish the distinction of being the handsomest
race in the world. The German is a mixture of various
anatomical types, including, in some parts, distinct traces
of Mongolian blood, which indicate that the raiding Huns
meddled, according to their custom, with the German
women, and bequeathed to a section of the nation the
Turanian cheek-bones, as well as certain moral characteristics. Lastly, the German race has never shown much
aptitude for governing and assimilating other peoples.
The French, by virtue of their greater sympathy, are far
more successful.

The French have their own form of this pseudo-science
in their doctrine of the persistence of national characteristics. Each nation may be summed up in a formula :
England, for example, is ' the country of will.' A few
instances may, no doubt, be quoted in support of this
theory. Julius Cæsar said : ' Duas res plerasque Gallia
industriosissime prosequitur, rem militarem et argute
loqui ' ; and these are still the characteristics of our gallant
allies. And Madame de Staël may be thought to have
hit off the German character very cleverly about the time
when Bismarck first saw the light. ' The Germans are
vigorously submissive. They employ philosophical reason-
ings to explain what is the least philosophic thing in the
world, respect for force and the fear which transforms that
respect into admiration.' But the fact remains that the
characters of nations frequently change, or rather that what
we call national character is usually only the policy of the
governing class, forced upon it by circumstances, or the
manner of living which climate, geographical position,
and other external causes have made necessary for the
inhabitants of a country.

To found patriotism on homogeneity of race is no wiser
than to bound it by frontier lines. As the Abbé Noël has
lately written about his own country, Belgium,

the race is not the nation. The nation is not a physiological
fact ; it is a moral fact. What constitutes a nation is the community of sentiments and ideals which results from a common

history and education. The variations of the cephalic index
are here of no great importance. The essential factor of the
national consciousness resides in a certain common mode of
conceiving the conditions of the social life.

Belgium, the Abbé maintains, has found this national
consciousness amid her sufferings ; there are no longer
any distinctions between French-speaking Belgians and
Walloons or Flemings. This is in truth the real basis
of patriotism. It is the basis of our own love for our
country. What Britain stands for is what Britain is.
We have long known in our hearts what Britain stands
for ; but we have now been driven to search our thoughts
and make our ideals explicit to ourselves and others.
The Englishman has become a philosopher *malgré lui*.
'Whatever the world thinks,' writes Bishop Berkeley,
'he who hath not much meditated upon God, the human
soul, and the *summum bonum*, may possibly make a thriving
earthworm, but will most indubitably make a sorry patriot
and a sorry statesman.' These words, which were quoted
by Mr. Arthur Balfour a few years ago, may seem to make
a large demand on the average citizen ; but in our quiet
way we have all been meditating on these things since
last August, and we know pretty well what our *summum
bonum* is for our country. We believe in chivalry and
fair play and kindliness—these things first and foremost ;
and we believe, if not exactly in democracy, yet in a government under which a man may think and speak the thing
he wills. We do not believe in war, and we do not believe
in bullying. We do not flatter ourselves that we are the
supermen ; but we are convinced that the ideas which we
stand for, and which we have on the whole tried to carry
out, are essential to the peaceful progress and happiness
of humanity ; and for these ideas we have drawn the
sword. The great words of Abraham Lincoln have been
on the lips of many and in the hearts of all since the beginning of the great contest : 'With malice towards none ;
with charity for all : with firmness in the right as God
gives us to see the right—let us strive on to finish the work
we are in.'
Patriotism thus spiritualised and moralised is the true

patriotism. When the emotion is once set in its right relations to the whole of human life and to all that makes human life worth living, it cannot become an immoral obsession. It is certain to become an immoral obsession if it is isolated and made absolute. We have seen the appalling perversion—the methodical diabolism—which this obsession has produced in Germany. It has startled us because we thought that the civilised world had got beyond such insanity ; but it is of course no new thing. Machiavelli said, ' I prefer my country to the salvation of my soul '—a sentiment which sounds noble but is not ; it has only a superficial resemblance to St. Paul's willingness to be ' accursed ' for the sake of his countrymen. Devil-worship remains what it was, even when the idol is draped in the national flag. This obsession may be in part a survival from savage conditions, when all was at stake in every feud ; but chiefly it is an example of the idealising and universalising power of the imagination, which turns every unchecked passion into a monomania. The only remedy is, as Lowell's Hosea Biglow reminds us, to bear in mind that

our true country is that ideal realm which we represent to ourselves under the names of religion, duty, and the like. Our terrestrial organisations are but far-off approaches to so fair a model ; and all they are verily traitors who resist not any attempt to divert them from this their original intendment. Our true country is bounded on the north and the south, on the east and west, by Justice, and when she oversteps that invisible boundary-line by so much as a hair's breadth, she ceases to be our mother, and chooses rather to be looked upon *quasi noverca*.

So Socrates said that the wise man will be a citizen of his true city, of which the type is laid up in heaven, and only conditionally of his earthly country.

The obsession of patriotism is not the only evil which we have to consider. We may err by defect as well as by excess. Herbert Spencer speaks of an ' anti-patriotic bias ' ; and it can hardly be disputed that many Englishmen who pride themselves on their lofty morality are suffering from this mental twist. The malady seems to

belong to the Anglo-Saxon constitution, for it is rarely
encountered in other countries, while we had a noisy pro-
Napoleonic faction a hundred years ago, and the Americans
had their 'Copperheads' in the Northern States during
the civil war. In our own day, every enemy of England,
from the mad Mullah to the mad Kaiser, has had his advocates at home ; and the champions of Boer and Boxer,
of Afridi and Afrikander, of the Mahdi and the Matabele,
have been usually the same persons. The English, it
would appear, differ from other misguided rascals in never
being right even by accident. But the idiosyncrasy of a
few persons is far less important than the comparative
insensibility of whole classes to the patriotic appeal, except
when war is actually raging. This is not specially characteristic of our own country. The German Emperor
has complained of his Social Democrats as ' people without
a fatherland ' ; and the cry ' À bas la patrie ' has been
heard in France.

It is usual to explain this attitude by the fact that
the manual workers ' have no stake in the country,' and
might not find their condition altered for the worse by
subjection to a foreign power. A few of our working-
men have given colour to this charge by exclaiming
petulantly that they could not be worse off under the
Germans ; but in this they have done themselves and
their class less than justice. The anti-militarism and
cosmopolitanism of the masses in every country is a profoundly interesting fact, a problem which demands no
superficial investigation. It is one result of that emancipation from traditional ideas, which makes the most important difference between the upper and middle classes on
the one side and the lower on the other. We lament that
the working-man takes but little interest in Christianity,
and rack our brains to discover what we have done to
discredit our religion in his eyes. The truth is that
Christianity, as a dogmatic and ecclesiastical system, is
unintelligible without a very considerable knowledge of
the conditions under which it took shape. But what are
the ancient Hebrews, and the Greeks and Romans, to the
working-man ? He is simply cut off from the means of

reading intelligently any book of the Bible, or of understanding how the institution called the Catholic Church,
and its offshoots, came to exist.  As our staple education
becomes more ' modern ' and less literary, the custodians
of organised religion will find their difficulties increasing.
But the same is true about patriotism.  Love of country
means pride in the past and ambition for the future.  Those
who live only in the present are incapable of it.  But our
working-man knows next to nothing about the past history
of England ; he has scarcely heard of our great men, and
has read few of our great books.  It is not surprising that
the appeal to patriotism leaves him cold.  This is an evil
that has its proper remedy.  There is no reason why a
sane and elevated love of country should not be stimulated
by appropriate teaching in our schools.  In America this
is done—rather hysterically ;  and in Germany—rather
brutally.  The Jews have always made their national history a large part of their education, and even of their
religion.  Nothing has helped them more to retain their self-
consciousness as a nation.  Ignorance of the past and
indifference to the future usually go together.  Those who
most value our historical heritage will be most desirous to
transmit it unimpaired.

But the absence of traditional ideas is by no means
an unmixed evil.  The working-man sees more clearly
than the majority of educated persons the absurdity of
international hatred and jealousy.  He is conscious of
greater solidarity with his own class in other European
countries than with the wealthier class in his own ;  and
as he approaches the whole question without prejudice,
he cannot fail to realise how large a part of the product
of labour is diverted from useful purposes by modern
militarism.  International rivalry is in his eyes one of the
most serious obstacles to the abolition of want and misery.
Tolstoy hardly exaggerates when he says : ' Patriotism to
the peoples represents only a frightful future ; the fraternity
of nations seems an ideal more and more accessible to
humanity, and one which humanity desires.'  Military
glory has very little attraction for the working-man.  His
humanitarian instincts appear to be actually stronger than

those of the sheltered classes. To take life in any circumstances seems to him a shocking thing ; and the harsh pro-
cedure of martial law and military custom is abhorrent
to him. He sees no advantage and no credit in territorial
aggrandisement, which he suspects to be prompted mainly
by the desire to make money unjustly. He is therefore
a convinced pacificist ; though his doctrine of human
brotherhood breaks down ignominiously when he finds his
economic position threatened by the competition of cheap
foreign labour. If an armed struggle ever takes place
between the nations of Europe (or their colonists) and the
yellow races, it will be a working-man's war. But on the
whole, the best hope of getting rid of militarism may lie in
the growing power of the working class. The poor, being
intensely gregarious and very susceptible to all collective
emotions, are still liable to fits of warlike excitement. But
their real minds are at present set against an aggressive
foreign policy, without being shut against the appeals of a
higher patriotism.

And yet the irritation which is felt against preachers
of the brotherhood of man is not without justification.
Some persons who condemn patriotism are simply lacking
in public spirit, or their loyalty is monopolised by some fad
or ' cause,' which is a poor substitute for love of country.
The man who has no prejudices in favour of his own family
and his own country is generally an unamiable creature.
So we need not condemn Molière for saying, ' L'ami du
genre humain n'est pas du tout mon fait,' nor Brunetière
for declaring that ' Ni la nature ni l'histoire n'ont en effet
voulu que les hommes fussent tous frères.' But French
Neo-catholicism, a bourgeois movement directed against
all the ' ideas of 1789,' seems to have adopted the most
ferocious kind of chauvinism. M. Paul Bourget wrote
the other day in the *Écho de Paris*, ' This war must be
the first of many, since we cannot exterminate sixty-five
million Germans in a single campaign ! ' The women and
children too ! This is not the way to revive the religion
of Christ in France.

The practical question for the future is whether there is
any prospect of returning, under more favourable auspices,

to the unrealised ideal of the Middle Ages—an agreement among the nations of Europe to live amicably under one system of international law and right, binding upon all, and with the consciousness of an intellectual and spiritual unity deeper than political divisions. ' The nations are the citizens of humanity,' said Mazzini ; and so they ought to be. Some of the omens are favourable. Militarism has dug its own grave. The great powers increased their armaments till the burden became insupportable, and have now rushed into bankruptcy in the hope of shaking it off. In prehistoric times the lords of creation were certain gigantic lizards, protected by massive armour-plates which could only be carried by a creature thirty to sixty feet long. Then they died, when neither earth, air, nor water could support them any longer. Such must be the end of the European nations, unless they learn wisdom. The lesson will be brought home to them by Transatlantic competition. The United States of America had already, before this war, an initial advantage over the disunited states of Europe, amounting to at least 10 per cent. on every contract ; after the war this advantage will be doubled. It remains to be seen whether the next generation will honour the debts which we are piling up. Disraeli used to complain of what he called ' Dutch finance,' which consists in ' mortgaging the industry of the future to protect property in the present.' Pitt paid for the great war of a hundred years ago in this manner ; after a century we are still groaning under the burden of his loans. We may hear more of the iniquity of ' Dutch finance ' when the democracies of the next generation have a chance of repudiating obligations which, as they will say, they did not contract. However that may be, international rivalry is plainly very bad business ; and there are great possibilities in the Hague Tribunal, if, and only if, the signatories to the conference bind themselves to use force against a recalcitrant member. The conduct of Germany in this war has shown that public opinion is powerless to restrain a nation which feels strong enough to defy it.

Another cause which may give patriots leisure to turn their thoughts away from war's alarms is that the ' swarming ' period of the European races is coming to an end. The unparalleled increase of population in the first three quarters of the 19th century has been followed by a progressive decrease in the birth-rate, which will begin to tell upon social conditions when the reduction in the death-rate, which has hitherto kept pace with it, shall have reached its natural limit. Europe with a stationary population will be in a much happier condition ; and problems of social reform can then be tackled with some hope of success. Honourable emulation in the arts of life may then take the place of desperate competition and antagonism. Human lives will begin to have a positive value, and we may even think it fair to honour our saviours more than our destroyers. The effects of past follies will then soon be effaced ; for nations recover much more quickly from wars than from internal disorders. External injuries are rapidly cured ; but ' those wounds heal ill that men do give themselves.' The greatest obstacle to progress is not man's inherited pugnacity, but his incorrigible tendency to parasitism. The true patriot will keep his eye fixed on this, and will dread as the state's worst enemies those citizens who at the top and bottom of the social scale have no other ambition than to hang on and suck the life-blood of the nation. Great things may be hoped from the new science of eugenics, when it has passed out of its tentative and experimental stage.

In the distant future we may reasonably hope that patriotism will be a sentiment like the loyalty which binds a man to his public school and university, an affection purged of all rancour and jealousy, a stimulus to all honourable conduct and noble effort, a part of the poetry of life. It is so already to many of us, and has been so to the noblest Englishmen since we have had a literature. If Henry V's speech at Agincourt is the splendid gasconade of a royal freebooter, there is no false ring in the scene where John of Gaunt takes leave of his banished son ; nor in Sir Walter Scott's ' Breathes there a man with soul so dead,' etc. ' If I forget thee, O Jerusalem, let my right hand forget her cunning.' We cannot quite manage to substitute London for Zion in singing psalms, though there are some places in England—Eton, Winchester, Oxford, Cambridge—which do evoke these feelings. These emotions of loyalty and devotion are by no means to be checked or despised. They have an infinite potency for good. In spiritual things there is no conflict between intensity and expansion. The deepest sympathy is, potentially, also the widest. He who loves not his home and country which he has seen, how shall he love humanity in general which he has not seen? There are, after all, few emotions of which one has less reason to be ashamed than the little lump in the throat which the Englishman feels when he first catches sight of the white cliffs of Dover.

# THE BIRTH-RATE

## (1917)

THE numbers of every species are determined, not by the procreative power of its members, which always greatly exceeds the capacity of the earth to support a progeny increasing in geometrical progression, but by two factors, the activity of its enemies and the available supply of food. Those species which survive owe their success in the struggle for existence mainly to one of two qualities, enormous fertility or parental care. The female cod spawns about 6,000,000 eggs at a time, of which at most one-third—perhaps much less—are afterwards fertilised. An infinitesimal proportion of these escapes being devoured by fish or fowl. An insect-eating bird is said to require for its support about 250,000 insects a year, and the number of such birds must amount to thousands of millions. As a rule there is a kind of equilibrium between the forces of destruction and of reproduction. If a species is nearly exterminated by its enemies, those enemies lose their food-supply and perish themselves. In some sheltered spot the survivors of the victims remain and increase till they begin to send out colonies again. In some species, such as the mice in La Plata, and the beasts and birds which devour them, there is an alternation of increase and decrease, to be accounted for in this way. But permanent disturbances of equilibrium sometimes occur. The rabbit in Australia, having found a virgin soil, multiplied for some time almost up to the limit of its natural fertility and is firmly established on that continent. The brown rat (some say) has exterminated our black rat and the Maori rat in New Zealand.

The microbe of the terrible disease which the crews of Columbus brought back to Europe, after causing a devastating epidemic at the end of the fifteenth century, established a kind of *modus vivendi* with its hosts, and has remained as a permanent scourge in Europe. Other microbes, like those of cholera and plague, emigrate from the lands where they are endemic, like a horde of Tartars, and after slaying all who are susceptible disappear from inanition. The draining of the fens has driven the anopheles mosquito from England, and our countrymen no longer suffer from 'ague.' Cleanlier habits are banishing the louse and its accompaniment typhus fever.

Fertility and care for offspring seem as a rule to vary inversely. The latter is the path of biological progress, and is characteristic of all viviparous animals. That any degree of parental attention is incompatible with the immense fecundity of the lower organisms needs no demonstration. Such fertility is not necessary to keep up the numbers of the higher species, which find abundant food in the swarming progeny of the lower types, and are not themselves exposed to wholesale slaughter. Speaking of fishes, Sutherland says :

Of species that exhibit no sort of parental care, the average of forty-nine gives 1,040,000 eggs to a female each year ; while among those which make nests or any apology for nests the number is only about 10,000. Among those which have any protective tricks, such as carrying the eggs in pouches or attached to the body, or in the mouth, the average number is under 1000 ; while among those whose care takes the form of uterine or quasi-uterine gestation which brings the young into the world alive, an average of 56 eggs is quite sufficient.

Man is no exception to these laws. His evolution has been steadily in the direction of diminishing fertility and increasing parental care. This does not necessarily imply that the modern European loves his children better than the savage loves his. It is grim necessity, not want of affection, which determines the treatment of children by their parents over a great part of the world, and through the greater part of human history. The homeless hunters, who represent the lowest stage of savagery, are now almost extinct. In these tribes the woman has to follow the man carrying her baby. Under such conditions the chances of rearing a large family are small indeed. Very different is the life of the grassland nomads, who roam over the Arabian plateau and the steppes of Central Asia. These tribes, who really live as the parasites of their flocks and herds, depending on them entirely for subsistence, often multiply rapidly. Their typical unit is the great patriarchal family, in which the *sheikh* may have scores of children by different mothers. These children soon begin to earn their keep, and are taken care of. If, however, the patriarch so chooses, Hagar with her child is cast adrift, to find her way back to her own people, if she can. The grasslands are usually almost as full as they can hold. A period of drought, or pressure by rivals, in former times sent a horde of these hardy shepherds on a raid into the nearest settled province ; and if, like the Tartars, they were mounted, they usually killed, plundered, and conquered wherever they went, until the discovery of gunpowder saved civilisation from the recurrent peril of barbarian inroads. Barbarians of another type, hunters with fixed homes, seldom increase rapidly, partly because the dangers of forest-life for young children are much greater than on the steppe.

In the primitive river-valley civilisations, such as Egypt and Babylonia, the conditions of increase were so favourable that a dense population soon began to press upon the means of subsistence. In Egypt the remedy was a centralised government which could undertake great irrigation works and intensive cultivation. In Babylonia, for the first time in history, foreign trade was made to support a larger population than the land itself could maintain. There was little or no infanticide in Babylonia, but the death-rate in these steaming alluvial plains has always been very high.

When we turn to poor and mountainous countries like Greece, the conditions are very different. It was an old belief among the Hellenes that in the days before the Trojan War ' the world was too full of people.' The increase was doubtless made possible by the trade which developed in the Minoan period, but the sources of food-supply were liable to be interfered with. Hence came the necessity for active colonisation, which lasted from the eighth to the sixth century B.C. This period of expansion came to an end when all the available sites were occupied. In the sixth century the Greeks found themselves headed off, in the west by Phœnicians and Etruscans, in the east by the Persian Empire. The problem of over-population was again pressing upon them. Incessant civil wars between Hellenes kept the numbers down to some extent; but Greek battles were not as a rule very bloody, and every healthy nation has a surprising capacity of making good the losses caused by war. The first effect of the check to emigration was that the old ideal of the ' self-sufficient life,' which meant the practice of mixed farming, had to be partially abandoned. The most flourishing States, and especially Athens, had to take to manufactures, which they exchanged for the food-products of the Balkan States and South Russia. The result was an increasing urbanisation, and a new population of free ' resident aliens.' Conservatives hated this change and wished to revive the old ideal of a small self-supporting State, with a maximum of 20,000 or 30,000 citizens. Plato, in his latest work, the ' Laws,' wishes his model city to be not too near the sea, the proximity of which ' fills the streets with merchants and shopkeepers, and begets dishonesty in the souls of men.' On the other side Isocrates, the most far-seeing of Athenian politicians, realised that the day of small city-states was over, and that the limited, ' self-sufficient ' community would not long maintain its independence. He urged his countrymen to pursue a policy of peaceful penetration in Western Asia, as the Greeks were soon to do under the successors of Alexander. But the prejudice against industrialism was very strong. Greece in the fifth century remained a poor country; her exports were not more than enough to pay for the food of her existing population; and that population had to be artificially restricted. The Greeks were an exceptionally healthy and long-lived race; their great men for the most part lived to ages which have no parallel until the nineteenth century. The infant death-rate from natural causes may have been rather high, as it is in modern Greece, but it was augmented by systematic

infanticide. The Greek father had an absolute right to
decide whether a new-comer was to be admitted to the
family. In Ephesus alone of Greek cities a parent was
compelled to prove that he was too poor to rear a child
before he was allowed to get rid of it.[1] Even Hesiod,
centuries earlier, advises a father not to bring up more than
one son, and daughters were sacrificed more frequently
than sons. The usual practice was to expose the infant
in a jar; anyone who thought it worth while might rescue
the baby and bring it up as a slave. But this was not often
done. At Gela, in Sicily, there are 233 ' potted ' burials
in an excavated graveyard, out of a total of 570.[2] The
proportion of female infants exposed must have been very
large. The evidence of literature is supported by such
letters as this from a husband at Oxyrhynchus : ' When—
good luck to you—your child is born, if it is a male, let it
live ; if a female, expose it.' [3] Besides infanticide, abortion
was freely practised, and without blame.[4] The Greek
citizen married rather late ; but as his bride was usually
in her 'teens this would not affect the birth-rate. Nor need
we attach much importance, as a factor in checking population, to the characteristic Greek vice, nor to prostitution,
which throughout antiquity was incredibly cheap and
visited by no physical penalty. As for slaves, Xenophon
recommends that they should be allowed to have children
as a reward for good conduct.[5]

A rapid decline in population set in under the successors
of Alexander. Polybius ascribes it to selfishness and a
high standard of comfort, which is doubtless true of the
upper and middle classes ;[6] but the depopulation of rural

[1] Myres, *Eugenics Review*, April, 1915.

[2] Wilamowitz-Moellendorff, *Kultur der Gegenwart*, 2, 4, 1.

[3] Cimon, Pericles, and Socrates all had three sons, and apparently
no daughters.—Zimmern, *The Greek Commonwealth*, p. 331.

[4] *Cf.* (*e.g.*) Plato, *Theaetetus*, 149.

[5] We may suppose that the disproportion of the sexes, caused
by female infanticide, was about rectified by the deaths of males
in battle and civic strife. We do not hear that the Greek had any
difficulty in finding a wife.

[6] Families, he says, were limited to one or two, ' in order to leave
these rich.'

Greece can hardly be so accounted for. Perhaps the forests were cut down, and the rainfall diminished. It was the general impression that the soil was far less productive than formerly. The decay of the Hellenic race was accelerated after the Roman conquest, until the old stock became almost extinct. This disappearance of the most gifted race that ever inhabited our planet is one of the strangest catastrophes of history, and is full of warnings for the modern sociologist. Industrial slavery, indifference to parenthood, and addiction to club-life were certainly three of the main causes, unless we prefer to regard the two last as symptoms of hopelessness about the future.

The same disease fell upon Italy, and was coincident not with the murderous war against Hannibal and the subsequent campaigns, costly though they were, in Spain, Syria, and Macedonia, but with the Hellenisation of social life. Lucan, under Nero, complains that the towns have lost more than half their inhabitants, and that the country-side lies waste. Under Titus it was estimated that, whereas Italy under the Republic could raise nearly 800,000 soldiers, that number was now reduced by one-half. Marcus Aurelius planted a large tribe of Marcomanni on unoccupied land in Italy. In the fourth century Bologna, Modena, Piacenza, and many other towns in North Italy were in ruins. The land of the Volscians and Aequians, once densely populated, was a desert even in Livy's time. Samnium remained the wilderness that Sulla had left it ; and Apulia was a lonely sheep-walk.

The causes of this depopulation have been often discussed, both in antiquity and in our own day. Slavery, infanticide, celibacy, wars and massacres, large estates, and pestilence have all been named as causes ; but I am inclined to think that all these influences together are insufficient to account for so rapid a decline. The toll of war was lighter by far than in periods when the population was rising ; infectious disease (unless we suppose, as some have suggested, that malaria became for the first time endemic under the Roman domination) invaded the empire in occasional and destructive epidemics, but a healthy population recovers from pestilence, as from war, with

virginity has lasted on, with much else that belongs to the later Hellenistic age, in Catholicism.

In the Middle Ages the population question slumbered. The miserable chaos into which the old civilisation sank after the barbarian invasions, the orgies of massacre and plunder, the almost total oblivion of medical science, and the pestiferous condition of the medieval walled town, which could be smelt miles away, averted any risk of over-population. Families were very large, but the majority of the children died. Millions were swept away by the Black Death ; millions more by the Crusades. Such books as that of Luchaire, on France in the reign of Philip Augustus, bring vividly before us the horrible condition of society in feudal times, and explain amply the sparsity of the population.

The early modern period contains another notable example of a sudden and unaccountable decline in population. The scene is Spain, which, after playing an active and very prominent part in the world's history, sank quickly into the lethargy from which it has never recovered. It may be noted that here, as in the case of Rome, the decay of population and energy followed a great influx of plundered wealth. On the other hand, the increase of population in our newly-planted North American colonies must have been extremely rapid for two or three generations.

The enormous multiplication of the European races since the middle of the eighteenth century is a phenomenon quite unique in history, and never likely to be repeated.[1] It was rendered possible by the new labour-saving inventions which immensely increased the exports which could be exchanged for food, and by the opening up of vast new food-producing areas. The chief method by which the increase was effected, especially in the later period, has been the lengthening of human life by improved sanitation and medical science.[2] Since 1865 the average duration

[1] The population of England and Wales is said to have been 4,800,000 in 1600, and 6,500,000 in 1750. It was 8,890,000 in 1801, 32,530,000 in 1901, and approximately 37,000,000 in 1914.

[2] Statistics are wanting for the early part of the industrial revolution, but my study of pedigrees leads me to think that the average duration of life was considerably increased in the eighteenth century.

of life in England and Wales has been raised by a little more
than one-third. Other European countries show the same
ratio of improvement. This astonishing result, so little
known and so seldom referred to, was bound to have a great
effect on the birth-rate. So long as the swarming period
continued at its height, a net annual increase of 15 or even
20 per thousand could be sustained ; but the expansion of
the European peoples has now passed its zenith, and a
tendency to revert to more normal conditions is almost
everywhere observable. One of the most advanced nations,
France, has already reached the equilibrium towards which
other civilised nations are moving. The old-established
families in the United States are believed to be actually
dwindling.

The student of international vital statistics will be struck
first by the very wide differences in the birth-rate of different
countries. He will then notice that the more backward
countries have on the whole a considerably higher birth-
rate than the more advanced. Thirdly, he will observe
the parallelism between the birth-rate and death-rate, which
makes the net increase in countries with a high birth-rate
very little larger than that of countries with a low birth-
rate. The following figures will illustrate these points ;
they are taken from the Registrar-General's Blue Book
for 1912.

|  | Birth-rate | Death-rate | Net rate of increase |
|---|---|---|---|
| United Kingdom . . | 23·9 | 13·8 | 10·1 |
| Australia . . . . | 28·7 | 11·2 | 17·5 |
| Austria . . . . | 31·3 | 20·5 | 10·8 |
| Belgium . . . . | 22·9 | 16·4 | 6·5 |
| France . . . . | 19·0 | 17·5 | 1·5 |
| Germany . . . . | 28·6 | 17·3 | 11·3 |
| Italy . . . . | 32·4 | 18·2 | 14·2 |
| New Zealand . . . | 26·5 | 8·9 | 17·6 |
| Norway . . . . | 25·4 | 13·4 | 12·0 |
| Roumania . . . | 43·4 | 22·9 | 20·5 |
| Russia . . . . | 44·0 | 28·9 | 15·1 |

It will be seen that Australia and New Zealand, with
low birth-rates and the lowest death-rates in the world

increase more rapidly than Russia with an enormous birth-rate and proportionately high death-rate. No one can doubt that our colonies achieve their increase with far less friction and misery than the prolific but short-lived Slavs. Civilisation in a high form is incompatible with such conditions as these figures disclose in Russia. The figures for Egypt and India are similar to the Russian, but in India, which is overfull, the mortality is greater than even in Russia, and the same is true of China, in which we are told that seven out of ten children die in infancy. It has been suggested that the fairest measure of a country's well-being, as regards its actual vitality, is the square of the death-rate divided by the birth-rate.

It is well known that a decline in the birth-rate set in about forty years ago in this country, and has gone on steadily ever since, till the fall now amounts to about one-third of the total births. It thus corresponds very nearly to the fall in the death-rate during the same period. It is also well known that this decline is not evenly distributed among different classes of the people. Until the decline began, large families were the rule in all classes, and the slightly larger families of the poor were compensated by their somewhat higher mortality. But since 1877 large families have become increasingly rare in the upper and middle classes, and among the skilled artisans. They are frequent in the thriftless ranks of unskilled labour, and in one section of well-paid workmen—the miners. The highest birth-rates at present are in the mining districts and in the slums. The lowest are in some of the learned professions. In the Rhondda Valley the birth-rate is still about forty, which is double the rate in the prosperous residential suburbs of London. In the seats of the texile industry the decline has been very severe, although wages are fairly good; among the agricultural labourers the rate is also low. It will be found that in all trades where the women work for wages the birth-rate has fallen sharply; the miner's wife does not earn money, and has therefore less inducement to restrict her family. In agricultural districts the housing difficulty is mainly responsible; in the upper and middle classes the heavy expense of education and the burden of rates and taxes are probably the main reasons why larger families are not desired. We may add that in almost all the professions old men are overpaid and young men under-paid. Mr. and Mrs. Whetham [1] have found that, before 1870, 143 marriages of men whose names appear in ' Who's Who ' resulted in 743 children, an average of 5·2 each ; after 1870 the average is only 3·08. Celibacy also is com-moner among the educated. ' From the reports issued by two Women's Colleges, it appears that, excluding those who have left college within three years or less, out of 3000 women only 22 per cent. have married, and the number of children born to each marriage is undoubtedly very small.' The writers consider that this state of things is extremely dangerous for the country, inasmuch as we are now breeding mainly from our worst stocks (the feeble-minded are very prolific), while our best families are stationary or dwindling. Without denying the general truth of this pessimistic conclusion,[2] it may be pointed out that the miners are, physically at least, above the average of the whole population, and that the very low birth-rate of residential districts is partly due to the presence in large numbers of unmarried domestic servants. The death-rate of the slums is also very high.

The fears of the eugenist about the quality of the popu-lation are far more reasonable than the invectives of the fanatic about its defective quantity. Of the latter class we may say with Havelock Ellis that ' those who seek to restore the birth-rate of half a century ago are engaged in a task which would be criminal if it were not based on ignorance, and which is in any case fatuous.' And yet I hope to show before the close of this article that for two or three generations the British Empire could absorb a considerable increase, and that the Government might with advantage stimulate this by schemes of colonisation. The lament of the eugenist resounds in all countries alike.

---

[1] *The Family and the Nation*, p. 143.

[2] The births per 1000 married men under fifty-five in the different classes are :—Upper and middle class, 119 ; Intermediate, 132 ; Skilled workmen, 153 ; Intermediate, 158 ; Unskilled workmen, 213.

The German complains that the Poles, whom he considers an inferior race, breed like rabbits, while the gifted exponents of *Kultur* only breed like hares. The American is nervous about the numbers of the negro ; he has more reason to be nervous about the fecundity of the Slav and South Italian immigrant. Everywhere the tendency is for the superior stock to dwindle till it becomes a small aristocracy. The Americans of British descent are threatened with this fate. Pride and a high standard of living are not biological virtues. The man who needs and spends little is the ultimate inheritor of the earth. I know of no instance in history in which a ruling race has not ultimately been ousted or absorbed by its subjects. Complete extermination or expropriation is the only successful method of conquest. The Anglo-Saxon race has thus established itself in the greater part of Britain, and in Australasia. In North America it has destroyed the Indian hunter, who could not be used for industrial purposes ; but the temptation to exploit the negro and the cheaper European races was too strong to be resisted, and Nature's heaviest penalty is now being exacted against the descendants of our sturdy colonists. We did not lose America in the eighteenth century ; we are losing it now. As for South Africa, the Kaffir can live like a gentleman (according to his own ideas) on six months' ill-paid work every year ; the Englishman finds an income of £200 too small. There is only one end to this kind of colonisation. The danger at home is that the larger part of the population is now beginning to insist upon a scale of remuneration and a standard of comfort which are incompatible with any survival-value. We all wish to be privileged aristocrats, with no serfs to work for us. Dame Nature cares nothing for the babble of politicians and trade-union regulations. She says to us what Plotinus, in a remarkable passage, makes her say : ' You should not ask questions ; you should try to understand. *I am not in the habit of talking.*' In Nature's school it is a word and a blow, and the blow first. Before the close of this article I will return to the eugenic problem, and will consider whether anything can be done to solve it.

At the present time, when an apparently internecine

conflict is raging between the British Empire and Germany, a more detailed comparison of the vital statistics of the two countries will be read with interest. In England and Wales the birth-rate culminated in 1876 at a little over 36, after slowly rising from 33 in 1850. From 1876 the line of decline is almost straight, down to the ante-war figure of about 24. In Prussia, owing partly to wars, the fluctuations have been violent. In 1850 the figure (omitting decimals) was 39 ; in 1855, 34 ; in 1859, 40 ; in 1871, 34 ; in 1875, nearly 41. From this date, as in England, the steady decline began. In 1907 the rate had fallen to 33 ; in 1913 (German Empire) to 27·5. Here we may notice the abnormally high rate in the years following the great war of 1870, a phenomenon which was marked also throughout Europe after the Napoleonic wars. We may also notice that the decline has been of late slightly more rapid in Germany, falling from a high birth-rate, than in England, where the maximum was never so high. Another fact which comes out when the German figures are more carefully examined is that urbanisation in Germany has a sterilising effect which is not operative in England. Prinzing gives the comparative figures of *legitimate* fertility for Prussia as follows :

|  | 1879–1882 | 1894–1897 |
|---|---|---|
| Berlin | 23·8 | 16·9[1] |
| Other great towns | 26·7 | 23·5 |
| Towns of 20,000 to 100,000 | 26·8 | 25·7 |
| Small towns | 27·8 | 25·9 |
| Country districts | 28·8 | 29·0 |

Now urbanisation is going on even more rapidly in Germany than in England. The death-rate in England and Wales rose from 21 in 1850 to 23·5 in 1854 ; after sharp fluctuations it reached 23·7 in 1864 ; since then it has declined to its present figure (in normal times) of 14. In Prussia after the war of 1870 and the small-pox epidemic of 1871, there has been a steady fall from 26 to 17·3 (German Empire in 1911). The net increase is only slightly larger (in proportion to the population) in Germany than in Eng-

---

[1] It must be remembered that the illegitimate birth-rate in Berlin is scandalously high.

land ; and the increase in our great colonies, especially in Australasia, is much higher than in Germany. There is therefore no reason to suppose that a rapid alteration is going on to our disadvantage.

It is widely believed that the Roman Catholic Church, by sternly forbidding the artificial limitation of families, is increasing its numbers at the expense of the non-Catholic populations. To some extent this is true. The Prussian figures for 1895–1900 give the number of children per marriage as :

> Both parents Catholic . . . 5
> Both parents Protestant . . . 4
> Both parents Jews . . . . 3·7

An examination of the entries in ' Who's Who ' gives about the same proportion for well-to-do families in England. The Catholic birth-rate of the Irish is nearly 40.[1] The French-Canadians are among the most prolific races in the world. On the other hand, their infant mortality is very high, and it is said that French-Canadian parents take these losses philosophically. It is quite a different question whether it is ultimately to the advantage of a nation which desires to increase its numbers to profess the Roman Catholic religion. The high birth-rates are all in unprogressive Catholic populations. When a Catholic people begins to be educated, the priests apparently lose their influence upon the habits of the laity, and a rapid decline in the births at once sets in. The most advanced countries which did not accept the Reformation, France and Belgium, are precisely those in which parental prudence has been carried almost to excess. We must also remember that the Dutch Boers, who are Protestants, but who live under simple conditions not unlike those of the French-Canadians, are equally prolific, as were our own colonists in the United States before that country was industrialised. The advantages in numbers gained by Roman Catholicism are likely to be confined to half-empty countries, where

---

[1] The crude birth-rate of Ireland is wholly misleading, because so many young couples emigrate before the birth of their first child.

there is really room for more citizens, and where social ambition and the love of comfort are the chief motives for restricting the family.

The population of a settled country cannot be increased at will; it depends on the supply of food. The choice is between a high birth-rate combined with a high death-rate, and a low birth-rate with a low death-rate. The great saving of life which has been effected during the last fifty years carries with it the necessity of restricting the births. The next question to be considered is how this restriction is to be brought about. The oldest methods are deliberate neglect and infanticide. In China, where authorities differ as to the extent to which female infants are exposed, the practice certainly prevails of feeding infants whom their mothers are unable to suckle on rice and water, which soon terminates their existence. Such methods would happily find no advocates in Europe. The very ancient art of procuring miscarriage is a criminal act in most civilised countries, but it is practised to an appalling extent. Hirsch, who quotes his authorities, estimates that 2,000,000 births are so prevented annually in the United States, 400,000 in Germany, 50,000 in Paris, and 19,000 in Lyons. In our own country it is exceedingly common in the northern towns, and attempts are now being made to prohibit the sale of certain preparations of lead which are used for this purpose. Alike on grounds of public health and of morality, it is most desirable that this mischievous practice should be checked. Its great prevalence in the United States is to be attributed mainly to the drastic legislation in that country against the sale and use of preventives, to which many persons take objection on moral or æsthetic grounds, but which is surely on an entirely different level from the destruction of life that has already begun. The 'Comstock' legislation in America has done unmixed harm. It is worse than useless to try to put down by law a practice which a very large number of people believes to be innocent, and which must be left to the taste and conscience of the individual. To the present writer it seems a *pis aller* which high-minded married persons should avoid if they can practise self-restraint. Whatever

injures the feeling of 'sanctification and honour' with
which St. Paul bids us to regard these intimacies of life,
whatever tends to profane or degrade the sacraments of
wedded love, is so far an evil.  But this is emphatically a
matter in which every man and woman must judge for
themselves, and must refrain from judging others.

In every modern civilised country population is restricted partly by the deliberate postponement of marriage.
In many cases this does no harm whatever ; but in many
others it gravely diminishes the happiness of young people,
and may even cause minor disturbances of health.  Moreover, it would not be so widely adopted but for the tolerance,
on the part of society, of the 'great social evil,' the opprobrium of our civilisation.  In spite of the failure hitherto
of priests, moralists, and legislators to root it out, and in
spite of the acceptance of it as inevitable by the majority
of Continental opinion, I believe that this abomination will
not long be tolerated by the conscience of the free and progressive nations.  It is notorious that the whole body of
women deeply resents the wrong and contumely done by
it to their sex, and that, if democracy is to be a reality, the
immolation of a considerable section of women drawn from
the poorer classes cannot be suffered to continue.  It is
also plain to all who have examined the subject that the
campaign against certain diseases, the malignity and wide
diffusion of which are being more fully realised every year,
cannot be successful through medical methods alone.  If
the institution in question were abolished, medical science
would soon reduce these scourges to manageable limits,
and might at last exterminate them altogether ; but while
it continues there is no hope of doing this.  I believe then
that the time will come when the trade in vice will cease ;
and if I am right, early marriages will become the rule in
all classes.  This will render the population question more
acute, especially as the diseases which we hope to extir-
pate are the commonest cause both of sterility and of
infant mortality.  Under this pressure, we must expect to
see preventive methods widely accepted as the least of
unavoidable evils.

When we reflect on the whole problem in its widest

aspects, we see that civilised humanity is confronted by a Choice of Hercules. On the one side, biological law seems to urge us forward to the struggle for existence and expansion. The nation in that case will have to be organised on the lines of greatest efficiency. A strong centralised government will occupy itself largely in preventing waste. All the resources of the nation must be used to the uttermost. Parks must be cut up into allotments ; the unproductive labours of the scholar and thinker must be jealously controlled and limited. Inefficient citizens must be weeded out ; wages must be low and hours of work long. Moreover, the State·must be organised for war ; for its neighbours, we must suppose, are following the same policy. Then the fierce extra-group competition must come to its logical arbitrament in a life and death struggle. And war between two over-peopled countries, for both of which more elbow-room is a vital necessity, must be a war of complete expropriation or extermination. It must be so, for no other kind of war can achieve its object. The horrors of the present conflict will be as nothing compared with a struggle between two highly-organised State socialisms, each of which knows that it must either colonise the territory of the other or starve. It is idle to pretend that such a necessity will never arise. Another century of increase in Europe like that of the nineteenth century would bring it very near. If this policy is adopted, we shall see all the principal States organising themselves with a perfection far greater than that of Germany to-day, but taking German methods as their model ; and the end will be the extermination of the smaller or looser organisations. Such a prospect may well fill us with horror ; and it is terrible to find some of the ablest thinkers of Germany, such as Ernst Troeltsch, writing calm elegies over ' the death of Liberalism ' and predicting the advent of an era of cut-throat international competition. Juvenal speaks of the folly of *propter vitam vivendi perdere causas ;* and who would care to live in such a world ? But does Nature care whether we enjoy our lives or not ?

The other choice is that which France has made for herself ; it is on the lines of Plato's ideal State. Each country is to be, as far as possible, self-sufficing. If it cannot grow sufficient food for itself, it must of course export its coal or its gold, or the products of its industry and ingenuity. But it must know approximately what ' the number of the State ' (as Plato said) should be. It must limit its population to that number, and the limit will be fixed, not at the maximum number who can live there anyhow, but at the maximum number who can ' live well.' The object aimed at will not be constant expansion, but well-being. The energies liberated from the pitiless struggle for existence will be devoted to making social life wiser, happier, more harmonious and more beautiful. Have we any reason to hope that this policy is not contrary to the hard laws which Nature imposes on every species in the world ?

In the first place, would such a State escape being devoured by some brutal ' expanding' neighbour ? What would have happened to France if she had stood alone in this war ? The danger is real; but we may answer that France, as a matter of fact, did not stand alone, because other nations thought her too precious to be sacrificed. And the completely organised competitive State which I have imagined would be a far more unlovely place than Germany, and more unpleasant to live in. The spectacle of a saner and happier polity next door would break up the purely competitive State from within; the strain would be too great for human nature. We cannot argue confidently from the struggle for existence among the lower animals to our own species. For a long time past, human evolution has been directed, not to living anyhow, but to living in a certain way. We are guided by ideals for the future, by purposes which we clearly set before ourselves, in a way which is impossible to the brutes. These purposes are common to the large majority of men. No State can long maintain a rigid and oppressive organisation, except under the threat of danger; and a nation which aims only at perfecting its own culture is not dangerous to its neighbours. It is probable that without the supposed menace of another military Power on its eastern flank German militarism would have begun to crumble.

In the second place, would the absence of sharp competition within the group lead to racial degeneration ? This is a difficult question to answer. Perhaps a diminution of pugnacity and of the means to gratify this instinct would not be a misfortune. But it is certainly true that, if the operation of natural selection is suspended, rational selection must take its place. Failing this, reversion to a lower type is inevitable. The infant science of eugenics will have much to say on this subject hereafter ; at present we are only discovering how complex and obscure the laws of heredity are. The State of the future will have to step in to prevent the propagation of undesirable variations, whether physical or mental, and will doubtless find means to encourage the increase of families that are well endowed by Nature.

Assuming that a nation as a whole prefers a policy of this kind, and aims at such an equilibrium of births and deaths as will set free the energies of the people for the higher objects of civilised life, how will it escape the caco-genic effects of family restriction in the better classes com-bined with reckless multiplication among the refuse which always exists in a large community ? This is a problem which has not yet been solved. Public opinion is not ready for legislation against the multiplication of the unfit, and it is not easy to see what form such legislation could take. Many of the very poor are not undesirable parents ; we must not confound economic prosperity with biological fitness. The ' submerged tenth ' should be raised, where it is possible, into a condition of self-respect and responsi-bility ; but they must not be allowed to be a burden upon the efficient; and the upper and middle classes should simplify their habits so far as to make marriage and parent-hood possible for the young professional man. Special care should be taken that taxation is so adjusted as not to penalise parenthood in the socially valuable middle class.

For some time to come we are likely to see, in all the leading nations, a restricted birth-rate, prompted by desire for social betterment, combined, however, with concessions to the rival policy of commercial expansion, growing num-bers, and military preparation. The nations will not cease to fear and suspect each other in the twentieth century, and any one nation which chooses to be a nuisance to Europe will keep back the progress and happiness of the rest. The prospect is not very bright; a too generous confidence might betray some nation into irretrievable disaster. But the bracing influence of national danger may perhaps be beneficial. For we have to remember the pitiable decay of the ancient classical civilisation, which was partly due, as we have found, to a desire for comfortable and easy living. There have been signs that many of our country-men no longer think the strenuous life worth while; part of our resentment against Germany resembles the annoy-ance of an old-fashioned firm, disturbed in its comfortable security by the competition of a young and more vigorous rival. It is even suggested that after the war we should protect ourselves against German competition by tariff walls. This abandonment of the free trade policy on which our prosperity is built would soon bring our over-populated island to ruin.

In conclusion, if we leave the distant future to fend for itself when the time comes, what should be our policy with regard to population for the next fifty years? I am led to an opinion which may seem to run counter to the general purport of this article. For though the British Isles are even dangerously full, so that we are liable to be starved out if we lose the command of the sea, the British Empire is very far from being over-populated. In Canada and Australasia there is probably room for nearly 200,000,000 people. These countries are remarkably healthy for Northern Europeans; there is no reason why they should not be as rich and powerful as the United States are now. We hope that we have saved the Empire from German cupidity —for the time; but we cannot tell how long we may be undisturbed. It would be criminal folly not to make the most of the respite granted us, by peopling our Dominions with our own stock, while yet there is time. This, however, cannot be done by casual and undirected emigration of the old kind. We need an Imperial Board of Emigration, the officials of which will work in co-operation with the Govern-ments of our Dominions. These Governments, it may be presumed, will be anxious, after the war, to strengthen the colonies by increasing their population and developing their resources. They, like ourselves, have had a severe fright, and know that prompt action is necessary. Systematic plans of colonisation should be worked out, and emigrants drafted off to the Dominions as work can be found for them. Young women should be sent out in sufficient numbers to keep the sexes equal. We know now that our young people who emigrate are by no means lost to the Empire. The Dominions have shown that in time of need they are able and willing to defend the mother country with their full strength. Indeed, a young couple who emigrate are likely to be of more value to the Empire than if they had stayed at home; and their chances of happiness are much increased if they find a home in a part of the world where more human beings are wanted. But without official advice and help emigration is difficult. Parents do not know where to send their sons, nor what training to give them. Mistakes are made, money is wasted, and bitter disappointment caused. All this may be obviated if the Government will take the matter up seriously. The real issue of this war is whether our great colonies are to continue British; and the question will be decided not only on the field of battle, but by the action of our Government and people after peace is declared. The next fifty years will decide for all time whether those magnificent and still empty countries are to be the home of great nations speaking our language, carrying on our institutions, and valuing our traditions. When the future of our Dominions is secure, the part of England as a World-Power will have been played to a successful issue, and we may be content with a position more consonant with the small area of these islands.

I believe, then, that if facilities for migration are given by Government action, it will be not only possible but desirable for the increase in the population of the Empire, taken as a whole, to be maintained during the twentieth century. It is, of course, possible that chemical discoveries and other scientific improvements may greatly increase the yield of food from the soil, and that in this way the final limit to the population of the earth may be further off than now seems probable. But within a few centuries, at most, this limit must be reached ; and after that we may hope that the world will agree to maintain an equilibrium between births and deaths, that being the most stable and the happiest condition in which human beings can live together.[1]

[1] The possible effect of the labour movement in diminishing the population is considered in the next Essay. The last two years have, in my opinion, made the outlook less favourable.

# THE FUTURE OF THE ENGLISH RACE

## (THE GALTON LECTURE, 1919)

IN the year 1890 Sir Charles Dilke ended his survey of
' Greater Britain' and its problems with the prediction
that ' the world's future belongs to the Anglo-Saxon, the
Russian, and the Chinese races.' This was in the heyday
of British imperialism, which was inaugurated by Seeley's
' Expansion of England' and Froude's ' Oceana,' and
which inspired Mr. Chamberlain to proclaim at Toronto
in 1887 that the ' Anglo-Saxon stock is infallibly destined
to be the predominant force in the history and civilisation
of the world.' It was an arrogant, but not truculent,
mood, which reached its climax at the 1897 Jubilee, and
rapidly declined during and after the Boer war. These
writers and statesmen were utterly blind to the German
peril, though the disciples of Treitschke were already
working out a theory about the future destinies of the
world, in which neither Great Britain nor Russia nor China
counted for very much. There were illusions on both
sides of the North Sea, which had to be paid for in blood.
In both countries imperialism was a sentiment curiously
compounded of idealism and bombast, and supported by
very doubtful science. In the case of Germany the dis-
tortion of facts was deliberate and monstrous. Not only
was every schoolboy brought up on cooked population
statistics and falsified geography, but the thick-set, brachy-
cephalous Central European persuaded himself that he
belonged to the pure Nordic race, the great blond beasts
of Nietzsche, which, as he was taught, had already produced nearly all the great men in history, and was now

about to claim its proper place as master of the world. Political anthropology is no genuine science. Race and nationality are catchwords for which rulers find that their subjects are willing to fight, as they fought for what they called religion four hundred years ago. In reality, if we want to find a pure race, we must visit the Esquimaux, or the Fuegians, or the Pygmies; we shall certainly not find one in Europe. Our own imperialists had their illusions too, and we are not rid of them yet, because we do not realise that the fate of races is decided, not in the council-chamber or on the battle-field, but by the same laws of nature which determine the distribution of the various plants and animals of the world. It may be that by approaching our subject from this side we shall arrive at a more scientific, if a more chastened, anticipation of our national future than was acceptable to the enthusiasts of expansion in the last twenty years of Queen Victoria's reign.

The history of the world shows us that there have been three great human reservoirs which from time to time have burst their banks and flooded neighbouring countries. These are the Arabian peninsula, the steppes of Central Asia, and the lands round the Baltic, the original home of the Germanic and Anglo-Saxon peoples. The invaders in each case were pastoral folk, who were driven from their homes by over-population, or drought and famine, or the pressure of enemies behind them. It is easy for nomads to ' trek,' even for great distances; and till the discovery of gunpowder they were the most formidable of foes. The Arabs and Northern Europeans have founded great civilisations; the Mongol hordes have been an unmitigated curse to humanity. The invaders never kept their blood pure. The famous Jewish nose is probably Hittite, and certainly not Bedouin. There are no pure Turks in Europe, and the Hungarians have lost all resemblance to Mongols. The modern Germans seem to belong mainly to the round-headed Alpine race, which migrated into Europe in early times from the Asiatic highlands. In England there is a larger proportion of Nordic blood, because the Anglo-Saxons partially exterminated the natives; but the old

Mediterranean race, which had made its way up the warm western coasts, still holds its own in Cornwall, Wales, Ireland, and the Western Highlands; and within the last hundred years, owing to frequent migrations, has mixed so thoroughly with the Anglo-Saxon stock that the English are becoming darker in each generation. This is not the result of a racial decay of the blonds, as the American, Dr. Charles Woodruff, supposes, but is to be accounted for by the fact that dark eyes seem to be a Mendelian dominant, and dark hair a more potent character than light. The inhabitants of these islands are nearly all long-headed, this being a characteristic of both the Nordic and Mediterranean races. The round-headed invaders, who perhaps brought with them the so-called Celtic languages at a remote period, and imposed them upon the inhabitants, seem to have left no other mark upon the population, though their type of head is prevalent over a great part of France.

The ability of races to flourish in climates other than their own is a question of supreme importance to historians and statesmen, and, it need not be said, to emigrants. But it is only lately that it has been studied scientifically, and the results are still tentative. German ethnologists, of what we may call the *œdicephalous* school, already referred to, regard it as one of the tragedies of nature that the noble Nordic race, to which they think they belong, dies out when it penetrates southwards. In accordance with this law, the yellow-haired Achæans decayed in Greece, the Lombards in North Italy, the Vandals in Spain and Africa. After a few generations of life in a warm climate the Aryan stock invariably disappears. We shall show reasons for thinking that this theory is much exaggerated; but there is undoubtedly some truth in it. It has been found to be impossible for white men to colonise India, Burma, tropical America, and West Africa. It has been said that 'there is in India no third generation of pure English blood.' It is notoriously difficult to bring up even one generation of white children in India. The French cannot maintain themselves without race admixture in Martinique and Guadaloupe, nor the Dutch in Java, though it is said that the expectation of life for a European in Java is as good as in his own country. It seems to be also true that the blond race suffers most in a hot climate. In the Philippines it was observed that the fair-haired soldiers in the American army succumbed most readily to disease. In Queensland the Italian colonists are said to stand the heat better than the English, and Mr. Roosevelt, among other items of good advice which he bestowed so liberally on the European nations, advised us to populate the torrid parts of Australia with immigrants from the Latin races. In Natal the English families who are settled in the country are said to be enervated by the climate ; and on the high plateaux of the interior our countrymen find it necessary to pay periodical visits to the coast, to be unbraced. The early deaths and not infrequent suicides of Rand magnates may indicate that the air of the Transvaal is too stimulating for a life of high tension and excitement. There are even signs that the same may be true in a minor degree of the United States of America. Both the capitalist and the working man, if they come of English stock, seem to wear out more quickly than at home ; and the sterility of marriages among the long settled American families is so pronounced that it can hardly be due entirely to voluntary restriction of parentage. The effects of an unsuitable climate are especially shown in nervous disorders, and are therefore likely to tell most heavily on those who engage in intellectual pursuits, and perhaps on women rather more than on men. The sterilising effects of women's higher education in America are incontrovertible, though this inference is hotly denied in England. At Holyoake College it was found that only half the lady graduates afterwards married, and the average family of those who did marry was less than two children. At Bryn Mawr only 43 per cent. married, and had 0·84 children each ; the average family per graduate was therefore 0·37. If it be objected that new immigrants and their children are healthy and vigorous in America, it may be truly answered that the effects of an unfavourable climate are manifested fully only in the third and later generations. The argument may be further supported by the fate of black men who try to settle in Europe. Their strongly pigmented skin, which seems to protect them from the actinic rays of the tropical sun, so noxious to Europeans, and their broad nostrils, which inhale a larger number of tubercle bacilli than the narrow nose-slits of the Northerner, are disadvantages in a temperate climate. In any case, of the many thousands of negro servants who lived in England in the eighteenth century, it would be difficult to find a single descendant.

But there are other factors in the problem which should make us beware of hasty generalisations. It is obvious that since the American Republic contains many climates in its vast area, there may be parts of it which are perfectly healthy for Anglo-Saxons, and other parts where they cannot live without degenerating. Very few athletes, we are told, come from south of the fortieth parallel of latitude. But the decline in the birth-rate is most marked in the older colonies, the New England States, where for a long period the English colonists, living mainly on the land, not only throve and developed a singularly virile type of humanity, but multiplied with almost unexampled rapidity. The same is true not only of the French Canadian farmers, but of the South African Boers, who rear enormous families in a climate very different from that of Holland. The inference is that Europeans living on the land may flourish in any tolerably healthy climate which is not tropical.

There are, in fact, two other causes besides climate which may prevent immigrants from multiplying in a new country. The first of these is the presence of microbic diseases to which the old inhabitants are wholly or partially immune, but which find a virgin soil in the bodies of the newcomers. The strongest example is the West Coast of Africa, of which Miss Mary Kingsley writes: 'Yet remember, before you elect to cast your lot with the West Coasters, that 85 per cent. of them die of fever, or return home with their health permanently wrecked. Also remember that there is no getting acclimatised to the Coast. There are, it is true, a few men out there who, although they have been resident in West Africa for years, have never had fever, but you can count them on the fingers of one hand.' There can be no acclimatisation where the weeding out is as drastic as this. Either the anopheles mosquito or the European must quit. There are parts of tropical America where the natives have actually been protected by the malaria, which keeps the white man at arm's length. But more often the microbe is on the side of the civilised race, killing off the natives who have not run the gauntlet of town-life. The extreme reluctance of the barbarians who overran the Roman Empire to settle in the towns is easily accounted for if, as is probable, the towns killed them off whenever they attempted to live in them. The difference is remarkable between the fate of a conquered race which has become accustomed to town-life, and that of one which has not. There are no ' native quarters ' in the towns of any country where the aborigines were nomads or tillers of the soil. To the North American Indian, residence in a town is a sentence of death. The American Indians were accustomed to none of our zymotic diseases except malaria. In the north they were destroyed wholesale by tuberculosis ; in Mexico and Peru, where large towns existed before the conquest, they fared better. Fiji was devastated by measles ; other barbarians by small-pox. Negroes have acquired, through severe natural selection, a certain degree of immunisation in America ; but even now it is said that ' every other negro dies of consumption.' There are, however, two races, both long accustomed to town-life under horribly insanitary conditions, which have shown that they can live in almost any climate. These are the Jews and the Chinese. The medieval Ghetto exterminated all who were not naturally resistant to every form of microbic disease ; the modern Jew, though often of poor physique, is hard to kill. The same may be said of the Chinaman, who, when at home, lives under conditions which would kill most Europeans.

The other factor, which is really promoting the gradual disappearance of the Anglo-Saxons from the United States, is of a very different character. The descendants of the old immigrants are on the whole the aristocracy of the country. Now it is a law which hardly admits of exceptions, that aristocracies do not maintain their numbers. The ruling race rules itself out ; nothing fails like success. Gibbon has called attention to the extreme respect paid to long descent in the Roman Empire, and to the strange fact that, in the fourth century, no ingenuity of pedigree makers could deny that all the great families of the Republic were extinct, so that the second-rate plebeian family of the Anicii, whose name did appear in the Fasti, enjoyed a prestige far greater than that of the Howards and Stanleys in this country. Our own peerage consists chiefly of parvenus. Only six of our noble families, it is said, can trace their descent in the male line without a break to the fifteenth century. The peerage of Sweden tells the same tale. According to Galton, the custom or law of primogeniture, combined with the habit of marrying heiresses who, as the last representatives of dwindling families, tend to be barren, is mainly responsible for this. Additional causes may be the greater danger which the officer-class incurs in war, and, in former times, the executioner's axe. In our own day the reluctance of rich and self-indulgent women to bear children is undoubtedly a factor in the infertility of the leisured class.

This brings us naturally to the second part of our discussion—the consideration of the causes which lead to the increase or decrease of population. It is the most important part of our inquiry ; for it is usually assumed that the British Isles will continue to send out colonists in large numbers, as it did in the last century, and the hopes of the imperialist that a large part of the world will speak English for all time depend on the untested assurance that the swarming-time of our race is not yet over. Our starting-point must be that the pressure of population upon the means of subsistence is a constant fact in the human race, as in every other species of animals and plants. There is no species in which the numbers are not kept down, far below the natural capacity for increase, by the limitation of available food. It may not always be easy to trace the connection between the appearance

of new lives and the passing away of old, nor to say whether
it is the birth-rate which determines the death-rate, or
the death-rate the birth-rate.  But it is well known that,
wherever statistics are kept, the numbers of births and of
deaths rise and fall in nearly parallel lines, so that the
net rate of increase hardly alters at all, unless some change,
which can easily be traced, occurs in the habits of the
people or in the amount of the food supply.  In civilised
countries the greater care taken of human life, and its
consequent prolongation, has reduced the birth-rate, just
as in the higher mammals we find a greatly diminished
fertility as compared with the lower, and a much higher
survival-rate among the offspring born.  The average
duration of life in this country has increased by about
one-third in the last sixty years, and the birth-rate has
fallen in almost exactly the same proportion.  The position
of a nation in the scale of civilisation may almost be gauged
by its births and deaths.  The order in Europe, beginning
with the lowest birth-rate, is France, Belgium, Sweden,
the United Kingdom, Switzerland, Norway, Denmark,
Holland, Germany, Spain, Austria, Italy, Hungary, the
Balkan States, Russia.  The order of death-rates, again
beginning at the bottom, is Holland, Denmark, Norway,
Sweden, Switzerland, the United Kingdom, Belgium,
Germany, France, Italy, Austria, Serbia, Spain, Bulgaria,
Hungary, Roumania, Russia.  These two lists, as will
be seen, correspond very nearly with the scale of descending civilisation, the only notable exception being the low
position of France in the second list.  This anomaly is
explained by the fact that France having a stationary
population, the death-rate in that country corresponds
nearly with the mean expectation of life, whereas in
countries where the population is increasing rapidly,
either by excess of births over deaths or by immigration,
the preponderance of young lives brings the death-rate
down.  We must, therefore, be on our guard against
supposing that countries with the lowest death-rates are
necessarily the most healthy.  In New Zealand, for
example, the death-rate is under 10 per 1000, the lowest
in the world ; and though that country is undoubtedly

healthy, no one supposes that the average duration of life in New Zealand is a hundred years. To ascertain whether a nation is long-lived, we must correct the crude death-rate by taking into account the average age of the population. When this correction has been made, a low death-rate, and the low birth-rate which necessarily accompanies it, is a sign that the doctors are doing their duty by keeping their patients alive. If our physicians desire more maternity cases, they must make more work for the undertaker. Large families almost always mean a high infant mortality ; and it is significant that a twelfth child has a very much poorer chance of survival than a first or second. The agitation for the endowment of motherhood and the reduction of infant mortality is therefore futile, because, while other conditions remain the same, every baby ' saved ' sends another baby out of the world or prevents him from coming into it. The number of the people is not determined by philanthropists or even by parents. Children will come somehow whenever there is room for them, and go when there is none. But other conditions do not remain the same, and it is in these other conditions that we must seek the causes of expansion or contraction in the numbers of a community.

At the end of the sixteenth century the population of England and Wales amounted to about five millions, and a hundred years later to about six. There is no reason to think that under the conditions then existing the country could have supported a larger number. The birth-rate was kept high by the pestilential state of the towns, and thus the pressure of numbers was less felt than it is now, since it was possible to have, though not to rear, unlimited families. Occasionally, from accidental circumstances, England was for a short time under-populated, and these were the periods when, according to Professor Thorold Rogers, Archdeacon Cunningham, and other authorities, the labourer was well off. The most striking example was in the half-century after the Black Death, which carried off nearly half the population. Wages increased threefold, and the Government tried in vain to protect employers by enforcing pre-plague rates. Not only were

wages high, but food was so abundant that farmers often
gave their men a square meal which was not in the contract.
The other period of prosperity for the working man, according to our authorities, was the second quarter of the
eighteenth century. It has not, we think, been noticed
that this also followed a temporary set-back in the population. In 1688 the population of England and Wales was
5,500,520 ; in 1710 it was more than a quarter of a million
less. The cause of this decline is obscure, but its effects
soon showed themselves in easier conditions of life,
especially for the poor. Such periods of under-saturation,
which some new countries are still enjoying, are necessarily
short. Population flows in as naturally as water finds
its level.

It was not till the accession of George III that the
increase in our numbers became rapid. No one until
then would have thought of singling out the Englishman
as the embodiment of the good apprentice. Meteren, in
the sixteenth century, found our countrymen ' as lazy
as Spaniards ' ; most foreigners were struck by our fond-
ness for solid food and strong drink. The industrial
revolution came upon us suddenly ; it changed the whole
face of the country and the apparent character of the
people. In the far future our descendants may look back
upon the period in which we are living as a strange episode
which disturbed the natural habits of our race. The first
impetus was given by the plunder of Bengal, which, after
the victories of Clive, flowed into the country in a broad
stream for about thirty years. This ill-gotten wealth
played the same part in stimulating English industries
as the ' five milliards,' extorted from France, did for
Germany after 1870. The half-century which followed was
marked by a series of inventions, which made England the
workshop of the world. But the basis of our industrial
supremacy was, and is, our coal. Those who are in the
habit of comparing the progressiveness of the North-
Western European with the stagnation or decadence of
the Latin races, forget the fact, which is obvious when it
has once been pointed out, that the progressive nations
are those which happen to have valuable coal fields.

Countries which have no coal are obliged to import it, paying the freight, or to smelt their iron with charcoal. This process makes excellent steel—the superiority of Swedish razors is due to wood-smelting—but it is so wasteful of wood that the Mediterranean peoples very early in history injured their climate by cutting down their scanty forests, thereby diminishing their rainfall, and allowing the soil to be washed off the hillsides. The coasts of the Mediterranean are, in consequence, far less productive than they were two thousand years ago. But in England, when the start was once made, all circumstances conspired to turn our once beautiful island into a chaos of factories and mean streets, reeking of smoke, millionaires, and paupers. We were no longer able to grow our own food ; but we made masses of goods which the manufacturers were eager to exchange for it ; and the population grew like crops on a newly-irrigated desert. During the nineteenth century the numbers were nearly quadrupled. Let those who think that the population of a country can be increased at will, reflect whether it is likely that any physical, moral, or psychological change came over the nation coincidently with the inventions of the spinning-jenny and the steam-engine. It is too obvious for dispute that it was the possession of capital wanting employment, and of natural advantages for using it, that called these multitudes of human beings into existence, to eat the food which they paid for by their labour. And it should be equally obvious that the existence of forty-six millions of people upon 121,000 square miles of territory depends entirely upon our finding a market for our manufactures abroad, for so only are we able to pay for the food of the people. It is most unfortunate that these exports must, with our present population, include coal, which, if we had any thought for posterity, we should guard jealously and use sparingly ; for in five hundred years at the outside our stock will be gone, and we shall sink to a third-rate Power at once. We are sacrificing the future in order to provide for an excessive and discontented population in the present. During the present century we have begun to be conscious that our foreign trade is threatened ; and so sensitive is the birth-rate to economic conditions that it has begun to curve very slightly downward in relation to the death-rate, instead of descending with it in parallel lines.[1] This may be partly due to the curtailment of facilities for emigration, owing to the filling up of the new countries. For emigration does not diminish the population of the country which the emigrants leave ; it only increases its birth-rate.

We are now in a position to enumerate the causes which actually lead to an increase in the population of a country. The first is an increase in the amount of food produced in the country itself. If the parks and gardens of the gentry were ploughed up or turned into allotments, a few hundred thousands would be added to the population of the United Kingdom, at the cost of one of the few remaining beauties which make our country attractive to the eye. The introduction of the potato into Ireland added several millions of squalid inhabitants to that ill-conditioned island, and when the crop failed, large numbers of them inflicted themselves on the United States, to the detriment of that country. The richest countries to-day are those which produce more food than they require, such as the United States, Canada, Australia, Roumania, and the Argentine. (We need hardly say that throughout this survey we are using the statistics of the years immediately before the war.) But this state of things cannot last long, for the net increase in such countries is invariably high, either by reason of a very high birth-rate, as in Roumania, or because newcomers flock in to enjoy a land of plenty. Another condition which leads to abnormally rapid increase is found when a civilised nation conquers and administers a backward country, introducing better methods of agriculture, and especially irrigation and the reclamation of waste lands. The alien Government also gives greater security, without raising the standard of living among the natives, since the dominant race usually monopolises the lucrative

---

[1] In the small islands round our coast increase has ceased for some decades. The vital statistics of these islands furnish an excellent illustration of automatic adjustment to a state of supersaturation.

careers. In this way we are directly responsible for increasing the population of Egypt from seven millions in 1883 to nine and three-quarter millions in 1899, an augmentation which, in the absence of immigration, illustrates the great natural fertility of the human race in the rare circumstances when unchecked increase is possible. Still more remarkable is the rise in the population of Java from five millions in 1825 to twenty-eight and a half millions in the first decade of this century. The cause of this increase is the augmented supply of food combined with a very low standard of living, a combination which is specially characteristic of Asia, where extreme super-saturation exists in India and China. A third cause is production of goods which can be exchanged for food grown abroad. This exchange, as we have seen, is stimulated by the presence of capital seeking employment. Our large towns are the creation of the capitalist, much more than if he had populated their depressing streets with his own children. Fourthly, a reduction in the standard of living of course makes a larger population possible. The misery of the working class in the generation after the Napoleonic Wars was a condition of the prosperity of our export trade at this period ; and conversely, the prosperity of our export trade was necessary to the existence of the new inhabitants. Capitalism is the cause of our dense population ; and the proletariat would infallibly cut their own throats by destroying it.

It is an important question whether a crowded population adds to the security of a nation or not. Numbers are undoubtedly of great importance in modern warfare. The French would have been less able to resist the Germans without allies in 1914 than they were in 1870. But we must not suppose that France could support a much larger population without reducing her standard of living to the point of under-feeding ; and an under-fed nation is incapable of the endurance required of first-class soldiers. A nation may be so much weakened in physique by under-feeding as to be impotent from a military point of view, in spite of great numbers ; this is the case in India and China. Deficient nourishment also diminishes the day's work. If European and American capital goes to China, and provides proper food for the workmen, we may have an early opportunity of discovering whether the supporters of the League of Nations have any real conscientious objection to violence and bloodshed. We may surmise that the European man, the fiercest of all beasts of prey, is not likely to abandon the weapons which have made him the lord and the bully of the planet. He has no other superiority to the races which he arrogantly despises. Under a régime of peace the Asiatic would probably be his master. To return from a short digression, we must note further that a nation with a low standard has no reserve to fall back upon ; it lives on the margin of subsistence, which may easily fail in war-time, especially if much food is imported when conditions are normal. It can hardly be an accident that in this war the nations with a high birth-rate broke up in the order of their fecundity, while France stood like a rock. The sacrifice of comfort to numbers, which we have seen to be possible by maintaining a low standard of living, not only diminishes the happiness of a nation, and keeps it low in the scale of civilisation ; it may easily prove to be a source of weakness in war.

The expedients often advocated to encourage denser population—which those who urge them thoughtlessly assume to be a good thing—such as endowment of parenthood, and better housing at the expense of the taxpayer —have no effect except to penalise and sterilise those who pay the doles, for the benefit of those who receive them. They are intensely dysgenic in their operation, for they cripple and at last eliminate just those stocks which have shown themselves to be above the average in ability. The process has already advanced a long way, even without the reckless legislation which is now advocated. The lowest birth-rates, less than half that of the unskilled labourers, are those of the doctors, the teaching profession, and ministers of religion. The position of this class, intellectually and often physically the finest in the kingdom, is rapidly becoming intolerable, and it is the wastrels who mainly benefit by their spoliation.

The causes of shrinkage in population are the opposites of those which we have found to promote its increase. The production of food may be diminished by the exhaustion of the soil, or by the progressive aridity caused by cutting down woods. The manufacture of goods to be exchanged for food may fall off owing to foreign competition, a result which is likely to follow from a rise in the standard of living, for the labourer then demands higher wages, and consumes more food per head, which of itself must check fertility, since the same amount of food will now support a smaller number. The delusion shared by the whole working class that they can make work for each other, at wages fixed by themselves, is ludicrous; a community cannot subsist ' by taking in each other's washing.' Or the supply of importable food may fail by the peopling up of the countries which grow it. Any conditions which make it no longer worth while to invest capital in business, or which destroy credit, have the same effect. One of the causes of the decay of the Roman Empire was the drain of specie to the East in exchange for perishable commodities. When trade is declining a general listlessness comes over the industrial world, and the output falls still further. There have been alleged instances of peoples which have dwindled and even disappeared from *taedium vitae*. This is said to have been the cause of the extinction of the Guanches of the Canary Islands; but the symptoms described rather suggest an outbreak of sleeping-sickness.

Paradoxical as it may seem, neither voluntary restriction of births, nor famine, nor pestilence, nor war, has much effect in reducing numbers. Birth-control, instead of diminishing the population, may only lower the death-rate. France in 1781, with a birth-rate of 39, had much the same net increase as in the years before the war with a birth-rate of 20. The parallel lines of the births and deaths in this country have already been mentioned. Famine and pestilence are followed at once by an increased number of births. India and China, though frequently ravaged by both these scourges, remain super-saturated. Of course, if the famine is chronic, the population must fall to the point where the food is sufficient; and a zymotic disease which has become endemic may be too strong for the natural fertility of the nation attacked, as has happened to several barbarous races; but an invasion of plague, cholera, or influenza has no permanent effect on the numbers of Europeans. War resembles plague in its action upon population. When, as in the late war, nearly the whole of the able-bodied men are on active service, the loss of population caused by cessation of births is greater than all the fatal casualties of the battle-field. A rough calculation gives the result that twelve million lives have been lost to the belligerent nations by the separation of husbands and wives during the war. And yet it may be predicted that these losses, added to the eight millions or so who have been killed, would be made good in a very few years but for the destruction of capital and credit which the war has caused. If we study the vital statistics of a country like Germany, which has engaged in several severe wars since births and deaths began to be registered, we shall find that the contour-line representing the fluctuations of the birth-rate indicates a steep ravine in the year or years while the war lasted, followed by a hump or high table-land for several years after. In a short time, as far as numbers are concerned, the war is as if it had never been. When we remember that the number of possible fathers is much reduced by casualties, this rise in the birth-rate after a war offers a strong confirmation of the thesis which we have been maintaining, that the ebb and flow of population are not affected by conscious intention, but by increased or diminished pressure of numbers upon subsistence. If the German people, who before the war consumed more food than was good for them, have been habituated by our blockade to a reasonable abstemiousness, we shall have contributed to the eventual increase of the German people, in spite of all their soldiers whom we killed in France, and the civilians whom we starved in Germany. And if our success leads to a greater consumption by our working class, our population will show a corresponding decline. Emigration, as we have seen, does not diminish the home

H

population by a single unit ; and so, while there are empty lands available for colonisation, it is by far the best method of adding to the numbers of our race.

It should now be possible to form a judgment on the prospects of the Anglo-Saxon race in various parts of the world. In India, Burma, New Guinea, the West Indian Islands, and tropical Africa there is no possibility of ever planting a healthy European population. These dependencies may grow food for us, or send us articles which we can exchange for food, but they are not, and never can be, colonies of Anglo-Saxons. The prospects of South Africa are very dubious. The white man is there an aristocrat, directing semi-servile labour. The white population of the gold and diamond fields will stay there till the mines give out, and no longer. Large tracts of the country may at last be occupied only by Kaffirs. The United States of America are becoming less Anglo-Saxon every year, and this process is likely to continue, since in unskilled labour the Italian and the Pole seem to give better value for their wages than the Englishman or born American, with his high standard of comfort. In Canada, the temperate part of Australia, New Zealand, and Tasmania the chances for a large and flourishing English-speaking population seem to be very favourable, though in these dominions the high standard of living is a check to population, and in the case of Australasia the possibility of foreign conquest, while these priceless lands are still half empty, cannot be altogether excluded.

Even more interesting to most of us is the future of our race at home. As regards quality, the outlook for the present is bad. We have seen that the destruction of the upper and professional classes by taxation directed expressly against them has already begun, and this victimisation is certain to become more and more acute, till these classes are practically extinguished. The old aristocracy showed a tendency to decay even when they were unduly favoured by legislation, and a little more pressure will drive them to voluntary sterility and extermination. Even more to be regretted is the doom of the professional aristocracy, a caste almost peculiar to our country. These families can often show longer, and usually much better pedigrees than the peerage ; the persistence of marked ability in many of them, for several generations, is the delight of the eugenist. They are perhaps the best specimens of humanity to be found in any country of the world. Yet they have no prospects except to be gradually harassed out of existence, like the *curiales* of the later Roman Empire. The power will apparently be grasped by a new highly privileged class, the aristocracy of labour. This class, being intelligent, energetic, and intensely selfish, may retain its domination for a considerable time. It is a matter of course that, having won its privilege of exploiting the community, it will use all its efforts to preserve that privilege and to prevent others from sharing it. In other words, it will become an exclusive and strongly conservative class, on a broader basis than the territorial and commercial aristocracies which preceded it. It will probably be strong enough to discontinue the system of State doles which encourages the wastrel to multiply, as he does multiply, much faster than the valuable part of the population. We are at present breeding a large parasitic class subsisting on the taxes and hampering the Government. The comparative fertility of the lowest class as compared with the better stocks has greatly increased, and is still increasing. The competent working-class families, as well as the rich, are far less fertile than the waste products of our civilisation. Dr. Tredgold found that 43 couples of the parasitic class averaged 7·4 children per family, while 91 respectable couples from the working class averaged only 3·7 per family. Mr. Sidney Webb examined the statistics of the Hearts of Oak Benefit Society, which is patronised by the best type of mechanic, and found that the birth-rate among its members has fallen 46 per cent. between 1881 and 1901 ; or, taking the whole period between 1880 and 1904, the falling off is 52 per cent. This decline proves that the period of industrial expansion in England is nearly over. It would be far better if our birth-rate were as low as that of France, as it would be but for the reckless propagation of the ' submerged tenth.' England being now a paradise for human refuse, the offscourings of Europe (170,000 in 1908) take the place of the better stocks, whose position is made artificially unfavourable. These doles are at present paid by the minority, and this method may be expected to continue until the looting of the propertied classes comes to an enforced end. This will not take long, for it is certain that the amount of wealth available for plunder is very much smaller than is usually supposed. It is easy to destroy capital values, but very difficult to distribute them. The time will soon arrive when the patient sheep will be found to have lost not only his fleece but his skin, and the privileged workman will then have to choose between taxing himself and abandoning socialism. There is little doubt which he will prefer. The result will be that the festering sore of our slum-population will dry up, and the gradual disappearance of this element will be some compensation, from the eugenic point of view, for the destruction of the intellectual class. This process will considerably, and beneficially, diminish the population : and there are several other factors which will operate in the same direction. High wage industry can only maintain itself against the competition of cheaper labour abroad by introducing every kind of labour-saving device. The number of hands employed in a factory must progressively diminish. And as, in spite of all that ingenuity can do, the competition of the cheaper races is certain to cripple our foreign trade, the trade unions will be obliged to provide for a shrinkage in their numbers. We may expect that every unionist will be allowed to place one son, and only one, in the privileged corporation. A man will become a miner or a railwayman ' by patrimony,' and it will be difficulty to gain admission to a union in any other way. The position of those who cannot find a place within the privileged circle will be so unhappy that most unionists will take care to have one son only. Another change which will tend to discourage families will be the increased employment of women as bread-winners. Nothing is more remarkable in the study of vital statistics than the comparative birth-rates of those districts in which women earn wages, and of those in which they do not. The rate of increase among the miners is as great as that of the reckless casual labourers, and the obvious reason is that the miner's wife loses nothing by having children, since she does not earn wages. Contrast with these high figures (running up to 40 per thousand) the very low birth-rates of towns like Bradford, where the women are engaged in the textile industry and earn regular wages in support of the family budget. If the time comes when the majority of women are wage-earners, we may even see the pressure of population entirely withdrawn. Thus in every class of the nation influences are at work tending to a progressive decrease in our national fertility. It must be remembered, however, that at present the annual increase, in peace time, is 9 or 10 per thousand, so that it may be some time before an equilibrium is reached. But if our predictions are sound, a positive decrease, and probably a rapid one, is likely to follow. For our ability to exchange our manufactures for food will grow steadily less, as the self-indulgent and 'work-shy' labourer succeeds in gaining his wishes. If the coal begins to give out, the retreat will become a rout.

We are witnessing the decline and fall of the social order which began with the industrial revolution 160 years ago. The cancer of industrialism has begun to mortify, and the end is in sight. Within 200 years, it may be—for we must allow for backwashes and cross-currents which will retard the flow of the stream—the hideous new towns which disfigure our landscape may have disappeared, and their sites may have been reclaimed for the plough. Humanitarian legislation, so far from arresting this movement, is more likely to accelerate it, and the same may be said of the insatiate greed of our new masters. It is indeed instructive to observe how cupidity and sentiment, which (with pugnacity) are the only passions which the practical politician needs to consider, usually defeat their own ends. The working man is sawing at the branch on which he is seated. He may benefit for a time a minority of his own class, but only by sealing the doom of the rest. A densely populated country, which is unable to feed itself, can never be a working-man's paradise, a land of short hours and high wages. And the sentimentalist, kind only to be cruel, unwittingly promotes precisely the results which he most deprecates, though they are often much more beneficial than his own aims. The evil that he would he does not ; and the good that he would not, that he sometimes does.

For, much as we must regret the apparently inevitable ruin of the upper and upper middle classes, to which England in the past has owed the major part of her greatness, we cannot regard the trend of events as an unmixed misfortune. The industrial revolution has no doubt had some beneficial results. It has founded the British Empire, the most interesting and perhaps the most successful experiment in government on a large scale that the world has yet seen. It has foiled two formidable attempts to place Europe under the heel of military monarchies. It has brought order and material civilisation to many parts of the world which before were barbarous. But these achievements have been counterbalanced by many evils, and in any case they have done their work. The aggregation of mankind in large towns is itself a misfortune ; the life of great cities is wholesome neither for body nor for mind. The separation of classes has become more complete ; the country may even be divided into the picturesque counties where money is spent, and the ugly counties where it is made. Except London and the sea-ports, the whole of the South of England is more or less parasitic. We must add that in the early days of the movement the workman and his children were exploited ruthlessly. It is true that if they had not been exploited they would not have existed ; but a root of bitterness was planted which, according to what seems to be the law in such cases, sprang up and bore its poisonous fruit about two generations later. It is a sinister fact that the worst trouble is now made by the youngest men. The large fortunes which were made by the manufacturers were not, on the whole, well spent. Their luxury was not of a refined type ; literature and art were not intelligently encouraged ; and even science was most inadequately supported. The great achievements of the nineteenth century in science and letters, and to a less degree in art, were independent of the industrial world,

and were chiefly the work of that class which is now sink-
ing helplessly under the blows of predatory taxation.
Capitalism itself has degenerated ; the typical millionaire
is no longer the captain of industry, but the international
banker and company promoter.  It is more difficult than
ever to find any rational justification for the accumulations
which are in the hands of a few persons.  It is not to
be expected that the working class should be less greedy
and unscrupulous than the educated ; indeed it is plain
that, now that it realises its power, it will be even more
so.   In some ways the national character has stood the
strain of these unnatural conditions very well.  Those
who feared that the modern Englishman would make a
poor soldier have had to own that they were entirely wrong.
But as long as industrialism continues, we shall be in a
state of thinly disguised civil war.  There can be no industrial peace while our urban population remains, because
the large towns are the creation of the system which their
inhabitants now want to destroy.  They can and will
destroy it, but only by destroying themselves.  When
the suicidal war is over we shall have a comparatively
small population, living mainly in the country and cultivating the fruits of the earth.  It will be more like the
England of the eighteenth century than the England which
we know.  There will be no very rich men ; and if the
birth-rate is regulated there should be no paupers.  It
will be a far pleasanter age to live in than the present, and
more favourable to the production of great intellectual
work, for life will be more leisurely, and social conditions
more stable.  We may hope that some of our best families
will determine to survive, *coûte que coûte,* until these
better times arrive.  We shall not attempt to prophesy
what the political constitution will be.  Every existing
form of government is bad ; and our democracy can hardly
survive the two diseases which generally kill democracies
—reckless plunder of the national wealth, and the impotence
of the central government in face of revolutionary and
predatory sectionalism.
  Meanwhile, we must understand that although the
consideration of mankind in the mass, and the calculation

of tendencies based on figures and averages, must lead
us to somewhat pessimistic and cynical views of human
nature, there is no reason why individuals, unless they
wish to make a career out of politics (since it is the sad fate
of politicians always to deal with human nature at its
worst), should conform themselves to the low standards
of the world around them.  It is only ' in the loomp '
that humanity, whether poor or rich, ' is bad.'  There
are materials, though far less abundant than we could
wish, for a spiritual reformation, which would smooth the
transition to a new social order, and open to us unfailing
sources of happiness and inspiration, which would not
only enable us to tide over the period of dissolution, but
might make the whole world our debtor.  No nation is
better endowed by nature with a faculty for sane idealism
than the English.  We were never intended to be a nation
of shopkeepers, if a shopkeeper is doomed to be merely
a shopkeeper, which of course he is not.  Our brutal
commercialism has been a temporary aberration ; the
quintessential Englishman is not the hero of Smiles' ' Self-
help ' ; he is Raleigh, Drake, Shakespeare, Milton, Johnson,
or Wordsworth, with a pleasant spice of Dickens.  He is,
in a word, an idealist who has not quite forgotten that he
is descended from an independent race of sea-rovers,
accustomed to think and act for themselves.  Mr. Havelock Ellis, one of the wisest and most fearless of our prophets
to-day, quotes from an anonymous journalist a prediction
which may come true : ' London may yet be the spiritual
capital of the world ; while Asia—rich in all that gold
can buy and guns can give, lord of lands and bodies, builder
of railways and promulgator of police regulations, glorious
in all material glories—postures, complacent and obtuse,
before a Europe content in the possession of all that
matters.'  For, as the Greek poet says, ' the soul's wealth
is the only real wealth.'  The spirit creates values, while
the demagogue shrieks to transfer the dead symbols of them.
' All that matters ' is what the world can neither give nor
take away.  The spiritual integration of society which
we desire and behold afar off must be illuminated by the
dry light of science, and warmed by the rays of idealism,

a white light but not cold. And idealism must be compacted as a religion, for it is the function of religion to prevent the fruits of the flowering-times of the spirit from being lost. Science has not yet come to its own in forming the beliefs and practice of mankind, because it has been so much excluded from higher education, and so much repressed by sentimentalism under the wing of religion. The nation that first finds a practical reconciliation between science and idealism is likely to take the front place among the peoples of the world. In England we have to struggle not only against ignorance, but against a deep-rooted intellectual insincerity, which is our worst national fault. The Englishman hates an idea which he has never met before, as he hates the disturber of his privacy in a steamship cabin; and he takes opportunities of making things unpleasant for those who utter indiscreet truths. As Samuel Butler says : ' We hold it useful to have a certain number of melancholy examples whose notorious failure shall serve as a warning to those who do not cultivate a power of immoral self-control which shall prevent them from saying, or even thinking, anything that shall not be to their immediate and palpable advantage.' To do our countrymen justice, it is often not self-interest, but a tendency to deal with the concrete instance, in disregard of the general law, that blinds them to the larger aspects of great problems. Those who are able to trace causes and effects further than the majority must expect to be unpopular, but they will not mind it, if they can do good by speaking. The logic of events will justify them, and science has a new weapon in official statistics which will register at once the disastrous effects upon wealth and trade which the insane theories of the demagogue will bring about. No agitator can explain away ascertained figures ; if we go down hill, we shall do it with our eyes open. It may be that reactions will be set up which will render the anticipations in this article erroneous. Things never turn out either so well or so badly as they logically ought to do. Prophecy is only an amusement ; what does concern us all deeply is that we should see in what direction we are now moving.

# BISHOP GORE AND THE CHURCH OF ENGLAND

## (1908)

THE strength and the weakness of the Anglican Church lie in the fact that it is not the best representative of any well-defined type of Christianity. It is not strictly a Protestant body; for Protestantism is the democracy of religion, and the Church of England retains a hierarchical organisation, with an order of priests who claim a divine commission not conferred upon them by the congregation. It is not a State Church as the Russian Empire has [1] a State Church. That is a position which it has neither the will nor the power to regain. Still less could it ever justify a claim to separate existence as a purely Catholic Church, independent of the Church of Rome. A community of Catholics whose claim to be a Catholic and not a Protestant Church is denied by all other Catholics, by all Protestants, and by all who are neither Catholics nor Protestants, could not long retain sufficient prestige to keep its adherents together. The destiny of such a body is written in the history of the 'Old Catholics,' who seceded from Rome because they would not accept the dogma of Papal infallibility. The seceders included many men of high character and intellect, but in numbers and influence they are quite insignificant. The Church of England has only one title to exist, and it is a strong one. It may claim to represent the religion of the English people as no other body can represent it. 'No Church,' Döllinger wrote in 1872, 'is so national, so deeply rooted in popular affection, so bound up with the institutions and manners of the country,

In 1908.

or so powerful in its influence on national character.' These words are still partly true, though it is not possible to make the assertion with so much confidence as when Döllinger wrote. The English Church represents, on the religious side, the convictions, tastes, and prejudices of the English gentleman, that truly national ideal of character, which has long since lost its adventitious connexion with heraldry and property in land. A love of order, seemliness, and good taste has led the Anglican Church along a middle path between what a seventeenth-century divine called ' the meretricious gaudiness of the Church of Rome and the squalid sluttery of fanatic conventicles.' A keen sense of honour and respect for personal uprightness, a hatred of cruelty and treachery, created and long maintained in the English Church an intense repugnance against the priestcraft of the Roman hierarchy, feelings which have only died down because the bitter memories of the sixteenth century have at last become dim. A jealous love of liberty, combined with contempt for theories of equality, produced a system of graduated ranks in Church government which left a large measure of freedom, both in speech and thought, even to the clergy, and encouraged no respect for what Catholics mean by authority. The Anglican Church is also characteristically English in its dislike for logic and intellectual consistency and in its distrust of undisciplined emotionalism, which in the seventeenth and eighteenth centuries was known and dreaded under the name of ' enthusiasm.' This type is not essentially aristocratic. It does not traverse the higher ideals of the working class, which respects and admires the qualities of the ' gentleman,' though it resents the privileges long connected with the name. But it has no attraction for what may be impolitely called the vulgar class, whose religious feelings find a natural vent in an unctuous emotionalism and sentimental humanitarianism. This class, which forms the backbone of Dissent and Liberalism, is instinctively antipathetic to Anglicanism. Nor does the Anglican type of Christianity appeal at all to the ' Celtic fringe,' whose temperament is curiously opposite to that of the English, not only in religion but in most other matters. The Irish and the Welsh are no more likely to become Anglicans than the lowland Scotch are to adopt Roman Catholicism. Whether Dissent is a permanent necessity in England is a more difficult question, in spite of the class differences of temperament above mentioned. If the Anglican organisation were elastic enough to permit the order of lay-readers to be developed on strongly Evangelical lines, the lower middle class might find within the Church the mental food which it now seeks in Nonconformist chapels, and might gain in breadth and dignity by belonging once more to a great historic body.

The Church of England, then, can justify its existence as English Christianity, and in no other way. It began its separate career with a series of (doubtless) illogical compromises, in the belief that there is an underlying unity, though not uniformity, in the religion as well as in the character of the English people, which would be strong enough to hold a national Church together. The dissenters from the Reformation settlement were numerically insignificant, and their existence was not regarded as a peril to the Church, for it was recognised that in a free country absolute agreement cannot be secured. The Roman Catholics, after some futile persecution, were allowed to remain loyal to their old allegiance in spiritual matters, while the Independents and similar bodies were anarchical on principle, and upheld the 'dissidence of Dissent' as a thing desirable in itself. But the defection of the Wesleyan Methodists was another matter. This was a blow to the Church of England as irreparable as the loss of Northern Europe to the Papacy. It finally upset the balance of parties in the Church, by detaching from it the larger number of the Evangelicals, particularly in the tradesman class. It gave a great stimulus to Nonconformity, which now became for the first time an important factor in the national life. Till the Wesleyan secession, the Nonconformists in England had been a feeble folk. From a return made to the Crown in 1700, it appeared that the Dissenters numbered about one in twenty of the population. Now they are as numerous as the Anglicans. Their prestige has also been largely augmented by their dominating position in the United States, where the Episcopal Church, long viewed with disfavour as tainted with British sympathies, has never recovered its lost ground, and is a comparatively small, though wealthy and influential sect. Within the Anglican communion, the inevitable religious revival of the nineteenth century began on Evangelical lines, but soon took a form determined by other influences than those which covered England with the ostentatiously hideous chapels of the Wesleyans. The extent of the revival has indeed been much exaggerated by the numerous apologists of the Catholic movement. The undoubted increase of professional zeal, activity, and efficiency among the clergy has been taken as proof of a corresponding access of enthusiasm among the laity, for which there is not much evidence. In spite of slovenly services and an easy standard of clerical duty, the observances of religion held a larger place in the average English home before the Oxford Movement than is often supposed, larger, indeed, than they do now, when family prayers and Bible reading have been abandoned in most households.

The Oxford Movement claimed to be, and was, a revival of the principles of Anglo-Catholicism, which had not been left without witness for any long period since the Reformation. The continuity is certain, as is the continuity of the Ritualism of our day with the Tractarianism of seventy years ago; but the development has been rapid, especially in the last thirty years. Those who can remember the High Churchmen of Pusey's generation, or their disciples who in many country parsonages preserved the faith of their Tractarian teachers whole and undefiled, must be struck by the divergence between the principles which they then heard passionately maintained, and those which the younger generation, who use their name and enjoy their credit, avow to be their own.

In the Tractarians the Nonjurors seemed to have come to life again, and one might easily find enthusiastic Jacobites among them. Unlike their successors, they showed no sympathy with political Radicalism. Their love for and loyalty to the English Church, which found melodious expression in Keble's poetry, were intense. They were not hostile to Evangelicalism within the Church, until the ultra-Protestant party declared war against them ; but they viewed Dissent with scorn and abhorrence. They would gladly have excluded Nonconformists from any status in the Universities, and opposed any measures intended to conciliate their prejudices or remove their disabilities. Archdeacon Denison, in his sturdy opposition to the ' conscience clause ' in Church schools, was a typical representative of the old High Church party. But still more bitter was their animosity against religious Liberalism. Even after the feud with the Evangelicals had developed into open war, Pusey was ready to join with Lord Shaftesbury and his party in united anathemas against the authors of ' Essays and Reviews.' The beginnings of Old Testament criticism evoked an outburst of fury almost unparalleled. When Bishop Gray, of Cape Town, solemnly ' excommunicated ' Bishop Colenso, of Natal, and enjoined the faithful to ' treat him as a heathen man and a publican,' for exposing the unhistorical character of portions of the Pentateuch, he became a hero with the whole High Church party, and even the more liberal among the bishops were cowed by the tempest of feeling which the case aroused. In the same period, many Oxford men can remember Bishop Wilberforce's attack upon Darwinism, and, somewhat later, Dean Burgon's University sermon which ended with the stirring peroration : ' Leave me my ancestors in Paradise, and I leave you yours in the Zoological Gardens ! ' From the same pulpit Liddon, a little before his death, uttered a pathetic remonstrance against the course which his younger disciples were taking about inspiration and tradition.

Reverence for tradition was a very prominent feature in the theology of the older generation. They spent an immense amount of time, learning, and ingenuity in establishing a *catena* of patristic and orthodox authority for their principles, reaching back to the earliest times, and handed down in this country by a series of Anglo-Catholic divines. This unbroken tradition was conceived of as purely static, a ' mechanical unpacking,' as Father Tyrrell puts it, of the doctrine once delivered to the Apostles.

The Church, according to their theory, was supernaturally guided by the Holy Ghost, and its decisions were consequently infallible, as long as the Church remained undivided. Thus the earlier General Councils, before the schism between East and West, may not be appealed against, and the Creeds drawn up by them can never be revised. Since the great schism, the infallible inspiration of the Church has been in abeyance, like an old English peerage when a peer leaves two or more daughters and no sons. This fantastic theory condemns all later developments, and leaves the Church under the weight of the dead hand. On the question of the Establishment the party was divided, some of its members attaching great value to the union of Church and State, while others made claims for the Church, in the matter of self-government, which were hardly compatible with Establishment. Their bond of union was their conviction of ' the necessity of impressing on people that the Church was more than a merely human institution ; that it had privileges, sacraments, a ministry, ordained by Christ Himself ; that it was a matter of highest obligation to remain united to the Church.' [1]

As compared with their successors, the Tractarians were academic and learned ; they preached thoughtful and carefully prepared sermons ; they cared little for ecclesiastical millinery, and often acquiesced in very simple and ' backward ' ceremonial. Their theory of the Church, their personal piety and self-discipline, were of a thoroughly medieval type, as may be seen from certain chapters in the life of Pusey. They fought the battle of Anglo-Catholicism, at Oxford and elsewhere, with a whole-hearted conviction that knew no misgivings or scruples. Oxford has not forgotten the election, as late as 1862, of an orthodox naval officer to a chair of history for which Freeman was a candidate.

A change of tone was already noticeable, according to Dean Church, soon after Newman's secession. Many High Churchmen, in speaking of the English Church, became apologetic or patronising or lukewarm. Progressive

---

[1] Palmer's *Narrative*, p. 20.

members of the party professed a distaste for the name
Anglican, and wished to be styled Catholics pure and simple.
The same men began to speak of their opponents in the
Church as Protestants; no longer as ultra-Protestants.
Other changes soon manifested themselves. The archæo-
logical side of the movement lost its interest; the appeal to
antiquity became only a convenient argument to defend
practices adopted on quite other grounds. The *epigoni*
of the Catholic revival are not learned; they know even
less of the Fathers than of their Bibles. Their chief
literature consists of a weekly penny newspaper, which
reflects only too well their prejudices and aspirations.
On the other hand, they are far busier than the older
generation. The movement has become democratic;
it has passed from the quadrangles of Oxford to the
streets and lanes of our great cities, where hundreds of
devoted clergymen are working zealously, without care for
remuneration or thought of recognition, among the poorest
of the populace. Of late years, the more energetic section
of the party has not only abandoned the ' Church and
King ' Toryism of the old High Church party, but has
plunged into socialism. The Mirfield community is said
to be strongly imbued with collectivist ideas; and the
Christian Social Union, which is chiefly supported by
High Churchmen, tends to become more and more a Union
of Christian Socialists, instead of being, as was intended
by its founders, a non-political association for the study
of social duties and problems in the light of the Sermon
on the Mount. This attitude is partly the result of a
close acquaintance with the sufferings of the urban proletariat, which moves the priests who minister among
them to a generous sympathy with their lot; and, partly,
it may be, to an unavowed calculation that an alliance
with the most rapidly growing political party may in time
to come be useful to the Church. Their methods of teaching
are also more democratic, though many of them make
the fatal mistake of despising preaching. They rely
partly on what they call ' definite Catholic teaching,'
including frequent exhortations to the practice of confession;
and partly on appeals to the eye, by symbolic ritual and

elaborate ceremonial. Their more ornate services are often admirably performed from a spectacular point of view, and are far superior to most Roman Catholic functions in reverence, beauty, and good taste. The extreme section of the party is contemptuously lawless, not only repudiating the authority of the Judicial Committee of the Privy Council, but flouting the bishops with studied insolence. A glaring instance is to be found in the correspondence between Mr. Athelstan Riley and the Bishop of Oxford, which followed the Report of the Royal Commission on ritual practices.

Doctrinally, the modern Ritualist is prepared to surrender the old theory of inspiration. He takes, indeed, but little interest in the Bible; his oracle is not the Book, but 'the Church.' What he means by the Church it is not easy to say. The old Anglican theory of the infallible undivided Church is not repudiated by him, but does not appeal to minds which look forward much more than backward; he is not yet, except in a few instances, disposed to accept the modern Roman Church as the arbiter of doctrine; and the English Church has no living voice to which he pays the slightest respect. The 'tradition of Western Catholicism' is a phrase which has a meaning for him, and he probably hopes for a reunion, at some distant date, of the Anglican Church with a reformed Rome. It is therefore essential, in his opinion, that no alteration shall take place in the formularies which we share with Rome; the Bible may be thrown to the critics, but the Creeds are inviolable. The Thirty-nine Articles he passes by with silent disdain. They are, he thinks not unjustly, a document to which no one, High, Low, or Broad, can now subscribe without mental reservations.

The theory of development in doctrine, which, in its latest application by 'Modernists' like Loisy and Tyrell, is now agitating the Roman Church, is exciting interest in a few of the more thoughtful Anglo-Catholics; but the majority are blind to the difficulties for which the theory of two kinds of truth is a desperate remedy. Nor is it likely, perhaps, that the plain Englishman will ever allow that an ostensibly historical proposition may be false as a matter of fact, but true for faith.

I

This party in the Church has a lay Pope, who represents the opinions of the more enterprising among the rank and file, and is president of their society, the English Church Union. It has the ably conducted weekly newspaper above referred to, and it has the general sympathy and support of the strongest man in the English Church, Charles Gore, Bishop of Birmingham. This prelate, partly by his personal qualities—his eloquence, high-minded disinterestedness, and splendid generosity, and partly by knowing exactly what he wants, and having full courage of his opinions, has at present an influence in the Anglican Church which is probably far greater than that of any other man. It is therefore a matter of public interest to ascertain what his views and intentions are, as an ecclesiastical statesman and reformer, and as a theologian.

Bishop Gore exercised a strong influence over the younger men at Oxford before the publication of ' Lux Mundi.' But it was his editorship of this book, and his contribution to it, which first brought his name into prominence as a leader of religious thought. The religious public, with rather more penetration than usual, fastened on the pages about inspiration, and the limitations of Christ's human knowledge, which are from the editor's own pen, as the most significant part of the book. The authors are believed to have been annoyed by the disproportionate attention paid to this short section. But in truth these pages indicated a new departure among the High Church party, a change more important than the acceptance of the doctrine of evolution, which was being made smoother for the religious public by the brilliant writings of Aubrey Moore. The acceptance of the verdict of modern criticism as to the authorship of the 110th Psalm, in the face of the recorded testimony of Christ that it was written by David, was a concession to ' Modernism ' which staggered the old-fashioned High Churchman. Liddon did not conceal his distress that such doctrine should have come out of the Pusey House. But the manifesto was well timed ; it enabled the younger men to go forward more freely, and sacrificed nothing that was in any way essential to the Anglo-Catholic position. Since the appearance of 'Lux Mundi,' the High Church clergy have been able without fear to avow their belief in the scientific theories associated with Darwin's name, and their rejection of the rigid doctrine of verbal inspiration, while the Evangelicals, who have not been emancipated by their leaders, labour under the reproach of extreme obscurantism in their attitude towards Biblical studies.

As Canon of Westminster, and then as Bishop of Worcester, and of Birmingham, Dr. Gore has written and spoken much, and has defined his position more closely in relation to Anglo-Catholicism, to Church Reform, and to the social question. It will be convenient to take these three heads separately.

This Bishop regards the excesses of the Ritualists as a deplorable but probably inevitable incident in a great movement. He quotes Newman's remonstrance against some hot-headed members of his adopted Church, who, 'having done their best to set the house on fire, leave to others the task of extinguishing the flames.'[1] But he reminds us that there has always been 'intemperate zeal' in the Church, from the time of St. Paul's letters to the Church at Corinth to our own day. 'It must needs be that offences come,' wherever persons of limited wisdom are very much in earnest. The remedy for extravagance is to give fair scope for the legitimate principle. In the case of the so-called Ritualist movement, the inspiring principle or motive is easily found. It is the idea of a visible Church, exercising lawful authority over its members.

This is the key to Bishop Gore's whole position. It rests on the conviction that Jesus Christ founded, and meant to found, a visible Church, an organised society. It is reasonable, the Bishop says, to suppose that He did intend this, for it is only by becoming embodied in the convictions of a society, and informing its actions, that ideas have reality and power. Christianity could never have lived if there had been no Christian Church. And, from the first, Christians believed that this society, the Catholic Church, was not left to organise itself on any model

[1] *Contemporary Review*, April 1899.

which from time to time might seem to promise the best results, but was instituted from above, as a Divine ordinance, by the authority of Christ Himself.[1] The witness of the early Christian writers is unanimous that the conception of a visible Church was a prominent feature in the Christianity of the sub-apostolic age, and it is plain that the civil power suspected the Christians just because they were so well organised. The Roman Empire was accustomed to tolerate superstitions, but it was part of her policy to repress *collegia illicita*. The witness of the New Testament points in the same direction. Jesus Christ committed His message, not to writing, but to a 'little flock' of devoted adherents. He instituted the two great sacraments (Bishop Gore will admit no uncertainty on this point) to be a token of membership and a bond of brotherhood. He instituted a *civitas Dei* which was to be wide enough to embrace all, but which makes for itself an exclusive claim. The 'heaven' of the first century was a city, a new Jerusalem; Christians are spoken of by St. Paul as citizens of a heavenly commonwealth. The distinction between the universal invisible Church and particular visible Churches is 'utterly unscriptural,' and was overthrown long ago by William Law in his controversy with Hoadley.

As for the 'Apostolical Succession,' Dr. Gore thinks that its principle is more important than the form in which it is embodied. The succession would not be broken if all the presbyters in the Church governed as a college of bishops; and if something of this kind actually happened for a time in the early Church no argument against the Apostolical Succession can be based thereon.[2] The principle is that no ministry is valid which is assumed, which a man takes upon himself, or which is delegated to him from below. That this theory is Sacerdotalism in a sense may be admitted. But it does not imply a *vicarious* priesthood, only a representative one. It does not deny the priesthood which belongs to the Church as a whole. The true sacerdotalism means that Christianity is the life of an organised

---

[1] *The Church and the Ministry*, pp. 9, 10.
[2] *Ibid.*, p. 74.

society, in which a graduated body of ordained ministers is made the instrument of unity. It is no doubt true that in such a Church unspiritual men are made to mediate spiritual gifts, but happily we may distinguish character and office. Nor must we be deterred from asserting our convictions by the indignant protests which we are sure to hear, that we are 'unchurching' the non-episcopal bodies.[1] We do not assert that God is tied to His covenant, but only that we are so.

Dr. Gore has no difficulty in proving that the sacerdotal theory of the Christian ministry took shape at an early date, and has been consistently maintained in the Catholic Church from ancient times to our own day. It is much more difficult to trace it back to the Apostolic age, even if, with Dr. Gore, we accept as certain the Pauline authorship of the Pastoral Epistles, which is still *sub judice*. The 'Didache' is a stumbling-block to those who wish to find Catholic practice in the century after our Lord's death; but that document is dismissed as composed by a Jewish Christian for a Jewish Christian community. After the second century, the apologists for the priesthood are in smooth waters.

The conclusion is that 'the various presbyterian and congregationalist organisations, in dispensing with the episcopal succession, violated a fundamental law of the Church's life.'[2] 'A ministry not episcopally received is invalid, that is to say, it falls outside the conditions of covenanted security, and cannot justify its existence in terms of the covenant.'[3] The Anglican Church is not asking for the cause to be decided all her own way; for she has much to do to recall herself to her true principles. 'God's promise to Judah was that she should remember her ways and should be ashamed, when she should receive her sisters Samaria and Sodom, and that He would give them to her for daughters, but not by her covenant.'[4] The ' covenant ' which the Church is to be content to forgo in order to recover Samaria and *Sodom* (the ' Free Churches ' can hardly be expected to relish this method of opening

---

[1] *The Church and the Ministry*, p. 110.   [2] *Ibid.*, p. 344.
[3] *Ibid.*, p. 345.   [4] *Ibid.*, p. 348.

negotiations) is apparently the covenant between Church and State. 'In the future the Anglican Church must be content to act as, first of all, part and parcel of the Catholic Church, ruled by her laws, empowered by her spirit.' The bishops are to be ready to maintain, at all cost, the inherent spiritual independence which belongs to their office.

Such a theory of the essentials of a true Church necessarily requires, as a corollary, a refutation of the Roman Catholic theory of orders, which reduces the Anglican clergy to the same level as the ministers of schismatical sects. Bishop Gore answers the objection that the Roman Church is the logical expression of his theory of the ministry, by saying that Roman Catholicism is not the development of the whole of the Church, but only of a part of it ; and moreover, that spiritually it does not represent the whole of Christianity as it finds expression in the first Christian age or in the New Testament.[1] The Roman Church is a one-sided outgrowth of the religion of Christ—a development of those qualities in Christianity with which the Latin genius has special affinity. It has committed itself to unhistorical doctrines, involving a deficient appreciation of the intellectual and moral claim of truth to be valued for its own sake no less than for its results. Much of its teaching can only be explained as the result of an ' over-reckless accommodation to the unregenerate natural instincts in religion.' [2] The fact that the largest section of Christendom has become what Rome now is, is no proof that theirs is the line of true development. We can see this clearly enough if we consider the case of Buddhism. The main existing developments of Buddhism are a mere travesty of the spirit of Sakya Muni.[3] In this way Dr. Gore anticipates and rejects the argument since then put forward by Loisy, and other Liberal Catholic apologists, that history has proved Roman Catholicism to be the proper development of Christ's religion. In short, the Anglican Church, which

---

[1] *The Mission of the Church*, p. 32.
[2] *Church Congress Report*, 1896, p. 143.
[3] *Ibid.*, p. 142.

indisputably possesses the Apostolic Succession, has no reason to go humbly to Rome to obtain recognition of her Orders.

So far, in reviewing Bishop Gore's published opinions, we are on familiar High Anglican ground. But what is the Bishop's seat of authority in doctrine ? He has shown himself willing, within limits, to apply critical methods to Holy Scripture. He has very little respect for the infallible Pope. And he would be the last to trust to private judgment—the *testimonium Spiritus Sancti* as understood by some Protestants. Where, then, is the ultimate Court of Appeal ? Bishop Gore finds it in the two earliest of the three Creeds, ' in which Catholic consent is especially expressed ; ' and in a half apologetic manner he adds that this Catholic basis has been ' generally understood ' to imply ' an unrealisable but not therefore unreal appeal to a General Council.' [1] No revision, therefore, of the Church's doctrinal formularies can be made except by the authority of a court which can never, by any possibility, be summoned ! The unique sanctity and obligation which Bishop Gore considers to attach to the Creeds have been asserted by him again and again with a vehemence which proves that he regards the matter as of vital importance. ' There must be no compromise as regards the Creeds. . . . If those who live in an atmosphere of intellectual criticism become incapable of such sincere public profession of belief as the Creed contains, the Church must look to recruit her ministry from classes still capable of a more simple and unhesitating faith.' [2] And, again, in his most recent book : ' I have taken occasion before now to make it evident that, as far as I can secure it, I will admit no one into this diocese, or into Holy Orders, to minister for the congregation, who does not *ex animo* believe the Creeds.' [3] Dr. Gore has not spared to stigmatise as morally dishonest those who desire to serve the Church as its ministers while harbouring doubts about the physical miracle known as the Virgin

[1] *Church Congress Report*, 1903, p. 15.
[2] *Ibid.*, p. 17.
[3] *The New Theology and the Old Religion*, p. 162.

Birth, and one of his clergy was a few years ago induced to resign his living by an aspersion of this kind, to which the Bishop gave publicity in the daily press.

Now it has been generally supposed that the Anglican clergy are bound to declare their adhesion not only to the Creeds, but to the Thirty-nine Articles, and to the infallible truth of Holy Scripture. Bishop Gore, however, holds that when a new deacon, on the day of his ordination, solemnly declares that he ' assents to the Thirty-nine Articles,' and that he ' believes the doctrine therein set forth to be agreeable to the word of God,' he ' can no longer fairly be regarded as bound to particular phrases or expressions in the Articles.' [1] And further, when the same new deacon expresses his ' unfeigned belief in all the canonical Scriptures of the Old and New Testaments,' ' that expression of belief can be fairly and justly made by anyone who believes heartily that the Bible, as a whole, records and contains the message of God to man in all its stages of delivery and that each one of the books contains some element or aspect of this revelation.' [2]

The Bishop himself has affirmed his personal belief that some narratives in the Old Testament are probably not historical. It may fairly be asked on what principle he is prepared to evade the plain sense and intention of a doctrinal test in two cases while stigmatising as morally flagitious any attempts to do the same in a third. For it is unquestionable that a general assent to the Articles does not mean that the man who gives that assent is free to repudiate any ' particular phrases or expressions ' which do not please him. A witness who admitted having signed an affidavit with this intention would cut a poor figure in a law court. And it is difficult to see how adhesion to the antiquated theory of inspiration could be demanded more stringently than by the form of words which was drawn up, as none can doubt, to secure it. These things being so, either the accusation of bad faith applies to the treatment which the Bishop justifies in the case of the Articles and the Bible, or it should not be brought against

---

[1] *Church Congress Report*, 1903, p. 16.    [2] *Ibid.*

those who apply to one clause in their vows the principle which is admitted and used in two others.

There are some honourable men who have abstained from entering the service of the Church on account of these requirements. But there are many others who recognise that knowledge grows and opinions change, while formularies for the most part remain unaltered ; and who consider that, so long as their general position is understood by those among whom they work, it would be overscrupulous to refuse an inward call to the ministry because they know that they will be asked to give a formal assent to unsuitably worded tests drawn up three centuries ago. Dr. Gore himself would probably have been refused ordination fifty years ago on the ground of his lax views on inspiration; and the Bishops who approved of the condemnation of Colenso, who condemned ' Essays and Reviews,' and who would have condemned ' Lux Mundi,' were more ' honest ' to the tests than their successors. But an obstinate persistence in that kind of honesty would have excluded from the ministry all except fools, liars, and bigots. Again, it might have been supposed that the laity also, who at their baptism and confirmation made the same declaration of belief in ' all the articles' of the Apostles' Creed, and who are bidden by the Church to repeat the same Creed every week, are in the same position as the clergy. But the Bishop again attempts to draw a distinction. ' The responsibility of joining in the Creed is left to the conscience of the layman,' but not to the conscience of the clergyman, nor, we suppose, of the choir.[1] This plea seems to us a very lame one. The Church of England has never thought of imposing severer doctrinal tests on the clergy than on the laity, and assent to the Creeds is as integral a part of the baptismal as of the ordination vows.

No loyal Christian wishes to impugn a doctrine which touches so closely the life of the Redeemer as the account of His miraculous conception, which appears, in our texts, in two books of the New Testament. If the tradition is as old as the Church, which is very doubtful, it must, from

---

[1] *The New Theology and the Old Religion*, p. 163.

the nature of the case, rest on the unsupported assertion of Mary, the mother of Jesus ; for Joseph could only testify that the child was not his. It is therefore useless to reinforce the Gospel narrative by appealing to ' Catholic tradition,' [1] as if it could add anything to the evidence. It is significant, however, of the Bishop's own feelings about tradition, that he quietly sets aside the plain statement of the Synoptic Gospels that Joseph and Mary had a large family of four sons and more than one daughter by their marriage. This statement, which is doubtless historical, became intolerable to the conscience of the Church during the long frenzy of asceticism, when marital relations were regarded as impure and degrading ; and in consequence the perpetual virginity of Mary, though contradicted in the New Testament, became as much an article of faith as her conception of Jesus by the Holy Ghost. We have no wish to criticise the arguments for the Virgin Birth which Dr. Gore has collected in his ' Dissertations.' But when a strenuous effort is made to exclude from the ministry of the Church all who cannot declare *ex animo* that they believe it to be a certain historical fact, it becomes a duty to point out that, on ordinary principles of evidence, the story must share the uncertainty which hangs over other strange and unsupported narratives. The Bishop expresses his doubt whether those who regard this miracle as unproven can be convinced of the Divinity of Christ. This only shows how difficult it is for an ecclesiastic in his high position to induce either clergy or laity to talk frankly to him. To most educated men there would be no difficulty in believing that the Son of God became incarnate through the agency of two earthly parents. The analogy of hybrids in the animal world is not felt to apply to the union of the human and divine natures, except by persons of very low intelligence. We should have preferred to be silent on this delicate subject, but for the fact that some men whom the Church can ill spare have been advised officially not to apply for ordination, on account of their views about this miracle. Fortunately, the practice of demanding

---

[1] *Dissertations*, pp. 41–49.

more specific declarations than the law requires has not been adopted in most dioceses.

The question of the miraculous element in religious truth has indeed reached an acute stage. The Catholic doctrine is and always has been that there are two 'orders'—the natural and the supernatural—on the same plane, and distinguishable from each other. The Catholic theologian is prepared to define what occurrences in the lives of the Saints are natural, and what supernatural. Miracles are of frequent occurrence, and are established by ordinary evidence. Three miracles have to be placed to the credit of each candidate for canonisation before he or she is entitled to bear the title of saint, and the evidence for these miracles is sifted by a commission. This theory has been practically abandoned in the English Church. There are few among our ecclesiastics and theologians who would spend five minutes in investigating any alleged supernatural occurrence in our own time. It would be assumed that, if true, it must be ascribed to some obscure natural cause. The result is that the miracles in the Creeds, or in the New Testament, are isolated as they have never been before. They seem to form an order by themselves, a class of fact belonging neither to the world of phenomena as we know it, nor to the world of spirit as we know it. From this situation has arisen the tendency, increasingly prevalent both in the Roman Church and in Protestant Germany, to distinguish 'truths of faith' from 'truths of fact.' The former, it is said, have a representative, symbolic character, and are only degraded by being placed in the same category as physical phenomena. This contention is open to very serious objections, but it at least indicates the actual state of the problem, viz. that to most educated men the miraculous element in Christianity seems to float between earth and heaven, no longer essentially connected with either, while on the other hand the majority of religious people, including a few men of high intelligence, find it difficult to realise their faith without the help of the miraculous. Supernaturalism, which from the scientific point of view is the most unsatisfactory of all theories, traversing as it does the first article in the creed of science—the uniformity of nature — gives, after all, a kind of crude synthesis of the natural and the spiritual, by which it is possible to live; it is, for many persons, an indispensable bridge between the world of phenomena and the world of spirit. But when the heavy-handed dogmatist requires a categorical assent to the literal truth of the miraculous, in exactly the same sense in which physical facts are true, a tension between faith and reason cannot be avoided. And it is in this literal sense that Bishop Gore requires all his clergy to assent to the miracles in the Creeds.

The fact is that the Catholic party in the Church are in a hopeless *impasse* with regard to dogma. They cannot take any step which would divide them from ' the whole Church,' and the whole Church no longer exists except as an ideal—it has long ago been shivered into fragments. The Roman Church is in a much better position. The Pope may at any time ' interpret ' tradition in such a manner as to change it completely—there is no appeal from his authoritative pronouncements ; but for the High Anglican there is no living authority, only the dead hand, and a Council which can never meet. It is much as if no important legislation could be passed in this country without a joint session of our Parliament and the American Congress. It is difficult to see any way of escape, except by accepting the principle of development in a sense which would repudiate the time-honoured ' appeal to antiquity.'

We have next to consider Bishop Gore as a Church Reformer. We have seen that he desires an autonomous Church, which can legislate for itself. The dead hand, which weighs so lightly upon him when it forbids any attempt to revise the formularies of the faith, seems to him intolerably heavy when it obliges the Church to conform to ' the laws, canons, and rubrics of the sixteenth and seventeenth centuries, which it cannot alter or add to.' [1] The only remedy, he thinks, is a really representative assembly, of bishops, presbyters, and laymen. In the early Church, as he points out, the laity were always recognised

---

[1] *Church Congress Report*, 1899, p. 63.

as constituent members of the government of the Church. In a democratic age, the laity as a body should exercise the powers which in the Middle Ages were delegated to, or usurped by, 'emperors, kings, chiefs and lords.' The parish ought to have the real control of the Church buildings, except the chancel; the Church servants ought to be appointed and removed by the parish meeting. It would be a step forward if these parish councils could be organised under diocesan regulation, and invested with the control of the parish finances, except the vicar's stipend; the right to object to the appointment of an unfit pastor; and some power of determining the ceremonial at the Church services. The diocesan synod should become a reality; there should also be provincial synods, which could become national by fusion. But in the last resort the declaration of the mind of the Church on matters of doctrine and morals ought to belong to the bishops.[1]

But who are the laity? 'By a layman,' he says, 'I mean one who fulfils the duties of Church membership— one who is baptised into the Church, who has been confirmed if he has reached years of discretion, and who is a communicant.' A roll of Church members, he suggests, should be kept in each parish, on which should be entered the name of each confirmed person, male or female. The names of those who had passed (say) two years without communicating should be struck off the roll. Further, names should be removable for any scandalous offences.[2]

It is easy to see that the 'communicant franchise' would work entirely in favour of that party in the Church which attaches the greatest importance to that Sacrament. It would exclude a large number of Protestant laymen who subscribe to Church funds, and who on any other franchise would have a share in its government. But we need not suspect Dr. Gore of any *arrière pensée* of this kind. His ideal of parochial life is one which must appeal to all who wish well to the Church. We will quote a few characteristic sentences:

[1] *Church Congress Report*, 1899, pp. 65–67.
[2] *Ibid.*, 1896, pp. 342–346.

'Are we to set to work to revive St. Paul's ideal of the life of a Church ? If so, what we need is not more Christians, but better Christians. We want to make the moral meaning of Church membership understood and its conditions appreciated. We want to make men understand that it costs something to be a Christian ; that to be a Christian, that is, a Churchman, is to be an intelligent participator in a corporate life consecrated to God, and to concern oneself, therefore, as a matter of course, in all that touches the corporate life, its external as well as its spiritual conditions. . . . We Christians are fellow-citizens together in the commonwealth that is consecrated to God, a commonwealth of mortal men with bodies as well as souls.'[1]

With regard to ritual, he will not allow that the disputes are unimportant. The vital question of self-government is at stake. From this point of view, a ' mere ceremony ' may mean a great deal. St. Paul, who said ' Circumcision is nothing,' also said, ' If ye be circumcised Christ shall profit you nothing.'[2] This is quite consistent with his hearty disapproval of the introduction of purely Roman ceremonial.

Does this ideal of a free Church in a free State involve disestablishment ? Not necessarily, Dr. Gore thinks. Why should not legal authority be entrusted to diocesan courts, with a right of appeal to a court of bishops, abolishing the jurisdiction of the Judicial Committee in spiritual cases ? It is the paralysis of spiritual authority, in his opinion, which pushes into prominence all extravagances, and conceals the vast amount of agreement which exists in essentials. ' We are weary of debating societies ; we want the healthy discipline of co-operative government.'[3] The policy of this self-governing Church is to be ' Liberal-Catholic,' a type which ' responds to the moral needs of our great race.'

Such is the scheme of Church reform towards which the Bishop is working ; and he has told us, in the sentence last quoted, what kind of Church he looks forward to see. But what kind of Church would it actually be, if his designs were carried out ? It would not be a national Church ;

---

[1] *Epistle to the Ephesians*, pp. 113, 114.
[2] *Contemporary Review*, April 1899.
[3] *Ibid.*

for his belief that Catholicism 'responds to the moral needs of our race' is contradicted by the whole history of modern England. The laity of England may not be quite 'as Protestant as ever they were,' though we often hear that they are so; but they show no disposition to become Catholics. Catholicism as we know it is Latin Christianity, and even in the Latin countries it is now a hothouse plant, dependent on a special education in Catholic schools and seminaries, with an *index librorum prohibitorum*. Such a system is impossible in England. Seminaries for the early training of future clergymen may indeed be established; but beds of exotics cannot be raised by keeping the gardeners in greenhouses while the young plants are in the open air. The 'Liberal Catholic' Church, accordingly, would shed, by degrees, the very large number of Churchmen who still call themselves Protestant. Nor would the adjective 'Liberal' secure the adhesion of the 'intellectuals.' Bishop Gore's Liberalism would exclude most of them as effectually as the most rigid Conservatism. It would also be a disestablished and disendowed Church; for surely it is building castles in the air to think of episcopal courts recognised by law. The prospect of disestablishment does not alarm the Bishop. Some of his utterances suggest that he would almost welcome it. Indeed, disestablishment is viewed with complacency by an increasing number of High Church clergy. They feel that they can never carry out their plans for de-Protestantising the Church while the Crown has the appointment of the bishops. For even if, as has lately been the case, their party gets more than its due share of preferment, there will always, under the existing system, be a sufficient number of Liberal and Evangelical bishops on the bench to make a consistent policy of Catholicising impossible. And the Catholic party are so admirably organised that they are confident in their power to carry their schemes under any form of self-government, even though the mass of the laity are untouched by their views. Moreover, the town clergy, among whom are to be found advocates of disestablishment, find in many places that the parochial idea has completely broken down. The unit is the congregation, no longer the parish, and the clergy are supported by pew-rents and voluntary offerings, not by endowments. In such parishes, disestablishment might, they think, give them greater liberty, and would make little difference to them in other ways. But in the country districts the case is very different. Thirty years after disestablishment, the quiet country rectory, nestling in its bower of trees and shrubs, with all that it has meant for centuries in English rural life, would in most villages be a thing of the past.

For these reasons, the Bishop's policy of reconstructing the Church of England as a self-governing body, professing definitely Catholic principles and enjoining Catholic practices, seems to us an impossible one. The chief gainer by it would be the Church of Rome, which would gather in the most consistent and energetic of the Anglo-Catholics, who would be dissatisfied at the contrast between the pretensions of their own Church and its isolated position. The non-episcopal bodies would also gain numerous recruits from among the ruins of the Evangelical and Liberal parties in the Church.

But, it may be said, this dismal forecast may be falsified if the Anglican Church can win the masses. The English populace are at present neither Protestant nor Catholic ; they are, if we count heads, mainly heathen. May not the working man, who has no leaning to dissent, unless it be the ' corybantic Christianity ' of the Salvation Army, be brought into the Church ?

Bishop Gore has always shown an earnest sympathy with the aspirations of the working class to improve their material condition. He is also profoundly impressed by the apparent discrepancy between the teachings of Christ about wealth and the principles which His professed disciples wholly follow and in part avow. These anxious questionings form the subject of a fine sermon which he preached at the Church Congress of 1906, on the text about the camel and the needle's eye. Jesus Christ chose to be born of poor and humble parents, in a land remote from the centre of political or intellectual influence, and in the circle of labouring men. He chose to belong to the class of the respectable artisan, and most of the twelve

Apostles came from the same social level. In His teaching He plainly associated blessedness with the lot of poverty, and extreme danger with the lot of wealth. All through the New Testament the assumption is that God is on the side of the poor against the rich. As Jowett once said, there is more in the New Testament against being rich, and in favour of being poor, than we like to recognise. And is not this the cause of our failure to win the masses ? Is it not because we are the Church of capital rather than of labour ? The Church ought to be a community in which religion works upward from below. The Church of England expresses that point of view which is precisely not that which Christ chose for His Church. The incomes of the bishops range them with the wealthier classes ; the clergy associate with the gentry and not with the artisans. We must acknowledge with deep penitence that we are on wrong lines. For himself, the Bishop admits that he has ' a permanently troubled conscience ' in the matter. Then, with that admirable courage and practicality which is the secret of much of his influence, he proceeds to indicate four ' lines of hopeful recovery.' First, the Church must get rid of the administration of poor relief. Where the charity of the Church is understood to mean the patronage of the rich, it can do nothing without disaster. All will be in vain till it has ceased to be a plausible taunt that a man or woman goes to church for what can be got. Secondly, we must give the artisans their true place in Church management, and must consult their tastes in all non-essentials. Thirdly, the clergy should ' concentrate themselves upon bringing out the social meaning of the sacraments,' and giving voice to the spirit of Christian brotherhood. Lastly, we ought to free the clerical profession entirely from any association of class.

The Bishop is not a Collectivist, but he has great sympathy with some of the aims of Socialism. In a ' Pan-Anglican Paper ' just issued, he discusses the attitude of the Church towards Socialism. Christianity, he says, must remain independent of State-Socialism, as of other organisations of society. Socialism would make a far deeper demand on character than most of its adherents realise. ' An experiment in State-Socialism, based on the average level of human character as it exists at present, would be doomed to disastrous failure.' (Bishop Creighton said the same thing more epigrammatically. ' Socialism will only be possible when we are all perfect, and then it will not be needed.') But what we have is no Socialistic State, but a great body of aspiration, based on a great demand for justice in human life. The indictment of our present social organisation is indeed overwhelming, and with this indictment Christianity ought to have the profoundest sympathy, for it is substantially the indictment of the Old Testament prophets. The prophets were on the side of the poor ; and so was our Lord. Where is the prophetic spirit in the Church to-day ? We need ' a tremendous act of penitence.' Our charities have been mere ambulance-work ; but ' the Christian Church was not created to be an ambulance-corps.' We have followed the old school of political economy instead of the prophets and Christ. Broadly, we may contrast two ideals of society : individualism, which means in the long run the right of the strong ; and socialism, which means that the society is supreme over the individual. ' On the whole, Christianity is with Socialism.'

This ' Pan-Anglican Paper ' is a fair representation of the views which are spreading rapidly among the High Church clergy. The party is in fact making a determined effort to enlist the sympathies of the working man with the Church, by offering him in return its sympathy and countenance in his struggle against capitalism. This is a phase of the movement which it is very difficult to judge fairly. Dr. Gore's sermon was calculated to give any Christian who heard it, whether Conservative or Liberal, ' a troubled conscience ; ' and his practical suggestions are as convincing as any suggestions that are not platitudes are likely to be. But in weaker hands this sympathy with the cause of Labour is in great danger of becoming one of the most insidious temptations that can attack a religious body. The Church of England has been freely accused of too great complaisance to the powers that be, when those powers were oligarchic. Some of the clergy are now trying to repeat, rather than redress, this error, by an obsequious attitude to King Working-man. But the Church ought to be equally proof against the *vultus instantis tyranni* and the *civium ardor prava iubentium.* The position of a Church which should sell itself to the Labour party would be truly ignominious. It would be used so long as the politicians of the party needed moral support and eloquent advocacy, and spurned as soon as its services were no longer necessary. The taunt of Helen to Aphrodite in the third book of the ' Iliad ' sounds very apposite when we read the speeches of some clerical ' Christian Socialists,' who find it more exciting to organise processions of the unemployed than to attend to their professional duties.

> ἧσο παρ' αὐτὸν ἰοῦσα, θεῶν δ' ἀπόεικε κελεύθου,
> μηδ' ἔτι σοῖσι πόδεσσιν ὑποστρέψειας Ὄλυμπον,
> ἀλλ' αἰεὶ περὶ κεῖνον ὀΐζυε καί ἑ φύλασσε,
> εἰς ὅ κέ σ' ἢ ἄλοχον ποιήσεται, ἢ ὅ γε δούλην.[1]

It is as a slave, not as an honoured help-mate, that the Social Democrats would treat any Christian body that helped them to overthrow our present civilisation. And rightly; for Christ's only injunction in the sphere of economics was, ' Take heed and beware of all covetousness.' He refused pointedly to have anything to do with disputes about the distribution of property; and in the parable of the Prodigal Son the demand, ' Give me the portion of goods that falleth to me,' is the prelude to a journey in that ' far country ' which is forgetfulness of God (*terra longinqua est oblivio Dei*). Christ unquestionably meant His followers to think but little of the accessories of life. He believed that if men could be induced to adopt the true standard of values, economic relations would adjust themselves. He promised His disciples that they should not want the necessaries of subsistence, and for the rest, He held that the freedom from anxiety, covetousness, and envy, which He enjoined as a duty, would also make their

[1] ' Go and sit thou by his side, and depart from the way of the gods ; neither let thy feet ever bear thee back to Olympas ; but still be vexed for his sake and guard him, till he make thee his wife— or rather his slave.'

life happy. This is a very different spirit from that which makes Socialism a force in politics.

Bishop Gore, we may be sure, will not willingly allow the High Church party to be entangled in corrupt alliances. When he handles what may be called applied Christianity, he does so in a manner which makes us rejoice at the popularity of his books. The little commentaries on the Sermon on the Mount, and on the Epistles to the Romans and Ephesians, are admirable. They are simple, practical, and profound. We subjoin a short analysis of the notes on the first part of the Sermon on the Mount, as an illustration of the teaching which runs all through the three commentaries.

The Sermon on the Mount is not the whole of Christianity. It is the climax of law, of the letter that killeth. The Divine requirement is pressed home with unequalled force upon the conscience; yet not in the form of mere laws of conduct, but as a type of character. It is promulgated not by an inaccessible God, but by the Divine Love manifested in manhood. The hard demand of the letter is closely connected with the promise of the Spirit. We are told that many of the precepts in the sermon were anticipated by Pagan and Jewish writers. But this we might have expected, since all men are rational and moral through fellowship with the Word, who is also the Reason of God. Christ is the light which in conscience and reason lightens every man throughout the history of the race. But the Sermon is comprehensive where other summaries are fragmentary, it is pure where they are mixed. It is teaching for grown men, who require principles, not rules. And it is authoritative, reinforced by the mysterious Person of the speaker. The Beatitudes are a description of character. Christ requires us, not to do such and such things, but to be such and such people. . . . True blessedness consists in membership of the kingdom of heaven, which is a life of perfect relationship with man and nature based on perfect fellowship with God. . . . The Beatitudes describe the Christian character in detail; in particular, they describe it as contrasted with the character of the world, which, in the religious sense, may be defined as human society as it organises itself apart from God. The first Beatitude enjoins detachment, such as His who emptied Himself, as having nothing and yet possessing all things. We are all to be detached; there are some whom our Lord counsels to be literally poor. ' Blessed

are they that mourn ' means that we are not to screen ourselves
from the common lot of pain. We must distinguish ' godly
sorrow ' from the peevish discontent and slothfulness which
St. Paul calls the sorrow of the world, and which in medieval
casuistry is named acedia. ' Blessed are the meek ' means
that we are not to assert ourselves unless it is our duty to do
so. The true Christian is a man who in his private capacity
cannot be provoked. On a general view of life, though not
always in particular cases, we must allow that we are not treated
worse than we deserve. The fourth Beatitude tells us that
if we want righteousness seriously, we can have it. The fifth
proclaims the reward of mercy, that is, compassion in action.
Pity which does nothing is only hypocrisy or emotional self-
indulgence. On the whole, we can determine men's attitude
to us by our attitude to them ; the merciful do obtain mercy.
' Purity of heart ' means singleness of purpose ; but in the
narrower sense of purity it is worth while to say that those
who profess to find it ' impossible ' to lead a pure life might
overcome their fault if they would try to be Christlike altogether,
instead of struggling with that one fault separately. ' Sincerum
est nisi vas, quodcunque infundis acescit.' On the seventh—
there are many kinds of false peace, which Christ came to break
up ; but fierce, relentless competition is an offence in a Christian
nation. The last shows what our reward is likely to be in this
world, if we follow these counsels. Where the Christ-character
is not welcomed, it is hated.

From the later sections a few characteristic comments
may be given in an abridged form.

We are apt to have rather free and easy notions of the Divine
fatherhood. To call God our Father, we must ourselves be
sons ; and it is only those who are led by the Spirit of God who
are the sons of God. . . . Ask for great things, and small things
will be given to you. This is exactly the spirit of the Lord's
Prayer. . . . Act for God. Direct your thoughts and intentions
Godward, and your intelligence and affections will gradually
follow along the line of your action. . . . You must put God
first, or nowhere. . . . It is a perilous error to say that we have
only to follow our conscience ; we have to enlighten our
conscience and keep it enlightened. . . . There is no greater
plague of our generation than the nervous anxiety which
characterises all its efforts. We ought to be reasonably careful,
and then go boldly forward in the peace of God. . . . Our Lord

did not mean to make of His disciples a new kind of Pharisee.
. . . ' Judge not,' means, Do not be critical. The condemnation
of one who is always finding fault carries no moral weight.
It is those who have the lowest and vaguest standards of what
is right who are often the most critical in judgment of other
people. . . . We ought so to limit our desires that what we
want for ourselves we can reasonably expect also for others. . . .
A man who wants to do his duty must always be prepared to
stand alone. . . . Christianity is not so much a statement of
the true end or ideal of human life, as a great spiritual instrument for realising the end.

These extracts will be sufficient to show what are the
characteristics of these little commentaries. They exhibit
extreme honesty of purpose, fearless acceptance of Christ's
teaching honestly interpreted, scorn of unreality and empty
words, and a determination never to allow preaching to be
divorced from practice. No more stimulating Christian
teaching has been given in our generation.

The valuable treatise on the Holy Communion, called
' The Body of Christ,' is too theological for detailed discussion in these pages. The points in which the Roman
Church has perverted and degraded the really Catholic
sacramental doctrine are forcibly exposed, and the true
nature of the sacrament is unfolded in a masterly and
beautiful manner.

A study of the whole body of theological writings from
the pen of this remarkable man leaves us with the conviction
that he is one of the most powerful spiritual forces in our
generation. It is the more to be regretted that in certain
points he seems to be hampered by false presuppositions
and misled by unattainable ideals. His loyalty to ' Catholic
truth,' as understood by the party in the Church to which
he consents to belong, prevents him from understanding
where the shoe really pinches among those of the younger
generation who are both thoughtful and devout. He
makes a fetish of the Creeds, documents which only represent
the opinions of a majority at a meeting ; and what manner
of meetings Church Councils sometimes were, is known
to history. He is still impressed with the grandeur of the
Catholic idea, as embodied in the Roman Church, and will

do nothing to preclude reunion, should a more enlightened policy ever prevail at the Vatican. But this country has done with the Roman Empire, in its spiritual as well as its temporal form. The dimensions of that proud dominion have shrunk with the expansion of knowledge ; new worlds have been opened out, geographical and mental, which never owned its sway ; the *caput orbis* has become provincial, and her authority is spurned even within her own borders. There is no likelihood of the English people ever again accepting ' Catholicism,' if Catholicism is the thing which history calls by that name. The movement which the Bishop hopes to lead to victory will remain, as it has been hitherto, a theory of the ministry rather than of the Church, and its strength will be confined, as it is now, mainly to clerical circles.

Catholicism and Protestantism (in so far as they are more than names for institutionalism and mysticism, which are permanent types) are both obsolescent phases in the evolution of the Christian religion. ' The time cometh when neither in this mountain nor yet at Jerusalem shall men worship the Father.'

A profound reconstruction is demanded, and for those who have eyes to see has been already for some time in progress. The new type of Christianity will be more Christian than the old, because it will be more moral. A number of unworthy beliefs about God are being tacitly dropped, and they are so treated because they are unworthy of Him. The realm of nature is being claimed for Him once more ; the distinction between natural and super-natural is repudiated ; we hear less frequent complaints that God ' does nothing ' because He does not assert Himself by breaking one of His own laws. The divinity of Christ implies—one might almost say it means—the eternal supremacy of those moral qualities which He exhibited in their perfection. ' Conversio fit ad Dominum ut Spiritum,' as Bengel said. The visible or Catholic Church is not the name of an institution which has the privilege of being governed by bishops. It is ' dispersed throughout the whole world,' under many banners and many disguises. Its political reunion is (Plato would say) an ἐν μύθῳ εὐχή, and is at present neither to be expected nor desired. Among those who are by right citizens of the spiritual kingdom, those only are in danger of exclusion from it who entrench themselves in a little fort of their own and erect barriers, which may make them their own prisoners, but which will not hinder the great commonwealth of seekers after truth from working out modern problems by modern lights, until the whole of our new and rich inheritance, intellectual, moral, and æsthetic, shall be brought again under the obedience of Christ.

# ROMAN CATHOLIC MODERNISM

## (1909)

THE Liberal movement in the Roman Church is viewed
by most Protestan's with much the same mixture of
sympathy and misgiving with which Englishmen regard
the ambition of Russian reformers to establish a constitutional government in their country. Freedom of thought
and freedom of speech are almost always desirable ; but
how, without a violent revolution, can they be established
in a State which exists only as a centralised autocracy,
held together by authority and obedience ? This sympathy, and these fears, are likely to be strongest in those
who have studied the history of Western Catholicism
with most intelligence. From the Edict of Milan to the
Encyclical of Pius X, the evolution which ended in
papal absolutism has proceeded in accordance with what
looks like an inner necessity of growth and decay. The
task of predicting the policy of the Vatican is surely not
so difficult as M. Renan suggested, when he remarked to
a friend of the present writer, ' The Church is a woman ;
it is impossible to say what she will do next.' For where
is the evidence of caprice in the history of the Roman
Church ? If any State has been guided by a fixed policy,
which has imposed itself inexorably on its successive rulers,
in spite of the utmost divergences in their personal
characters and aims, that State is the Papacy.

Beneath all the eddies which have broken the surface,
the great stream has flowed on, and has flowed in one
direction. The same logic of events which transformed
the constitutional principate of Augustus into the sulta-

nate of Diocletian and Valentinian, has brought about a parallel development in the Church which inherited the traditions, the policy, and the territorial sphere of the dead Empire. The second World-State which had its seat on the Seven Hills has followed closely in the footsteps of the first. It is not too fanciful to trace, as Harnack has done, the resemblance in detail—Peter and Paul in the place of Romulus and Remus ; the bishops and arch-bishops instead of the proconsuls ; the troops of priests and monks as the legionaries ; while the Jesuits are the Imperial bodyguard, the protectors and sometimes the masters of the sovereign. One might carry the parallel further by comparing the schism between the Eastern and Western Churches, and the later defection of northern Europe, with the disruption of the Roman Empire in the fourth century ; and in the sphere of thought, by com-paring the scholastic philosophy and casuistry with the *Summa* of Roman law in the Digest.[1]

The fundamental principles of such a government are imposed upon it by necessity. In the first place, pro-gressive centralisation, and the substitution of a graduated hierarchy for popular government, came about as inevitably in the Catholic Church as in the Mediterranean Empire of the Cæsars. The primitive colleges of presbyters soon fell under the rule of the bishops, the bishops under the patriarchs ; and then Rome suffered her first great defeat in losing the Eastern patriarchates, which she could not subjugate. The truncated Church, no longer ' universal,' found itself obliged to continue the same policy of cen-tralisation, and with such success that, under Innocent III, the triumph of the theocracy seemed complete. The Papacy dominated Europe *de facto*, and claimed to rule the world *de jure*. Boniface VIII, when the clouds were already gathering, issued the famous Bull ' Unam sanctam,' in which he said : ' Subesse Romano pontifici omnes

---

[1] Bishop Creighton always emphasised this view of Roman Catholicism. ' The Roman Church,' he wrote, ' is the most com-plete expression of Erastianism, for it is not a Church at all, but a state in its organisation ; and the worst form of state—an autocracy.' (*Life and Letters*, ii. 375.)

humanas creaturas declaramus, definimus, et pronuntiamus omnino esse de necessitate salutis.' The claim is logical. A theocracy (when religion is truly monotheistic) [1] must claim to be universal *de jure*; and its ruler must be the infallibly inspired and autocratic vicegerent of the Almighty. He is the rightful lord of the world, whether he gives a continent to the King of Spain by a stroke of the pen, or whether his secular jurisdiction is limited by the walls of his palace. In the fourteenth century the Pope is already called ' dominus deus noster '—precisely the style in which Martial adulates Domitian. In the Bull of Pius V (1570) the claim of universal dominion is reiterated ; it is asserted that the Almighty,

' cui data est omnis in caelo et in terra potestas, unam sanctam catholicam et apostolicam ecclesiam, extra quam nulla est salus, uni soli in terris, videlicet apostolorum principi Petro Petrique successori Romano pontifici in potestatis plenitudine tradidit gubernandam.'

But the final victory of infallibilism was the achievement of the nineteenth-century Jesuits, who completed the dogmatic apotheosis of the Pope at the moment when the last vestiges of his temporal power were being snatched from him.

Now a government of this type is always in want of money. The spiritual Roman Empire was as costly an institution as the court and the bureaucracy of Diocletian and his successors. The same necessity which suppressed democracy in the Church drove it to elaborate an oppressive system of taxation, in which every weakness of human nature was systematically exploited for gain, and every morsel of divine grace placed on a tariff. But this method of raising revenue is only possible while the priests can persuade the people that they really control a treasury of grace, from which they can make or withhold grants at their pleasure. It stands or falls with a non-ethical and magical view of the divine economy which is hardly compatible with a high level of culture or morality. The

---

[1] In contrast with ' henotheism ' or ' monolatry,' such as the worship of the early Hebrews.

Catholic Church has thus been obliged, for purely fiscal reasons, to discourage secular education, particularly of a scientific kind, and to keep the people, so far as possible, in the mental and moral condition most favourable to such transactions as the purchase of indulgences and the payment of various insurances against hell and purgatory.

Another necessity of absolute government is the repression of free criticism directed against itself. Heresy and schism in an autocratic Church take the place of treason against the sovereign. Cyprian, in the third century, had already laid down the principles by which alone the central authority could be maintained.

'Ab arbore frange ramum ; fractus germinare non poterit. A fonte praecide rivum ; praecisus arescit. . . . Quisquis ab ecclesia separatus adulterae iungitur, a promissis ecclesiae separatur. Alienus est, hostis est. Habere non potest Deum patrem, qui ecclesiam non habet matrem.'

Schismatics are therefore rebels, whose lives are forfeit under the laws of treason. Heretics are in no better case ; for the Church is the only infallible interpreter both of Scripture and of tradition ; and to differ from her teaching is as disloyal as to secede from her jurisdiction. Even Augustine could say, ' I should not believe the Gospel, if the authority of the Church did not determine me to do so ' ; a statement which a modern ultramontane has capped by saying, ' Without the authority of the Pope, I should not place the Bible higher than the Koran.' Bellarmine claims an absolute monopoly of inspiration for the Roman Church on the ground that Rome alone has preserved the apostolic succession beyond dispute.[1] As for the treatment which heretics deserve, the same authority is very explicit.

' In the first place, heretics do more mischief than any pirate or brigand, because they slay souls ; nay more, they subvert the foundations of all good and fill the commonwealth with

---

[1] ' Nunc defecit certa successio in omnibus ecclesiis apostolicis, praeterquam in Romana, et ideo ex testimonio huius solius ecclesiae sumi potest certum argumentum ad probandas apostolicas traditiones.' Bellarmine, *De Verbo Dei scripto et non scripto*, IV, ix, 10.

the disturbances which necessarily follow religious differences. In the second place, capital punishment inflicted on them has a good effect on very many persons. Many whom impunity was making indifferent are roused by these executions to consider what is the nature of the heresy which attracts them, and to take care not to end their earthly lives in misery and lose their future happiness. Thirdly, it is a kindness to obstinate heretics to remove them from this life. For the longer they live, the more errors they devise, the more men they pervert, and the greater damnation they acquire for themselves.' [1]

In all matters which are not essential for the safety of the autocracy, an absolutist Church will consult the average tastes of its subjects. If the populace are at heart pagan, and hanker after sensuous ritual, dramatic magic, and a rich mythology, these must be provided. The 'intellectuals,' being few and weak, may be safely rebuffed or disregarded until their discoveries are thoroughly popularised. The pronouncements of the Roman Inquisition in the case of Galileo are typical.

'The theory that the sun is in the centre of the world, and stationary, is absurd, false in philosophy, and formally heretical, because it is contrary to the express language of Holy Scripture. The theory that the earth is not the centre of the world, nor stationary, but that it moves with a daily motion, is also absurd and false in philosophy, and, theologically considered, it is, to say the least, erroneous in faith.'

The exigencies of despotic government thus supply the key to the whole policy and history of the Papacy. 'The worst form of State' can only be bolstered up by the worst form of government. There should therefore be no difficulty in distinguishing between the official policy of the Roman See—which has been almost uniformly odious—and the history of the Christian religion in the Latin countries, which has added new lustre to human nature. The Catholic saints did not fly through the air, nor were their hearts pierced with supernatural darts, as the mendacious hagiology of their Church would have us believe ; but they have a better title to be remembered

[1] Bellarmine, *De Laicis*, III, xxi, 22.

by mankind, as the best examples of a beautiful and precious kind of human excellence.

The papal autocracy has now reached its Byzantine period of decadence. During the Middle Ages Catholicism suited the Latin races very well on the whole. Their ancestral paganism was allowed to remain substantially unchanged—the *nomina*, but not the *numina* were altered ; their awe and reverence for the *caput orbis*, ingrained in the populations of Europe by the history of a thousand years, made submission to Rome natural and easy ; a host of myths ' abounding in points of attachment to human experience and in genial interpretations of life, yet lifted beyond visible nature and filling a reported world believed in on faith,' [1] adorned religion with an artistic and poetical embroidery very congenial to the nations of the South. But a monarchy essentially Oriental in its constitution is unsuited to modern Europe. Its whole scheme is based on keeping the laity in contented ignorance and sub- servience ; and the laity have emancipated themselves. The Teutonic nations broke the yoke as soon as they attained a national self-consciousness. They escaped from a system which had educated, but never suited them. Nor has the shrinkage been merely territorial. The Pyrrhic victories over Gallicanism, Jansenism, Catholic democracy (Lamennais), historical theology (Döllinger and the Old Catholics), each alienated a section of thinking men in the Catholic countries. The Roman Church can no longer be called Catholic, except in the sense in which the kingdom of Francis II remained the Holy Roman Empire. It is an exclusive sect, which preserves much more political power than its numbers entitle it to exert, by means of its excellent discipline, and by the sinister policy of fomenting ˜political disaffection. Examples of this last are furnished by the contemporary history of Ireland, of France, and of Poland.

These considerations are of primary importance when we try to answer the questions : To what extent is the Roman Church fettered by her own past ? Is there any

[1] Santayana, *Reason in Religion*, p. 108.

insuperable obstacle to a modification of policy which might give her a new lease of life ? We have seen how much importance is attached to the Church's title-deeds. Is tradition a fatal obstacle to reform ? Theoretically, the tradition which she traces back to the apostles gives her a fixed constitution. So the Catholic Church has always maintained. ' Regula quidem fidei una omnino est, sola immobilis et irreformabilis.' [1] The rule of faith may be better understood by a later age than an earlier, but there can be no additions, only a sort of unpacking of a treasure which was given whole and entire in the first century. In reality, of course, there has been a steady evolution in conformity to type, the type being not the ' little flock ' of Christ or the Church of the Apostles, but the absolute monarchy above described. It has long been the *crux* of Catholic apologetics to reconcile the theoretical immobility of dogma with the actual facts.

The older method was to rewrite history. It was convenient, for example, to forget that Pope Honorius I had been anathematised by three ecumenical councils. The forged Decretals gave a more positive sanction to absolutist claims ; and interpolations in the Greek Fathers deceived St. Thomas Aquinas into giving his powerful authority to infallibilism. This method cannot be called obsolete, for the present Pope recently informed the faithful that ' the Hebrew patriarchs were familiar with the doctrine of the Immaculate Conception, and found consolation in the thought of Mary in the solemn moments of their life.' [2] But such simple devices are hardly practicable in an age when history is scientifically studied. Moreover, other considerations, besides controversial straits, have suggested a new theory of tradition. A Cæsar who, like the kings of the Medes and Persians, is bound by the laws of his predecessors, is not absolute. Acceptance of the theory of development in dogma would relieve the Pope from the weight of the dead hand.

The new apologetic is generally said to have been inaugurated by Cardinal Newman. His work ' The

[1] Tertullian, *De Virg. Vel.*, 1.
[2] Encyclical of October 27, 1904.

Development of Christian Doctrine,' is no doubt an epoch-making book, though the idea of tradition as the product of the living spirit of a religious society, preserving its moral identity while expressing itself, from time to time, in new forms, was already familiar to readers of Schleiermacher. Newman gives us several ' tests ' of true development. These are—preservation of type ; continuity of principles ; power of assimilation ; logical sequence ; anticipation of results ; tendency to conserve the old ; chronic vigour. These tests, he considered, differentiate the Roman Church from all other Christian bodies, and prove its superiority. The Church has its own genius, which lives and works in it. This is indeed the Holy Spirit of God, promised by Jesus Christ. Through the operation of this spirit, old things become new, and fresh light is shed from the sacred pages of Scripture. Catholic tradition is, in fact, the glorified but ever-present Christ Himself, reincarnating Himself, generation after generation, in the historical Church. It is unnecessary to enquire whether there is apostolic authority for every new dogma, for the Church is the mouthpiece of the living Christ.

This theory marks, on one side, the complete and final apotheosis of the Pope and the hierarchy, who are thereby made independent even of the past history of the Church. Pius IX was not slow to realise that the only court of appeal against his decisions was closed in 1870. ' La tradizione sono io,' he said, in the manner of Louis XIV. The Pope is henceforth not the interpreter of a closed cycle of tradition, but the pilot who guides its course always in the direction of the truth. This is to destroy the old doctrine of tradition. The Church becomes the source of revelation instead of its custodian. On the other side, it is a perilous concession to modern ideas. There is an obvious danger that, as the result of this doctrine, the dogmas of the Church may seem to have only a relative and provisional truth ; for, if each pronouncement were absolutely true, there would be no real development, and the appearance of it in history would become inexplicable.

This new and, in appearance, more liberal attitude towards modern ideas of progress has raised the hopes of

many in the Roman Church whose minds and consciences
are troubled by the ever-widening chasm which separates
traditional dogma from secular knowledge.  While dogma
was stationary—*immobilis et irreformabilis*—there seemed
to be no prospect except that the progress of human knowledge would leave theology further and further behind,
till the rupture between Catholicism and civilisation
became absolute.  The idea that the Church would ever
modify her teaching to bring it into harmony with modern
science seemed utterly chimerical.  But if the static
theory of revelation is abandoned, and a dynamic theory
substituted for it ; if the divine part of Christianity resides,
not in the theoretical formulations of revealed fact, but
in the living and energising spirit of the Church ; why
should not dogmatic theology become elastic, changing
periodically in correspondence with the development of
human knowledge, and no longer stand in irreconcilable
contradiction with the ascertained laws of nature ?

Thus the dethronement of tradition by the Pope con-
tributed to make the Modernist movement possible.  The
Modernists have even claimed Newman as on their side.
This appeal cannot be sustained.  ' The Development of
Christian Doctrine ' is mainly a polemic against the high
Anglican position, and an answer to attacks upon Roman
Catholicism from this side.  Anglicanism at that time
had committed itself to a thoroughly stationary view of
revelation.  Its ' appeal to antiquity '—a period which, in
accordance with a convenient theory, it limited to the
councils of the ' undivided Church '—was intended to
prove the catholicity and orthodoxy of the English Church,
as the faithful guardian of apostolic tradition, and to condemn the medieval and modern accretions sanctioned by
the Church of Rome.  The earlier theory of tradition left
the Roman Church open to damaging criticism on this
side ; no ingenuity could prove that all her doctrines
were ' primitive.'  Even in those early days of historical
criticism, it must have been plain to any candid student
of Christian ' origins ' that the Pauline Churches were far
more Protestant than Catholic in type.  But Newman
had set himself to prove that ' the Christianity of history

L

is not Protestantism; if ever there were a safe truth, it is this.' Accordingly, he argues that 'Christianity came into the world as an idea rather than an institution, and had to fit itself with armour of its own providing.' Such expressions sound very like the arguments of the Modernists; but Newman assuredly never contemplated that they would be turned against the policy of his own Church, in the interests of the critical rationalism which he abhorred. His attitude towards dogma is after all not very different from that of the older school. 'Time was needed' (he says) 'for the elucidation of doctrines communicated once. for all through inspired persons'; his examples are purgatory and the papal supremacy. He insists that his 'tests' of true development are only controversial, 'instruments rather than warrants of right decisions.' The only real 'warrant' is the authority of the infallible Church. It is highly significant that one of the features in Roman Catholicism to which he appeals as proving its unblemished descent from antiquity is its exclusiveness and intolerance.

'The Fathers (he says complacently) anathematised doctrines, not because they were old, but because they were new; for the very characteristic of heresy is novelty and originality of manifestation. Such was the exclusiveness of the Christianity of old. I need not insist on the steadiness with which that principle has been maintained ever since.'

The Cardinal is right; it is quite unnecessary to insist upon it; but, when the Modernists claim Newman as their prophet, it is fair to reply that, if we may judge from his writings, he would gladly have sent some of them to the stake.

The Modernist movement, properly so called, belongs to the last twenty years, and most of the literature dates from the present century. It began in the region of ecclesiastical history, and soon passed to biblical exegesis, where the new heresy was at first called 'concessionism.' The scope of the debate was enlarged with the stir produced by Loisy's 'L'Évangile et l'Église' and 'Autour d'un Petit Livre'; it spread over the field of Christian origins generally, and problems connected with them, such as the growth of ecclesiastical power and the evolution of dogma. For a few years the orthodox in France generally spoke of the new tendency as *loisysme*.  It was not till 1905 that Édouard Le Roy published his ' Qu'est-ce qu'un dogme ? ' which carried the discussion into the domain of pure philosophy, though the studies of Blondel and Laberthonnière in the psychology of religion may be said to involve a metaphysic closely resembling that of Le Roy. Mr. Tyrrell's able works have a very similar philosophical basis, which is also assumed by the group of Italian priests who have remonstrated with the Pope.[1]  M. Loisy protests against the classification made in the papal Encyclical which connects biblical critics, metaphysicians, psychologists, and Church reformers, as if they were all partners in the same enterprise.  But in reality the same presuppositions, the same philosophical principles, are found in all the writers named ;  and the differences which may easily be detected in their writings are comparatively superficial.  The movement appears to be strongest in France, where the policy of the Vatican has been uniformly unfortunate of recent years, and has brought many humiliations upon French Catholics.  Italy has also been moved, though from slightly different causes.  In the protests from that country we find a tone of disgust at the constitution of the Roman hierarchy and the character of the papal *entourage,* about which Italians are in a position to know more than other Catholics.  Catholic Germany has been almost silent ;  and Mr. Tyrrell is the only Englishman whose name has come prominently forward.

It will be convenient to consider the position of the Modernists under three heads :  their attitude towards New Testament criticism, especially in relation to the life of Christ ;  their philosophy ;  and their position in the Roman Catholic Church.

The Modernists themselves desire, for the most part, that criticism rather than philosophy should be regarded as the starting-point of the movement.  ' So far from our

---

[1] In *The Programme of Modernism,* and *Quello che vogliamo.*

philosophy dictating our critical method, it is the critical method that has of its own accord forced us to a very tentative and uncertain formulation of various philosophical conclusions. . . . This independence of our criticism is evident in many ways.'[1] The writers of this manifesto, and M. Loisy himself, appear not to perceive that their critical position rests on certain very important philosophical presuppositions ; nor indeed is any criticism of religious origins possible without presuppositions which involve metaphysics. The results of their critical studies, as bearing on the life of Christ, we shall proceed to summarise, departing as little as possible from the actual language of the writers, and giving references in all cases. It must, however, be remembered that some of the group, such as Mr. Tyrrell, have not committed themselves to the more extreme critical views, while others, such as the Abbé Laberthonnière, the most brilliant and attractive writer of them all, hold a moderate position on the historical side. It is perhaps significant that those who are specialists in biblical criticism are the most radical members of the school.

The Gospels, says M. Loisy, are for Christianity what the Pentateuch is for Judaism. Like the Pentateuch, they are a patchwork and a compound of history and legend. The differences between them amount in many cases to unmistakable contradictions. In Mark the life of Jesus follows a progressive development. The first to infer His Messiahship is Simon Peter at Cæsarea Philippi ; and Jesus Himself first declares it openly in His trial before the Sanhedrin. In Matthew and Luke, on the contrary, Jesus is presented to the public as the Son of God from the beginning of His ministry ; He comes forward at once as the supreme Lawgiver, the Judge, the anointed of God. The Fourth Gospel goes much further still. His heavenly origin, His priority to the world, His co-operation in the work of creation and salvation, are ideas which are foreign to the other Gospels, but which the author of the Fourth Gospel has set forth in his prologue, and, in part, put into

---

[1] *The Programme of Modernism*, p. 16.

the mouth of John the Baptist.[1] The difference between
the Christ of the Synoptic Gospels and the Christ of John
may be summed up by saying that ' the Christ of the
Synoptics is historical, but is not God ; the Johannine
Christ is divine, but not historical.'[2] But even Mark
(according to M. Loisy) probably only incorporates the
document of an eye-witness ; his Gospel betrays Pauline
influence.[3] The Gospel which bears his name is later than
the destruction of Jerusalem, and was issued, probably
about A.D. 75, by an unknown Christian, not a native of
Palestine, who wished to write a book of evangelical in-
struction in conformity with the ideas of the Hellenic-
Christian community to which he belonged.[4] The tradition
connecting it with Peter may indicate that it was composed
at Rome, but has no other historical value.[5]

The Gospel of Matthew was probably written about
the beginning of the second century by a non-Palestinian
Jew residing in Asia Minor or Syria. He is before all things
a Catholic ecclesiastic, and may well have been one of the
presbyters or bishops of the churches in which the institution of a monarchical episcopate took root.[6] The narratives
peculiar to Matthew have the character rather of legendary
developments than of genuine reminiscences. The historical value of these additions is *nil*. As a witness to
fact, Matthew ranks below Mark, and even below Luke.[7]
In particular, the chapters about the birth of Christ seem
not to have the slightest historical foundation. The fictitious character of the genealogy is proved by the fact
that Jesus seems not to have known of His descent [from
David]. The story of the virgin birth turns on a text from
Isaiah. Of this part of the Gospel, Loisy says, ' rien n'est
plus arbitraire comme exégèse, ni plus faible comme
narration fictive.'[8] Luke has taken more pains to compose a literary treatise than Mark or Matthew. The

---

[1] *The Programme of Modernism*, pp. 50–54.
[2] Loisy, *Simples Réflexions*, p. 168.
[3] *Ibid. L'Évangile et l'Église*, pp. 3–5
[4] *Ibid. Les Évangiles Synoptiques*, p. 119.
[5] *Ibid.*        [6] *Ibid.* p. 143.
[7] *Ibid.* pp. 138, 139.      [8] *Ibid.* p. 104.

authorities which he follows seem to be—the source of our
Mark, the so-called Matthew *logia*, and some other source
or sources. But he treats his material more freely than
Matthew. ' The lament of Christ over the holy city, His
words to the women of Jerusalem, His prayer for His
executioners, His promise to the penitent thief, His last
words, are very touching traits, which may be in conformity with the spirit of Jesus, but which have no
traditional basis.' [1] ' The fictitious character of the
narratives of the infancy is less apparent in the Third
Gospel than in the First, because the stories are much
better constructed as legend, and do not resemble a *midrash*
upon Messianic prophecies. " Le merveilleux en est moins
banal et moins enfantin. Il paraît cependant impossible
de leur reconnaître une plus grande valeur de fond." ' [2]

The Gospel of Luke was probably written (not by a
disciple of St. Paul) between 90 and 100 A.D. ; but the
earliest redaction, which traced the descent of Jesus from
David through Joseph, has been interpolated in the interests of the later idea of a virgin birth. The first two
chapters are interesting for the history of Christian beliefs,
not for the history of Christ. As for the Fourth Gospel,
it is enough to say that the author had nothing to do with
the son of Zebedee, and that he is in no sense a biographer
of Christ, but the first and greatest of the Christian mystics. [3]

The result of this drastic treatment of the sources
may be realised by perusing chapter vii of Loisy's ' Les
Évangiles Synoptiques.' The following is a brief analysis
of this chapter, entitled ' La Carrière de Jésus.' Jesus
was born at Nazareth about four years before the Christian
era. His family were certainly pious, but none of His
relatives seems to have accepted the Gospel during His
lifetime. Like many others, the young Jesus was attracted
by the terrifying preaching of John the Baptist, from whom
He received Baptism. When John was imprisoned He
at once attempted to take his place. He began to preach

[1] Loisy, *Les Évangiles Synoptiques*, p. 166.
[2] *Ibid.* p. 169.
[3] *Ibid. Le Quatrième Évangile*, passim.

round the lake of Galilee, and was compelled by the persistent demands of the crowd to ' work miracles.' This mission only lasted a few months ; but it was long enough for Jesus to enrol twelve auxiliaries, who prepared the villages of Galilee for His coming, travelling two and two through the north of Palestine. Jesus found His audience rather among the *déclassés* of Judaism than among the Puritans. The staple of His teaching was the advent of the ' kingdom of God '—the sudden and speedy coming of the promised Messiah. This teaching was acceptable neither to Herod Antipas nor to the Pharisees ; and their hostility obliged Jesus to fly for a short time to the Phœnician territory north of Galilee. But a conference between the Master and His disciples at Cæsarea Philippi ended in a determination to visit the capital and there proclaim Jesus as the promised Messiah. As they approached Jerusalem, even the ignorant disciples were frightened at the risks they were running, but Jesus calmed their fears by promising that they should soon be set on twelve thrones judging the twelve tribes of Israel. ' Jésus n'allait pas à Jérusalem pour y mourir.' [1]

The doomed prophet made his public entry into Jerusalem as Messiah, and, as a first act of authority, cleared the temple courts by an act of violence, in which He was doubtless assisted by His disciples. For some days after this He preached daily about the coming of the kingdom, and foiled with great dexterity the traps which His enemies laid for Him. ' But the situation could only end in a miracle or a catastrophe, and it was the catastrophe which happened.' [2] Jesus was arrested, after a brief scuffle between the satellites of the High Priest and the disciples ; and the latter, without waiting to see the end, fled northwards towards their homes. When brought before Pilate, Jesus probably answered ' Yes ' to the question whether He claimed to be a king ; but ' la parole du Christ johannique, Mon royaume n'est pas de ce monde, n'aurait jamais pu être dite par le Christ

---

[1] Loisy, *Les Évangiles Synoptiques*, p. 214.
[2] *Ibid.* p. 21?.

d'histoire.' This confession led naturally to His immediate execution ; after which

'on peut supposer que les soldats détachèrent le corps de la croix avant le soir et le mirent dans quelque fosse commune, où l'on jetait pêle-mêle les restes des suppliciés. Les conditions de sépulture furent telles qu'au bout de quelques jours il aurait été impossible de reconnaître la dépouille du Sauveur, quand même on l'aurait cherchée.' [1]

The disciples, however, had been too profoundly stirred by hope to accept defeat. None of them had seen Jesus die ; and though they knew that He was dead, they hardly realised it. Besides, they were fellow-countrymen of those who had asked whether Jesus was not Elijah, or even John the Baptist, come to life again. What more natural than that Peter should see the Master one day while fishing on the lake ? 'The impulse once given, this belief grew by the very need which it had to strengthen itself.' Christ 'appeared also to the eleven.' So it was that their faith brought them back to Jerusalem, and Christianity was born.

'The supernatural life of Christ in the faithful and in the Church has been clothed in an historical form, which has given birth to what we might somewhat loosely call the Christ of legend.' So the Italian manifesto sums up the result of this reconstruction or denudation of the Gospel history.[2] 'Such a criticism,' say the authors not less frankly than truly, 'does away with the possibility of finding in Christ's teaching even the embryonic form of the Church's later theological teaching.' [3]

Readers unfamiliar with Modernist literature will probably have read the foregoing extracts with utter amazement. It seems hardly credible that such views should be propounded by Catholic priests, who claim to remain in the Catholic Church, to repeat her creeds, minister at her altars, and share her faith. What more, it may well be asked, have rationalist opponents of Christianity

---

[1] Loisy, *Les Évangiles Synoptiques*, p. 223.
[2] *The Programme of Modernism*, pp. 82, 83.
[3] *Ibid.* p. 90.

ever said, in their efforts to tear up the Christian religion by the roots, than we find here admitted by Catholic apologists ? What is left of the object of the Church's worship if the Christ of history was but an enthusiastic Jewish peasant whose pathetic ignorance of the forces opposed to Him led Him to the absurd enterprise of attempting a *coup d'état* at Jerusalem ? Is not Jesus reduced by this criticism to the same level as Theudas or Judas of Galilee ? and, if this is the true account, what sentiment can we feel, when we read His tragic story, but compassion tinged with contempt ?

And on what principles are such liberties taken with our authorities ? What is the criterion by which it is decided that Christ said, ' I am a king,' but not ' My kingdom is not of this world ' ? Why must the resurrection have been only a subjective hallucination in the minds of the disciples ? To these questions there is a plain answer. The non-intervention of God in history is an axiom with the Modernists. ' L'historien,' says M. Loisy, ' n'a pas à s'inspirer de l'agnosticisme pour écarter Dieu de l'histoire ; il ne l'y rencontre jamais.' [1] It would be more accurate to say that, whenever the meeting takes place, ' the historian ' gives the Other the cut direct.

But now comes in the peculiar philosophy by which the Modernists claim to rehabilitate themselves as loyal and orthodox Catholics, and to turn the flank of the rationalist position, which they have seemed to occupy themselves. The reaction against Absolutism in philosophy has long since established itself in Germany and France. In England and Scotland the battle still rages ; in America the rebound has been so violent that an extreme form of anti-intellectualism is now the dominant fashion in philosophy. It would have been easy to predict—and in fact the prediction was made—that the new world-construction in terms of will and action, which disparages speculative or theoretical truth and gives the primacy to what Kant called the practical reason, would be eagerly

[1] Loisy, *Simples Réflexions*, p. 211.

welcomed by Christian apologists, hard-pressed by the discoveries of science and biblical criticism. Protestants, in fact, had recourse to this method of apologetic before the Modernist movement arose. The Ritschlian theology in Germany (in spite of its ' static ' view of revelation), and the *Symbolo-fidéisme* of Sabatier and Ménégoz, have many affinities with the position of Tyrrell, Laberthonnière, and Le Roy.

It is exceedingly difficult to compress into a few pages a fair and intelligible statement of a *Weltansicht* which affects the whole conception of reality, and which has many ramifications. There is an additional difficulty in the fact that few of the Modernists are more than amateurs in philosophy. They are quick to see the strategic possibilities of a theory which separates faith and knowledge, and declares that truths of faith can never come into collision with truths of fact, because they ' belong to different orders.' It suits them to follow the pragmatists in talking about ' freely chosen beliefs,' and ' voluntary certainty '; Mr. Tyrrell even maintains that ' the great mass of our beliefs are reversible, and depend for their stability on the action or permission of the will.' But philosophy is for them mainly a controversial weapon. It gives them the means of justifying their position as Catholics who wish to remain loyal to their Church and her formularies, but no longer believe in the miracles which the Church has always regarded as matters of fact. Nevertheless, an attempt must be made to explain a point of view which, to the plain man, is very strange and unfamiliar.

Two words are constantly in the mouth of Modernist controversialists in speaking of their opponents. The adherents of the traditional theology are ' intellectualists,' and their conception of reality is ' static.' The meaning of the latter charge may perhaps be best explained from Laberthonnière's brilliantly written essay, ' Le Réalisme Chrétien et l'Idéalisme Grec.' The Greeks, he says, were insatiable in their desire to *see*, like children. Blessedness, for them, consisted in a complete vision of reality ; and, since thought is the highest kind of vision, salvation

was conceived of by them as the unbroken contemplation
of the perfectly true, good, and beautiful. Hence arose the
philosophy of ' concepts '; they idealised nature by considering it *sub specie æternitatis*. Reality resided in the un-
changing ideas ; the mutable, the particular, the individual
was for them an embarrassment, a ' scandal of thought.'
The sage always tries to escape from the moving world
of becoming into the static world of being. But an ideal
world, so conceived, can only be an abstraction, an im-
poverishment of reality. Such an idealism gives us neither
a science of origins nor a science of ends. Greek wisdom
sought eternity and forgot time ; it sought that which
never dies, and found that which never lives.

' An abstract doctrine, like that of Greek philosophy or of Spinoza,
consists always in substituting for reality, by simplification,
ideas or concepts which they think statically in their logical
relations, regarding them at the same time as adequate repre-
sentations and as essences immovably defined.' [1]

Hellenised Christianity, proceeds our critic, regarded
the incarnation statically, as a fact in past history. But
the real Christ is an object of faith. ' He introduces into
us the principles of that which we ought to be. That
which He reveals, He makes in revealing it.' In other
words, Christ, and the God whom He reveals, are a power
or force rather than a fact. ' A God who has nothing to
become has nothing to do.' God is not the idea of ideas,
but the being of beings and the life of our life. He is not
a supreme notion, but a supreme life and an immanent
action. He is not the ' unmoved mover,' but He is in the
movement itself as its principle and end. While the Greeks
conceived the world *sub specie æternitatis*, God is conceived
by modern thought *sub specie temporis*. God's eternity is
not a sort of arrested time in which there is no more life ;
it is, on the contrary, the maximum of life.

It is plain that we have here a one-sided emphasis
on the dynamic aspect of reality no less fatal to sound
philosophy than the exclusively static view which has

[1] Laberthonnière, *Le Réalisme Chrétien et l'Idéalisme Grec*,
pp. 44, 45.

been falsely attributed to the Greeks. A little clear thinking ought to be enough to convince anyone that the two aspects of reality which the Greeks called στάσις and κίνησις are correlative and necessary to each other. A God who is merely the principle of movement and change is an absurdity. Time is always hurling its own products into nothingness. Unless there is a being who can say, ' I am the Lord, I change not,' the ' sons of Jacob ' cannot flatter themselves that they are ' not consumed.'[1] But Laberthonnière and his friends are not much concerned with the ultimate problems of metaphysics; what they desire is to shake themselves free from ' brute facts ' in the past, to be at liberty to deny them as facts, while retaining them as representative ideas of faith. If reality is defined to consist only in life and action, it is a meaningless abstraction to snip off a moment in the process, and ask, ' Did it ever really take place ? ' This awkward question may therefore be ignored as meaningless and irrelevant, except from the ' abstract ' standpoint of physical science.

The crusade against ' intellectualism ' serves the same end. M. Le Roy and the other Christian pragmatists have returned to the Nominalism of Duns Scotus. The following words of Frassen, one of Scotus' disciples, might serve as a motto for the whole school :

' Theologia nostra non est scientia. Nullatenus speculativa est, sed simpliciter practica. Theologiae obiectum non est speculabile, sed operabile. Quidquid in Deo est practicum est respectu nostri.'

M. Le Roy also seems to know only these two categories. Whatever is not ' practical '—having an immediate and obvious bearing on conduct—is stigmatised as ' theoretical ' or ' speculative.' But the whole field of scientific study lies outside this classification, which, pretends to be exhaustive. Science has no ' practical ' aim, in the narrow sense of that which may serve as a guide to moral action ; nor does it deal with ' theoretical ' or ' speculative ' ideas,

[1] *Malachi*, ii 6.

except provisionally, until they can be verified. The aim of science is to determine the laws which prevail in the physical universe ; and its motive is that purely disinterested curiosity which is such an embarrassing phenomenon to pragmatists. And since the faith which lies behind natural science is at least as strong as any other faith now active in the world, it is useless to frame categories in such a way as to exclude the question, ' Did this or that occurrence, which is presented as an event in the physical order, actually happen, or not ? ' The question has a very definite meaning for the man of science, as it has for the man in the street. To call it ' theoretical ' is ridiculous.

What M. Le Roy means by ' interpreting dogmas in the language of practical action ' may be gathered from his own illustrations. The dogma, ' God is our Father,' does not define a ' theoretical relation ' between Him and us. It signifies that we are to behave to Him as sons behave to their father. ' God is personal ' means that we are to behave to Him as if He were a human person. ' Jesus is risen ' means that we are to think of Him as if He were our contemporary. The dogma of the Real Presence means that we ought to have, in the presence of the consecrated Host, the same feelings which we should have had in the presence of the visible Christ. ' Let the dogmas be interpreted in this way, and no one will dispute them.' [1]

The same treatment of dogma is advocated in Mr. Tyrrell's very able book ' Lex Orandi.' The test of truth for a dogma is not its correspondence with phenomenal fact, but its ' prayer-value.' This writer, at any rate before his suspension by the Society of Jesus, to which he belonged, is less subversive in his treatment of history than the French critics whom we have quoted. Although in apologetics the criterion for the acceptance of dogmas must, he thinks, be a moral and practical one, he sometimes speaks as if the ' prayer-value ' of an ostensibly historical proposition carried with it the necessity of its truth as matter of fact.

[1] Le Roy, *Dogme et Critique*, p. 26.

'Between the inward and the outward, the world of reality and the world of appearances, the relation is not merely one of symbolic correspondence. The distinction that is demanded by the dualism of our mind implies and presupposes a causal and dynamic unity of the two. We should look upon the outward world as being an effectual symbol of the inward, in consequence of its natural and causal connection therewith.'[1]

But Mr. Tyrrell does not seem to mean all that these sentences might imply. He speaks repeatedly, in the 'Lex Orandi,' of the 'will-world' as the only real world.

'The will (he says) cannot make that true which in itself is not true. But it can make that a fact relatively to our mind and action which is not a fact relative to our understanding. . . . It rests with each of us by an act of will to create the sort of world to which we shall accommodate our thought and action. . . . It does not follow that harmony of faith with the truths of reason and facts of experience is the best or essential condition of its credibility. . . . Abstractions (he refers to the world as known to science) are simple only because they are barren forms created by the mind itself. Faith and doubt have a common element in the deep sense of the insufficiency of the human mind to grasp ultimate truths. . . . The world given to our outward senses is shadowy and dreamy, except so far as we ascribe to it some of the characteristics of will and spirit. . . . The world of appearance is simply subordinate to the real world of our will and affections.'

Because the 'abstract' sciences cannot and do not attempt to reach ultimate truth, it is assumed that they are altogether 'barren forms.' This is the error of much Oriental mysticism, which denies all value to what it regards as the lower categories. In his later writings Mr. Tyrrell objects to being classed with the American and English pragmatists—the school of Mr. William James. But the doctrine of these passages is ultra-pragmatist. The will, which is illegitimately stretched to include feeling,[2] is

---

[1] *Lex Orandi*, p. 165 (abridged).

[2] This is not carelessness on the part of the writer. Paulsen also says (*Introduction to Philosophy*, p. 112), ' It is impossible to separate feeling and willing from each other. . . . Only in the highest stage of psychical life, in man, does a partial separation of feeling from willing occur.' But it is the highest stage of psychical

treated as the creator as well as the discerner of reality. The 'world of appearance' is plastic in its grasp. It is this metaphysical pragmatism which is really serviceable to Modernism. If the categories of the understanding can be so disparaged as to be allowed no independent truth, value, or importance, all collisions between faith and fact may be avoided by discrediting in advance any conclusions at which science may arrive. Assertions about 'brute fact' which are scientifically false may thus not be untrue when taken out of the scientific plane, because outside that plane they are harmless word-pictures, soap-bubbles blown off by the poetical creativeness of faith. Any assertion about fact which commends itself to the will and affections and which is proved by experience to furnish nutriment to the spiritual life, may be adhered to without scruple. It is not only useful, but true, in the only sense in which truth can be predicated of anything in the higher sphere.

The obvious criticism on this notion of religious truth as purely moral and practical is that it is itself abstract and one-sided. The universe as it appears to discursive thought, with its vast system of seemingly uniform laws, which operate without much consideration for our wishes or feelings, must be at least an image of the real universe. We cannot accept the irreconcilable dualism between the will-world and the world of phenomena which the philosophical Modernists assume. The dualism, or rather the contradiction, is not in the nature of things, nor in the constitution of our minds, but in the consciousness of the unhappy men who are trying to combine two wholly incompatible theories. On the critical side they are pure rationalists, much as they dislike the name. They claim, as we have seen, to have advanced to philosophy through criticism. But the Modernist critics start with very well-defined presuppositions. They ridicule the notion that

---

life, the human, with which we are alone concerned; and in this stage it is both possible and necessary to distinguish between feeling and willing. Some Voluntarists, hard pressed by facts, try to make ' will ' cover the whole of conscious and subconscious life, with the exception of logical reasoning, which is excluded as a sort of pariah !

'God is a personage in history'; they assume that for the historian 'He cannot be found anywhere'; that He is as though He did not exist. On the strength of this presupposition, and for no other reason, they proceed to rule out, without further investigation, all alleged instances of divine intervention in history. Unhampered by any of the misgivings which predispose the ordinary believer to conservatism, they follow the rationalist argument to its logical conclusions with startling ruthlessness. And then, when the whole edifice of historical religion seems to have been overthrown to the very foundations, they turn round suddenly and say that all their critical labours mean nothing for faith, and that we may go on repeating the old formulas as if nothing had happened.

The Modernists pour scorn on the scholastic 'faculty-psychology,' which resolves human personality into a syndicate of partially independent agents; but, in truth, their attempt to blow hot and cold with the same mouth seems to have involved them in a more disastrous self-disruption than has been witnessed in the history of thought since the fall of the Nominalists. In a sceptical and disillusioned age their disparagement of 'intellectualism,' or rather of discursive thought in all its operations, might find a response. But in the twentieth century the science which, as critics, they follow so unswervingly will not submit to be bowed out of the room as soon as matters of faith come into question. Our contemporaries believe that matters of fact are important, and they insist, with ever-increasing emphasis, that they shall not be called upon to believe, as part of their religious faith, anything which, as a matter of fact, is not true. The Modernist critic, when pressed on this side, says that it is natural for faith to represent its ideas in the form of historical facts, and that it is this inevitable tendency which causes the difficulties between religion and science. A sane criticism will allow that this is very largely true, but will not, we are convinced, be constrained to believe with M. Loisy that the historical original of the Christian Redeemer was the poor deluded enthusiast whom he portrays in ' Les Évangiles Synoptiques.'

However this may be—and it must remain a matter of opinion—the very serious question arises, whether it is really natural for faith to represent its ideas in the form of historical facts when it knows that these facts have no historical basis. The writers with whom we are dealing evidently think it is natural and inevitable, and we must assume that they speak from their own spiritual experience. But this state of mind does not seem to be a very common one. Those who believe in the divinity of Christ, but not in His supernatural birth and bodily resurrection, do not, as a rule, make those miracles the subject of their meditations, but find their spiritual sustenance in communion with the Christ who is the same yesterday, to-day, and for ever. Those who regard Jesus only as a prophet sent by God to reveal the Father, generally pray only to the God whom He revealed, and cherish the memory of Jesus with no other feelings than supreme gratitude and veneration. Those, lastly, who worship in God only the Great Unknown who makes for righteousness, find myths and anthropomorphic symbols merely disturbing in such devotions as they are still able to practise. In dealing with convinced Voluntarists it is perhaps not disrespectful to suggest that the difficult position in which they find themselves has produced a peculiar activity of the will, such as is seldom found under normal conditions.

We pass to the position of the Modernists in the Roman Catholic Church. It is well known that the advisers of Pius X have committed the Papacy to a wholesale condemnation of the new movement. The reasons for this condemnation are thus summed up by a distinguished ecclesiastic of that Church [1]:

'Why has the Pope condemned the Modernists? (1) Because the Modernists have denied that the divine facts related in the Gospel are historically true. (2) Because they have denied that Christ for most of His life knew that He was God, and that He ever knew that He was the Saviour of the world. (3) Because they have denied the divine sanction and the perpetuity

[1] Mgr. Moyes, in *The Nineteenth Century*, December, 1907.

M

of the great dogmas which enter into the Christian creed.
(4) Because they have denied that Christ Himself personally
ever founded the Church or instituted the Sacraments.  (5)
Because they deny and subvert the divine constitution of the
Church, by teaching that the Pope and the bishops derive their
powers, not directly from Christ and His Apostles, but from the
Christian people.'

The official condemnation is contained in two documents—the decree of the Holy Inquisition, ' Lamentabili
sane exitu,' July 3, 1907, and the Encyclical, ' Pascendi
dominici gregis,' September 8, 1907.  These pronouncements are intended for Catholics ; and their tone is that
of authoritative denunciation rather than of argument.
In the main, the summary which they give of Modernist
doctrines is as fair as could be expected from a judge who
is passing sentence ; but the papal theologians have not
always resisted the temptation to arouse prejudice by
misrepresenting the views which they condemn.  We have
not space to analyse these documents, nor is it necessary
to do so.  It will be more to the purpose to consider
whether, in spite of their official condemnation, the
Modernists are likely in the future to make good their
footing in the Roman Church.

Even before the Encyclical the Modernists had used
very bold language about the authority of the Church.

'The visible Church (writes Mr. Tyrrell in his " Much-abused
Letter ") is but a means, a way, a creature, to be used where
it helps, to be left where it hinders. . . . Who have taught us
that the consensus of theologians cannot err, but the theologians
themselves ?  Mortal, fallible, ignorant men like ourselves !
. . . Their present domination is but a passing episode in the
Church's history. . . . May not history repeat itself ? [as in
the transition from Judaism to Christianity].  Is God's arm
shortened that He should not again out of the very stones raise
up seed to Abraham ?  May not Catholicism, like Judaism,
have to die in order that it may live again in a greater and
grander form ?  Has not every organism got its limits of
development, after which it must decay and be content to survive in its progeny ?  Wine-skins stretch, but only within
measure ; for there comes at last a bursting-point when new
ones must be provided.'

In a note he explains: 'The Church of the Catacombs became the Church of the Vatican; who can tell what the Church of the Vatican may not turn into?'

It is thus on a very elastic theory of development that the Modernists rely. 'The differences between the larval and final stages of many an insect are often far greater than those which separate kind from kind.' And so this Proteus of a Church, which has changed its form so completely since the Gospel was first preached in the subterranean galleries of Rome, may undergo another equally startling metamorphosis and come to believe in a God who never intervenes in history. We may here remind our readers of Newman's tests of true development, and mark the enormous difference.

Mr. Tyrrell's 'Much-abused Letter' reaches, perhaps, the high-water mark of Modernist claims. Not all the writers whom we have quoted would view with complacency the prospect of the Catholic Church dying to live again, or being content to live only in its progeny. The proverb about the new wine-skins is one of sinister augury in such a connection. If the Catholic Church is really in such an advanced stage of decay that it must die before it can live, why do those who grasp the situation wish to keep it alive? Are they not precisely pouring their new wine into old bottles? Mr. Tyrrell himself draws the parallel with Judaism in the first century. Paul, he says, 'did not feel that he had broken with Judaism.' But the Synagogue did feel that he had done so, and history proved that the Synagogue was right.

Development, however great the changes which it exhibits, can only follow certain laws; and the development of the Church of Rome has steadily followed a direction opposite to that which the Modernists demand that it shall take. Newman might plausibly claim that the doctrines of purgatory and of the papal supremacy are logically involved in the early claims of the Roman Church. The claim is true at least in this sense, that, given a political Church organised as an autocracy, these useful doctrines were sure, in the interests of the government, to be promulgated sooner or later. But there is

not the slightest reason to suppose that the next development will be in the direction of that peculiar kind of
Liberalism favoured by the Modernists. It is difficult
to see how the Vatican could even meet the reformers
half-way without making ruinous concessions. 'This supernatural mechanism,' M. Loisy says in his last book,
'Modernism tends to ruin completely.' Just so; but
the Roman Church lives entirely on the faith in supernatural mechanism. Her sacramental and sacerdotal
system is based on supernatural mechanism—on divine
interventions in the physical world conditioned by human
agency; her theology and books of devotion are full of
supernatural mechanism; the lives of her saints, her
relics and holy places, the whole literature of Catholic
mysticism, the living piety and devotion of the faithful,
wherever it is still to be found, are based entirely on
that very theory of supernaturalistic dualism which the
Modernist, when he acts as critic, begins by ruling out
as devoid of any historical or scientific actuality. The
attractiveness of Catholicism as a cult depends almost
wholly on its frank admission of the miraculous as a matter
of daily occurrence. To rationalise even contemporary
history as M. Loisy has rationalised the Gospels would
be suicide for Catholicism.

It is tempting to give a concrete instance by way of
illustrating the impassable chasm which divides Catholicism as a working system from the academic scheme of
transformation which we have been considering.

' The French Catholics (writes the *Times* correspondent in Paris on
June 25, 1908) are awaiting with concern the report of a special
commission on a mysterious affair known as the Miraculous
Hailstones of Remiremont. On Sunday, May 26, 1907, during
a violent storm that swept over that region of the Vosges, among
the great quantity of hailstones that fell at the time a certain
number were found split in two. On the inner face of each of
the halves, according to the local papers that appeared the next
day, was the image of the Madonna venerated at Remiremont
and known as Notre Dame du Trésor. The local Catholics
regarded it as a reply to the municipal council's veto of the
procession in honour of the Virgin. So many people testified

to having seen the miraculous hailstones that the bishop of Saint-Dié instituted an inquiry ; 107 men, women, and children were heard by the parish priest, and certain well-known men of science [names given] were consulted. The report has just been published in the *Semaine Religieuse*, and concludes in favour of the absolute authenticity of the fact under inquiry. . . . The last word rests with the bishop, who will decide according to the conclusions of the report of the special commission.'

This is Catholicism in practice. Those who think to reform it by their contention that supernatural interventions can never be matters of fact, are liable to the reproach which they most dislike—that of scholastic intellectualism, and neglect of concrete experience.

This denial of the supernatural as a factor in the physical world seems to us alone sufficient to make the position of the Modernists in the Roman Church untenable. That form of Christianity stands or falls with belief in miracles. It has always sought to bring the divine into human life by intercalating acts of God among facts of nature. Its whole sacred literature, as we have said, is penetrated through and through by the belief that God continually intervenes to change the course of events. What would become of the cult of Mary and the saints if it were recognised that God does not so interfere, and that the saints, if criticism allows that they ever existed, can do nothing by their intercessions to avert calamity or bring blessing ? The Modernist priest, it appears, can still say ' Ora pro nobis ' to a Mary whose biography he believes to be purely mythical. At any rate, he can tell his consultants with a good conscience that if they pray to Mary for grace they will receive it. But what is the good of this make-believe ? And, if it is part of a transaction in which the worshipper pays money for assistance which he believes to be miraculous and only obtainable through the good offices of the Church, is it even morally honest ? The worshipper may be helped by his subjective conviction that his cheque on the treasury of merit has been honoured; but if, apart from the natural effects of suggestion, nothing has been given him but a mere *placebo*, is the sacerdotal office one which an honourable man would wish to fill ?

We have no wish whatever to make any imputation against the motives of the brave men who have withstood the thunders of the Vatican, and who in some cases have been professionally ruined by their courageous avowal of their opinions. Perhaps none but a Catholic priest can understand how great the sacrifice is when one in his position breaks away from the authority of those who speak in the name of the Church, and deliberately incurs the charge, still so terrible in Catholic ears, of being a heretic and a teacher of heresy. Not one man in twenty would dare to face the storm of obloquy, hatred, and calumny which is always ready to fall on the head of a heretical priest. The Encyclical indicates the measures which are to be taken officially against Modernists. Pius X ordains that all the young professors suspected of Modernism are to be driven from their chairs in the seminaries; that infected books are to be condemned indiscriminately, even though they may have received an *imprimatur*; that a committee of censors is to be established in every diocese for the revision of books; that meetings of liberal priests or laymen are to be forbidden; that every diocese is to have a vigilance committee to discover and inform against Modernists; and that young clerical Modernists are to be put 'in the lowest places,' and held up to the contempt of their more orthodox or obsequious comrades. But this persecution is as nothing compared with the crushing condemnation with which the religious world, which is his only world, visits this kind of contumacy; the loss of friendships, the grief and shame of loved relatives, and the haunting dread that an authority so august as that which has condemned him cannot have spoken in vain. Assuredly all lovers of truth must do homage to the courage and self-sacrifice of these men. The doubt which may be reasonably felt and expressed as to the consistency of their attitude reflects no disc edit on them personally. Nevertheless, the alternative must be faced, that a 'modernised' Catholicism must either descend to deliberate quackery, or proclaim that the bank from which the main part of her revenues is derived has stopped payment.

What will be the end of the struggle, and in what condition will it leave the greatest Church in Christendom ? There are some who think that the Church will grow tired of the attitude of Canute, and will retreat to the chair which Modernism proffers, well above high-water mark. But the policy of Rome has never been concession, but repression, even at the cost of alienating large bodies of her supporters ; and we believe that in the present instance, as on former occasions, the Vatican will continue to proscribe Modernism until the movement within her body is crushed. She can hardly do otherwise, for the alternative offered is not a gradual reform of her dogmas, but a sweeping revolution. This we have made abundantly clear by quotations from the Modernists themselves. If the Vatican once proclaimed that such views about supernaturalism as those which we have quoted are permissible, a deadly wound would be inflicted on the faith of simple Catholics all over the world. The Vicar of Christ would seem to them to have apostatised. The whole machinery of piety, as practised in Catholic countries, would be thrown out of gear. Nor is there any strong body of educated laymen, such as exists in the Protestant Churches, who could influence the Papacy in the direction of Liberalism. Not only are the laity taught that their province is to obey, and never to call in question the decisions of ecclesiastics, but the large majority of thoughtful laymen have already severed their connection with the Church, and take no interest in projects for its reform. Everything points to a complete victory for the Jesuits and the orthodox party ; and, much as we may regret the stifling of free discussion, and the expulsion of earnest and conscientious thinkers from the Church which they love, it is difficult to see how any other policy could be adopted.

Of the Modernists, a few will secede, others will remain in the Church, though in open revolt against the Vatican ; but the majority will be silenced, and will make a lip-submission to authority. The disastrous results of the rebellion, and of the means taken to crush it, will be apparent in the deterioration of the priesthood. Modern thought, it will be said, has now been definitely condemned by the Church; war has been openly declared against progress. Many who, before the crisis of the last few years, believed it possible to enter the Roman Catholic priesthood without any sacrifice of intellectual honesty, will in the future find it impossible to do so. We may expect to see this result most palpable in France, where men think logically, and are but little influenced by custom and prejudice. Unless the Republican Government blows the dying embers into a blaze by unjust persecution, it is to be feared that Catholicism in that country may soon become ' une quantité négligeable.' The prospects of the Church in Italy and Spain do not seem very much better. In fact the only comfort which we can suggest to those who regret the decline of an august institution, is that decadent autocracies have often shown an astonishing toughness. But as head of the universal Church, in any true sense of the word, Rome has finished her life.

A more vital question, for those at least who are Christians, but not Roman Catholics, is in what shape the Christian religion will emerge from the assaults upon traditional beliefs which science and historical criticism are pressing home. We have given our reasons for rejecting the Modernist attempt at reconstruction. In the first place, we do not feel that we are required by sane criticism to surrender nearly all that M. Loisy has surrendered. We believe that the kingdom of God which Christ preached was something much more than a patriotic dream. We believe that He did speak as never man spake, so that those who heard Him were convinced that He was more than man. We believe, in short, that the object of our worship was a historical figure. Nothing has yet come to light, or is likely to come to light, which prevents us from identifying the Christ of history with the Christ of faith, or the Christ of experience.

But, if too much is surrendered on one side, too much is taken back on the other. The contention that the progress of knowledge has left the traditional beliefs and cultus of Catholics untouched is untenable. It is not too much to say that the whole edifice of supernaturalistic

dualism under which Catholic piety has sheltered itself
for fifteen hundred years has fallen in ruins to the ground.
There is still enough superstition left to win a certain
vogue for miraculous cures at Lourdes, and split hailstones at Remiremont.  But that kind of religion is doomed,
and will not survive three generations of sound secular
education given equally to both sexes.  The craving for
signs and wonders—that broad road which attracts so
many converts and wins so rapid a success—leads religion at last to its destruction, as Christ seems to have
warned His own disciples.  Science has been the slowly
advancing Nemesis which has overtaken a barbarised
and paganised Christianity.  She has come with a winnow-
ing fan in her hand, and she will not stop till she
has thoroughly purged her floor.  She has left us the
divine Christ, whatever may be the truth about certain
mysterious events in His human life.  But assuredly she
has not left us the right to offer wheedling prayers to
a mythical Queen of Heaven ; she has not left us the
right to believe in such puerile stories as the Madonna-
stamp on hailstones, in order to induce a comfortably
pious state of mind.

The dualism alleged to exist between faith and knowledge will not serve.  Man is one, and reality is one ; there
can no more be two ' orders of reality ' not affecting
each other than there can be two faculties in the human
mind working independently of each other.  The universe
which is interpreted to us by our understanding is not
unreal, nor are its laws pliant to our wills, as the pragmatists do vainly talk.  It is a divinely ordered system,
which includes man, the roof and crown of things, and
Christ, in whom is revealed to us its inner character and
meaning.  It is not the province of faith either to flout
scientific knowledge, or to contaminate the material on
which science works by intercalating what M. Le Roy
calls ' transhistorical symbols '—myths in fact—which
do not become true by being recognised as false, as the new
apologetic seems to suggest.  Faith is not the born story-
teller of Modernist theology.  Faith is, on the practical
side, just the resolution to stand or fall by the noblest

hypothesis; and, on the intellectual side, .it is a progressive initiation, by experiment which ends in experience, into the unity of the good, the true, and the beautiful, founded on the inner assurance that these three attributes of the divine nature have one source and conduct to one goal.

The Modernists are right in finding the primary principle of faith in the depths of our undivided personality. They are right in teaching that faith develops and comes into its own only through the activity of the whole man. They are right in denying the name of faith to correct opinion, which may leave the character untouched. As Hartley Coleridge says :

> ' Think not the faith by which the just shall live
> Is a dead creed, a map correct of heaven,
> Far less a feeling fond and fugitive,
> A thoughtless gift, withdrawn as soon as given.
> It is an affirmation and an act
> That bids eternal truth be present fact.'

For all this we are grateful to them. But we maintain that the future of Christianity is in the hands of those who insist that faith and knowledge must be confronted with each other till they have made up their quarrel. The crisis of faith cannot be dealt with by establishing a *modus vivendi* between scepticism and superstition. That is all that Modernism offers us ; and it will not do. Rather we will believe, with Clement of Alexandria, that πιστὴ ἡ γνῶσις, γνωστὴ δὲ ἡ πίστις.

If this confidence in the reality of things hoped for and the hopefulness of things real be well-founded, we must wait in patience for the coming of the wise master-builders who will construct a more truly Catholic Church out of the fragments of the old, with the help of the material now being collected by philosophers, psychologists, historians, and scientists of all creeds and countries. When the time comes for this building to rise, the contributions of the Modernists will not be described as wood, hay, or stubble. They have done valuable service to biblical criticism, and in other branches, which will be always recognised. But the building will not (we venture to prophesy) be erected on their plan, nor by their Church. History shows few examples of the rejuvenescence of decayed autocracies. Nor is our generation likely to see much of the reconstruction. The churches, as institutions, will continue for some time to show apparent weakness ; and other moralising and civilising agencies will do much of their work. But, since there never has been a time when the character of Christ and the ethics which he taught have been held in higher honour than the present, there is every reason to expect that the next ' Age of Faith,' when it comes, will be of a more genuinely Christian type than the last.

# CARDINAL NEWMAN

## (1912)

THE life of Newman was divided into two nearly equal portions by his change of religion in October 1845. For the
earlier half of his career we have long had his own narrative ;
and Newman is a prince of autobiographers. It was his
wish that the ' Apologia ' should be the final and authoritative account of his life in the Church of England, and
of the steps by which he was led to transfer his allegiance
to another communion. The voluminous literature of
the Tractarian movement, which includes large collections
of Newman's own letters, has confirmed the accuracy of
his narrative, and has made any further description of that
strange episode in English University life superfluous.
With the ' Apologia ' and Dean Church's ' Oxford Movement ' before him, the reader needs no more. Mr. Wilfrid
Ward has therefore been well advised to adhere loyally to
the Cardinal's wishes, by confining himself to the last half
of Newman's life, after a brief summary of his childhood,
youth, and middle age till 1845. Nevertheless, it is misleading to give the title ' The Life of Cardinal Newman '
to a work which is only, as it were, the second volume of
a biography. There are very few men, however long-lived,
who have not done much of their best work before the
age of forty-five, and Newman was certainly not one of the
exceptions. From every point of view, except that of the
Roman Catholic ecclesiastical historian, Newman's Anglican
career was far more interesting and important than his
residence at Birmingham. He will live in history, not as
the recluse of Edgbaston, nor as the wearer of the Cardinal's

hat which fell to his lot, almost too late to save the credit of the Vatican, when he had passed the normal limit of human life, but as the real founder and leader of nineteenth century Anglo-Catholicism, the movement which he created and then tried in vain to destroy. The projects and failures and successes of his later life seem very pale and almost petty when compared with the activities of the years while he was making a chapter of English history. His greatest book, though it was written many years after his secession, is the record of a drama which ended in the interview with Father Dominic the Passionist. It is ' The History of my Religious Opinions ' ; and after 1845 his religious opinions had, as he says himself, no further history. The incomparable style which will give him a permanent place among the masters of English prose was the product of his life at Oxford, where he lived in a society of highly cultivated men, whose writings show many of the same excellences as his own. Newman's English is only the Oriel manner at its best. Such an instrument could hardly have been forged at the Birmingham Oratory, where his associates, who had followed him from Littlemore, were of such an inferior type that Mark Pattison, who knew them, was surprised that he could be satisfied with their company. His best sermons and his best poetry belong to his Anglican period. ' The Dream of Gerontius,' with all its tender grace, is far less virile than ' Lead, kindly Light,' and other short poems of his youth. Moreover, his record as a Roman ecclesiastic is one of almost unrelieved failure. If he had died eighteen years after his secession, when he already looked upon himself as an old man whose course was nearly run, he would have been regarded as one who had sacrificed a great career in the Church of England for neglect and obscurity. From the first he was distrusted by the ' Old Catholics ' (the old Roman Catholic families in England), and suspected at the Vatican, where Talbot assiduously represented him as ' the most dangerous man in England.' When Manning, Archdeacon of Chichester, followed his example and joined the Roman Church, Newman was confronted with a still more subtle and relentless opponent, whose hostility was never relaxed till the accession of a

Liberal Pope made it no longer possible to resist the bestowal of tardy honours upon a feeble octogenarian. The recognition came in time to soothe his decline, but too late to enable him to leave his mark upon the administration of the Roman Church.

The main events in a very uneventful career are narrated at length in Mr. Ward's volumes. After his 'conversion' Newman first resided in a small community at Maryvale (Oscott) but soon left it on a journey to Rome, where he spent some time at the Collegio di Propaganda, and had a foretaste of the distrust with which Pius IX and his advisers always regarded him. His plan at this time was to found a theological seminary at Maryvale; and in this scheme he had the support of Wiseman, the ablest Roman ecclesiastic in the United Kingdom. But the 'Essay on Development,' with its unscholastic language and unfamiliar line of apologetic, seriously alarmed the theologians at Rome; and Newman, accepting the first of many rebuffs, abandoned this project in favour of another. He resolved to join the Oratorians, an order founded by St. Philip Neri, and obtained permission to modify, in his projected establishment, the rules of the Order, which, among other things, prescribed frequent floggings in public. He visited Naples, and came back a believer in the liquefaction of the saint's blood. The amazing letter to Henry Wilberforce, written from Santa Croce, shows that he was the most docile and credulous of converts. Even the Holy House at Loreto caused him no difficulty. 'He who floated the ark on the surges of a world-wide sea, and inclosed in it all living things, who has hidden the terrestrial paradise, who said that faith might remove mountains . . . could do this wonder also.' It 'may have been'; 'everybody believes it in Rome'; therefore Newman 'has no doubt'!

The new Oratory was placed by Papal brief at Birmingham. The first members of it were his friends who had left the English Church with him. Recruits soon came in, and branch houses were talked of. But for many years Newman had reason to complain of neglect and want of sympathy. He even found empty churches when he preached in London. In conjunction with Faber, he next

started a series of ' Lives of the Saints,' in which the most
absurd ' miracles ' were accepted without question as true.
The ' Old Catholics,' who had no stomach for such food,
protested ; and Newman, this time thoroughly irritated,
had to admit another failure. The Oratory, however, and
its London offshoot under Faber were prosperous, and the
churches where Newman preached were not long empty.
In 1850 we find him in better spirits. He employed his
energies in a series of clever lectures on ' Anglican Difficulties,' in which he ridiculed the Church of his earlier vows
with all the refined cruelty of which he was a master. But
he was soon in trouble again. One Dr. Giacinto Achilli,
formerly a Dominican friar, gave lectures in London upon
the scandals of the Roman Inquisition, which had imprisoned him for attacking the Catholic faith and fomenting
sedition. The temper of the British public at this time
made it ready to believe anything to the discredit of the
Roman Church, and Achilli became a popular hero. Wiseman published a libellous article upon him in the *Dublin
Review*, which passed unnoticed. But when Newman
repeated the charges of profligacy in a public lecture, Achilli
brought an action for libel, which in costs and expenses
cost Newman £12,000. The money however was paid, and
much more than paid, by his co-religionists. This trial
was quickly followed by the inauguration of a scheme for
founding a Catholic University in Ireland, the avowed
object of which was to withdraw young Catholics from the
liberalising influences of mixed education. This scheme
was sure to appeal strongly to Newman. Liberalism had
come in with a rush at Oxford, after the dissipation of the
' long nightmare ' (as Mark Pattison calls it) while the
University was dominated by religious medievalism. The
Oxford of Newman had become the Oxford of Jowett.
The ablest of Newman's young friends and disciples, such
as Mark Pattison and J. A. Froude, were now in the opposite
camp, full of anger and disgust at the seductive influences
from which they had just escaped. Newman, as might be
expected, was anxious to protect Catholic students from
similar dangers, and accepted the post of Rector of the
proposed Catholic University. He intended it to provide

philosophical defences of Catholicity and Revelation, and create a Catholic literature.' The lectures in which he expounded his ideals at Dublin were a great success, and he returned to England full of hope. With a curious inability to read the character of one who was to be his worst enemy, he offered Manning the post of Vice-Rector. Manning's refusal was followed by his failure to obtain the support of Ward, Henry Wilberforce, and others ; and Catholic opinion in Ireland was much divided. For three or four years Newman was engaged in ineffectual efforts to push his scheme forward. At last, in 1855, he was installed as Rector, and began his work at Dublin. A fine church was built at St. Stephen's Green with the surplus of the Achilli subscriptions, and Newman produced some excellent literary work in the form of University lectures and sermons. But the whole movement was viewed with distrust by the Irish ecclesiastics, who, as he said in a moment of impatience, ' regard any intellectual man as being on the road to perdition.' There was a cloud over his work from first to last. He had been promised a bishopric, without which he was made to feel himself in an inferior position by the Irish prelates ; but the promise was not fulfilled. The Irish objected to one or two English professors on his staff, because they were English. Dr. Cullen, the ruling spirit in the Irish hierarchy, was a narrow conservative, who wished to use Newman merely as an instrument against progressive tendencies in Church and State. In 1857 he resigned an impossible task, and returned to Birmingham.

New undertakings followed, no more successful than the abortive university scheme. There was to be a new translation of the Bible, and a new Catholic magazine called the *Rambler*. The former enterprise was already well advanced when the general indifference of the Catholic public caused it to be abandoned. The *Rambler*, the contributors to which used a freedom of discussion unpalatable to Roman ecclesiastics, struggled on amid a storm of criticism till 1859, when Newman, who was then himself editor, resigned, and one more humiliating failure was registered. The management of the magazine passed into other hands.

The Oratory School at Birmingham, a much less contentious undertaking, was successfully launched in the same year.

In 1860 came the emancipation of the States of the Church by Cavour and Victor Emmanuel. Newman referred to the Piedmontese as ' sacrilegious robbers,' but his advocacy of the temporal power was not strong enough to please the Vatican, while the strength of Manning's language left nothing to be desired. Newman became more unpopular than ever. His reputation suffered by his former connection with the *Rambler* and his supposed connection with the *Home and Foreign Review*, which Acton intended to represent the views of progressive Catholics, till it also was snuffed out by the hierarchy. The five years from 1859 to 1864 are considered by Mr. Ward to have been the saddest in Newman's life. He felt, truly enough, that the dominant party had no sympathy with his aims, and that he was treated as ' some wild incomprehensible beast, a spectacle for Dr. Wiseman to exhibit to strangers, as himself being the hunter who captured it.' ' All through my life I have been plucked,' he writes to an old Oxford friend. There was even in his mind at this time a wistful yearning after the friends and the Church that he had left—a feeling, doubtless transient, but significant, which his biographer has allowed to show itself in a few pages of his book. After reminding himself, in his diary, of the warning against those who, after putting their hand to the plough, ' look back,' he proceeds to look back, because he cannot help it.

' I live more and more in the past, and in hopes that the past may revive in the future. . . . I think, as death comes on, his cold breath is felt on soul as on body, and that, viewed naturally, my soul is half dead now, whereas then [in his Protestant days] it was in the freshness and fervour of youth. . . . I say the same of my state of mind from 1834 to 1845, when I became a Catholic. It is a time past and gone—it relates to a work done and over. " Quis mihi tribuat, ut sim iuxta menses pristinos, secundum dies, quibus Deus custodiebat me ? Quando splendebat lucerna eius super caput meum, et ad lumen eius ambulabam in tenebris ? " . . . I have no friend at Rome ; I have laboured in England, to be misrepresented, backbitten and scorned. I have laboured in Ireland, with a door ever shut

in my face. . . . Contemporaneously with this neglect on the
part of those for whom I laboured, there has been a drawing
towards me on the part of Protestants.  Those very books and
labours which Catholics did not understand, Protestants did.
I am under the temptation of looking out for, if not courting,
Protestant praise. . . . What I wrote as a Protestant has had
far greater power, force, meaning, success, than my Catholic
works.'

Such reflections might seem to indicate a disposition to
return to the Anglican fold.  But a man must have van-
quished pride in its most insidious form before he can leave
the Church of Rome for any other.  The aristocratic *hauteur*
of the *civis Romanus* among barbarians lives on in the
sentiment of the Roman Catholic towards Protestants.
When Newman was publicly charged with intending to
return to Anglicanism, this spirit broke out in a disagree-
able and insulting manner.

The bitterness of these five years of neglect, in which he
had been eating his heart in silence, must be remembered
in connexion with the famous Kingsley controversy, which
in 1864 roused him to put on his armour and fight for
his reputation.  There had always been an element of
combativeness in Newman's disposition.  ' *Nescio quo
pacto*, my spirits most happily rise at the prospect of
danger,' he wrote early in life.  And when he could
persuade himself that not only his honour but that of
the Church was at stake, he could feel and show the true
Catholic ferocity, the cruellest spirit on earth.  ' A
heresiarch,' he had written even in his Anglican days,
' should meet with no mercy. He must be dealt with
by the competent authority as if he were embodied evil.
To spare him is a false and dangerous pity. It is to
endanger the souls of thousands, and it is uncharitable
towards himself' !  This was the temper, soured by
defeat and not mellowed by age, which Charles Kingsley
in an evil moment for himself chose wantonly to provoke.  At Christmas 1863 there appeared in *Macmillan's
Magazine* a review of Froude's ' History of England,' in
which Kingsley wrote ' Truth for its own sake has never
been a virtue with the Roman clergy.  Father Newman

informs us that it need not be, and on the whole ought not
to be—that cunning is the weapon which Heaven has
given to the saints wherewith to withstand the brute male
force of the wicked world.' This charge was in fact based
on a careless reading, or an imperfect recollection, of the
twentieth discourse in 'Sermons on Subjects of the Day.'
The discourse in question is a somewhat nauseous glorification of the servile temper, but it only says that the
meekness of the saints is (by Divine providence) so successful
that it is always mistaken for craft. The *imputation* of
cunning is therefore a note of sanctity in its victim. Kingsley ought to have read the sermon again, and withdrawn
unreservedly from an untenable position. But he thought
that something less than a complete apology would serve ;
and so gave Newman the opportunity of his life. When
the withdrawal which he offered was rejected, Kingsley
made matters ten times worse for himself by an ill-con-
sidered pamphlet called ' What then does Dr. Newman
mean ? ' In this effusion he vents all his scorn and hatred
for Catholicism—for its tortuous tactics, its monstrous
credulity and appetite for miracles, which must proceed,
according to him, either from infantile folly or from
deliberate imposture. Forgetting altogether that he has to
defend himself against a specific charge of slander, he offers
his great opponent the choice between writing himself down
a knave or a fool—a knave if he pretends to believe in the
Holy Coat and the blood of St. Januarius, a fool if he does
believe in them.

The coarseness of this attack upon an elderly man of
saintly character and acknowledged intellectual eminence,
who had to all appearance blighted a great career by
honestly obeying his conscience, offended the British public,
which was now fully disposed to give a respectful and
favourable hearing to whatever Newman might care to
say in reply. In a Catholic country it would have been
useless for a Protestant, however falsely attacked, to appeal
to Catholic public opinion for justice ; but Newman understood the English character, and saw his splendid chance.

The famous defence was, from every point of view except
the highest, a complete triumph. And although Hort was

strictly accurate in describing the treatment of Kingsley
as 'horribly unchristian,' it is demanding too much of
human nature to expect a master of fence, when wantonly
attacked with a bludgeon, to abstain from the pleasure of
pricking his adversary scientifically in the tender parts of
his body. The bitterest passages were excised in later
editions; and the 'Apologia' remains a masterpiece of
autobiography, and a powerful defence of Catholicism. To
Newman this appeared to be the turning-point in his fortunes. He felt strong enough to administer a severe snub
to Monsignor Talbot, his old enemy, who, hearing of the success of the 'Apologia,' invited him to preach at Rome. Then
at once he threw himself into a great scheme for founding
an Oratory at Oxford. Eight and a half acres were bought
between Worcester College, the Clarendon Press, the Ob-
servatory, and Beaumont Street, a magnificent site, which
the Oratorians acquired for only £8400. But here again
he was thwarted. W. G. Ward opposed the scheme with
all his might, insisting on the necessity of 'preserving the
purity of a Catholic atmosphere throughout the whole
course of education.' The whole tendency of the Ultramontane movement was to secure, before all other things,
a body of militant young Catholics to fight the battles of
the Church. Newman was willing to support the English
Church in its warfare against unbelief; to the Ultramontane
a Protestant is as certainly damned as an atheist, and is
more mischievous as being less amenable to Catholic
influence. Manning and Talbot seem to have given the
project its *coup de grâce* at Rome, and Newman sold the
land which he had bought. He was bitterly disappointed;
but the growth of public esteem had given him self-confi-
dence, and he did not again fall into despondency, though
he had a strange presentiment of approaching death, which
prompted his last famous poem, 'The Dream of Gerontius.' A second attempt to go to Oxford was thwarted
by enemies at Rome and in England in 1866-7. The extreme party, with Manning, now Archbishop, at their head,
seemed to be victorious all along the line. They were able
to proceed to their supreme triumph in the Vatican Council
which issued the dogma of Papal Infallibility. Newman,

while others were intriguing and haranguing, was quietly
engaged in preparing his subtlest and (on one side) his most
characteristic work, ' The Grammar of Assent,' an attempt
at a Catholic apologetic on a ' personalist,' as opposed to
an ' intellectualist ' basis. He declined to take an active
part in the theological conferences about infallibility, being
by this time well aware how little weight such arguments
as he could bring were likely to have at Rome. He was
disgusted at the insolent aggressiveness of the Ultramontanes, but he had no wish to combat it. The situation was
hopeless, and he knew it. The death of several friends
increased the sense of isolation, and during the years 1875
to 1879 his silence and depression were very noticeable to
those who lived with him. His dearest friend, Ambrose
St. John, was one of several who died about this time. But
Trinity College, Oxford, made him an honorary fellow in
1877, an honour which seemed to prognosticate the far
higher distinction which was soon to be conferred upon
him.

The death of Pius IX in 1878 brought to an end the long
reign of obscurantism at the Vatican, and with the election
of Leo XIII Newman emerged from the cloud under which
he had remained for more than a generation. The new
Pope lost no time in making him a Cardinal, though even
now the prize seemed to be on the point of slipping through
his fingers. He valued the honour immensely as setting
the official seal of approbation on his life's work, and the
last ten years of his life were quietly happy. He was able
to mingle actively in affairs of public interest, and to write
long letters, till near the end. He died on August 11,
1890, in his ninetieth year, and was buried, by his own
request, in the same grave with his friend Ambrose
St. John.

Why is it that this sad, isolated, broken life, in which
the young man renounces the creed of the boy, and the elder
man pours scorn upon the loyalties of his prime ; which
found its last haven in a society which wished to make a
tool of him but distrusted him too much for even this pitiful
service, has still an absorbing interest for our generation ?
For it is not only in England that Newman's fame lives

and grows. In France there is a cult of Newman, which has produced biographies by Bremond and Faure, as well as a history of the Catholic Revival in England by Thureau-Dangin. In England, besides Dean Church's ' Oxford Movement,' we have biographies by R. H. Hutton and W. Barry, and appreciations or depreciations by E. Abbott, Leslie Stephen, Froude, Mark Pattison, and several others.

The interest is mainly personal and psychological. Newman's writings, and his life, are a ' human document ' in a very peculiar degree. Bremond is right in calling attention to the *autocentrism* of Newman. ' Although (he says) the words " I " and " me " are relatively rare in Newman's writings, whether as preacher, novelist, controversialist, philosopher, or poet, he always reveals and always describes himself.' Even his historical portraits are reconstructed from his inner consciousness ; hence their historical falsity —all ages are mixed in his histories—and their philosophical truth. In a sense he was the most reserved of men. We do not know whether he had any ordinary temptations ; we do not know whether he ever fell in love. But the texture of his mind and the growth of his opinions have been laid bare to us with the candour of a saint and the accuracy of a dissector or analyst. He reminds us of De Quincey, who also could tell the story of his own life, but no other, and whose style, like his own, was modelled on the literary traditions of the eighteenth century.

He has left us, in the ' Apologia,' a picture of his precocious and dreamy boyhood, when he lived in a world of his own, peopled by angels and spirits, a world in which the supernatural was the only nature. He was lonely and reserved, then as always. It is not for nothing that in his sermons he expatiates so often on the impenetrability of the human soul. A nature so self-centred has always something hard and inhuman about it ; he was loved, but loved little in return. And yet he craved for more affection than he could reciprocate. ' I cannot ever realise to myself,' he wrote once, ' that anyone loves me.' It is a common feeling in imaginative, withdrawn characters. Deepseated in his nature was a reverence for the hidden springs of thought, action, and belief. When he spoke of ' conscience,' as he did continually, he meant, not the faculty which decides ethical problems, but the undivided soul-nature which underlies the separate activities of thought, will, and feeling. In this sense the epigrammatist was right who said that ' to Newman his own nature was a revelation which he called conscience.' He ' followed the gleam,' uncertain whither it would lead him. The poem ' Lead, kindly Light ' is the most intimate self-revelation that he ever made. This mental attitude, which he took early in life, became the foundation of his ' personalist ' philosophy, and of the anti-intellectualism which was the negative side of it. But this reliance on the inner light, which nearly made a mystic of him, was clouded by a haunting fear of God's wrath, which imparts a gloomy tinge to his Anglican sermons, and which, while he was halting between the English Church and Rome, plied him with the very unmystical question ' Where shall I be most *safe ?* ' an argument which he had used repeatedly and without scruple in his parochial sermons.[1]

It is nevertheless true that this self-centred spirit was, at least in early life, impressionable and open to the influence of others. His friendship with Hurrell Froude and Keble affected his opinions considerably : and still more potent was the pervading intangible influence of Oxford—the academic atmosphere. It cannot indeed be said that the University was at this time in a healthy condition. Mark Pattison has described with caustic contempt the intellectual lethargy of the place, and the miserable quality of the lectures. Oxford was still *de facto* a close clerical corporation, and in most colleges ' clubbable men ' rather than scholars were chosen for the fellowships. Oriel won its unique position by breaking through this tradition, and also by making originality rather than success in the university examinations the main qualification for election. But even at Oriel, and among the ablest men, there was great ignorance of much that was being thought and written elsewhere. Knowledge of German was rare. Even the classics were not read in a humanistic spirit. ' Of the world of

---

[1] Cf. e.g. *Parochial and Plain Sermons,* vi. 259.

wisdom and sentiment—of poetry and philosophy, of social and political experience, contained in the Latin and Greek classics, and of the true relation of the degenerate and semi-barbarous Christian writers of the fourth century to that world—Oxford, in 1830, had never dreamt.'[1] Theological prejudice in fact distorted the whole outlook of the resident fellows, and confounded all estimation of relative values. Newman never, all through his life, took a step towards overcoming this early prejudice. He imagined a golden age of the Church, or several golden ages, and found them in ' the first three centuries,' in the time of Alfred the Great or of Edward the Confessor, or in the seventeenth century. He was only sure that the sixteenth century was made of much baser metal. This unhistorical idealisation of the past, even of a barbarous past, was very characteristic of Newman and his friends. They bequeathed to the Anglican Church the strange legend of an age of pure doctrine and heroic practice, to which it should be our aim to ' return.' The real strength of this legend lies in the fact that it has no historical foundation. The ideal which is presented as a return or a revival is nothing of the kind, but a creation of our own time, projected by the imagination into the past, from which it comes back with a halo of authority. Newman had his full share of these illusions. In his youth and prime he was more of an Englishman than an Anglican. He despised foreigners, unless they were Catholic saints, could not bear the sight of the *tricolor*, and hated all the ' ideas of the Revolution.' His dictum, ' Luther is dead, but Hildebrand and Loyola are alive,' throws a flood of light upon the contents of his mind, as does the truly British prejudice which caused him to be horrified at the sight of ships coaling at Malta ' on a holy day.' His range of ideas was so much restricted that Bremond, a sincere admirer, says that his imagination lived on ' une poignée de souvenirs d'enfant.' How tragic was the fate which caught this loyal Englishman and more than loyal Oxonian in the meshes of a cosmopolitan institution in which England counted for little and Oxford for nothing at all !

[1] Mark Pattison, *Memoirs*, p. 97.

The Reform of 1832 seemed to threaten the English Church with destruction. Arnold in this year wrote ' The Church, as it now stands, no human power can save.' The bishops were stunned and bewildered by the unexpected outbreak of popular hostility. Old methods of defence were plainly useless ; some new plan of campaign must be devised against the double assault of political radicalism and theological liberalism. To Newman both alike were of the devil ; theological liberalism especially was only specious infidelity. He never had the slightest inkling that a deep religious earnestness and love of truth underlay the revolt against orthodox tradition. His fighting instincts were aroused. When Keble attributed the scheme for suppressing some Irish bishoprics to ' national apostasy,' he rushed to arms in defence of Church privileges and property. In the first Tract (1833) he says :

' A notion has gone abroad that the people can take away your power. They think they have given it and can take it away. They have been deluded into a notion that present palpable usefulness, produceable results, acceptableness to your flocks—that these and such-like are the tests of your Divine commission. Enlighten them in this matter. Exalt our holy fathers the Bishops, as the representatives of the Apostles, and the Angels of the Churches, and magnify your office, as being ordained by them to take part in their ministry.'

That was the keynote of the whole Tractarian movement. A weapon was needed to smite liberalism. Nothing but a compact and powerful organisation could repel the foe. God must have provided such an organisation : a Divine society, certain of ultimate victory, must exist somewhere. Newman and his friends hoped to find it in the Anglican Church ; and such was the power of their contagious zeal and confident enthusiasm, that the immediate danger was actually staved off, and the Establishment was allowed a new lease of life. But the national Church of England was not constituted to resist the national will, and the attempt to reorganise it on Catholic lines was foredoomed to failure. And so, since the assumption that a great institutional fighting Church *must* exist was never even questioned, when Anglicanism failed him there was no other refuge but Rome.

He was certainly more logical than his friends who remained behind. Anglo-Catholicism has its theoretical basis in a definition of Catholicity which is repudiated by all other Catholics ; its traditions are largely legendary. But it is an eclectic system well suited to the English character, and the distorted view of history which Newman bequeathed to the party has enabled it to borrow much that is good from different sides, without any sense of inconsistency. The idea of a Divine society has been and is the inspiration of thousands of ardent workers in the Anglican Church. It lifted the religion of many Englishmen from the somewhat gross and bourgeois condition in which the movement found it, to a pure and unworldly idealism. And, unlike most other religious revivals, especially in this country, it has remained remarkably free from unhealthy emotionalism and hysterics. The social atmosphere of Oxford, always alien to mawkish sentiment, penetrated the whole movement, and maintained in it for many years a certain sanity and dignity which, while they doubtless prevented it from spreading widely in the middle class, made the Tractarians respected by men of taste and education. But these influences could not be permanent. The goodwill of the Tractarian firm (if we may so express it) has now been acquired by men with very different aims and methods. The ablest members of the party are plunging violently into social politics, while the rank and file in increasing numbers are fluttering round the Roman candle, into which many of them must ultimately fall.

The progress of the movement between 1833 and 1845 was almost entirely in the direction of teaching the clergy to ' magnify their office.' The other part of the scheme, the combat against theological liberalism, fell quite into the background. The main reason for this was that during those strange years the theologians so completely dominated Oxford that liberalism could hardly raise its head, and was despised as well as hated. Only after Newman's secession could the regeneration of the University begin. Then indeed liberalism came in like a flood, though it was a very shallow flood in some cases. This was the day of the self-satisfied young rationalist, 'écarté par une plaisanterie des croyances dont la raison d'un Pascal ne réussit pas à se dégager,' as Renan says—an orgy of facile free thought which after a generation was chastised by another clerical reaction.

If Newman could have foreseen the victory of his party in the English Church, he might perhaps have been content to remain in it. We cannot tell. But it is doubtful whether he would have taken Pusey's place as leader of the party. Newman's influence was disturbing and subtly disintegrating to every cause for which he laboured. His startling candour often seemed like treachery. He could not work with others, and broke with nearly all his friends, retaining only his disciples. He confessed himself a bad judge of character. It is doubtful, after all, whether he was much injured by the jealousy and almost instinctive fear which he inspired among the Roman Catholic hierarchy. If he had been allowed to take the place due to his abilities, his character, and his reputation, what could he have done that he was unable to do at Edgbaston ? We cannot fancy him plunged in crooked ecclesiastical intrigue, like that *Inglese italianato*, Cardinal Manning. Still less can we fancy him haranguing strikers, and stealing the credit of composing a trade dispute. No doubt he suffered under the sense of injury ; but probably he did what was in him to do. If the Roman Church would not use him as a tool, it was probably because he would not have been a good tool. There are some mistakes which that Church seldom makes ; it knows how to choose its men.

What will be the verdict of history on the type of Catholicism which Newman represented ? He was kept out in the cold by a conservative Pope, and honoured by a liberal Pope. Which was right, from the point of view of Catholic interests and policy ? This is perhaps the most important question which the life of Newman raises ; for it affects our anticipations of the future even more than our judgments of the past. Is Newman a safe or a possible guide for Catholics in the twentieth century ?

Newman was no metaphysician ; he confesses it himself.

'My turn of mind,' he says, 'has never led me towards metaphysics; rather it has been logical, ethical, practical.'[1] For metaphysics requires an initial act of faith in human reason, and Newman had not this faith. Even in his Anglican days he uttered many astonishing things in contempt of reason. 'What is intellect itself (he asks) but a fruit of the Fall, not found in paradise or in heaven, more than in little children, and at the utmost but tolerated by the Church, and only not incompatible with the regenerate mind ? . . . Reason is God's gift, but so are the passions. . . . Eve was tempted to follow passion and reason, and she fell.'[2] 'Faith does not regard degrees of evidence.'[3] 'Faith and humility consist, not in going about to prove, but in the outset confiding in the testimony of others.' 'The more you set yourself to argue and prove, in order to discover truth, the less likely you are to reason correctly.'[4] The amazing crudity of this avowed obscurantism is likely to make the orthodox apologist writhe, and to move the rationalist to contemptuous laughter. In this and many other cases, Newman seems to love to caricature himself, and to put his beliefs in that form in which they outrage common sense most completely. We can imagine nothing more calculated to drive a young and ingenuous mind into flippant scepticism than a course of Newman's sermons. The *reductio ad absurdum* of his arguments is not left to the reader to make; it is innocently provided by the preacher.

And yet Newman's central position is not absurd, or only becomes absurd when it is applied to justify belief in gross superstition. He holds that what he calls 'reasoning' deals only with abstractions, and is not the faculty on which we rely in forming 'judgments.' These judgments, to which we give our 'assent,' and by which we regulate our conduct, are affirmations of the basal personality. And these have an authority far greater than can ever arise out of the logical manipulation of concepts. 'There is no ultimate test of truth besides the testimony borne to the

[1] *Stray Essays*, p. 94.  [2] *Parochial and Plain Sermons*, v. 112.
[3] *Ibid*. vi. 259.  [4] *Ibid*. vi. 340.

truth by the mind itself.' The ' mind itself,' the concrete
personality, is concerned with realities, while the intellect,
which for him corresponds very nearly with the discursive
reason (διάνοια) of the Greek philosophers, is at home only
in mathematics and, up to a certain point, in logic. The
concepts of the intellect have no existence outside it. ' The
mind has the gift, by an act of creation, of bringing before
it abstractions and generalisations which have no counterpart, no existence, out of it.' [1] Parenthetically, we may
remark that passages like this show how wide of the truth
Mr. Barry is when he speaks of Newman as a ' thorough
Alexandrine.' To deny the existence of universals, to regard them as mere creations of the mind, is rank blasphemy
to a Platonist ; and the Alexandrines were Christian Pla-
tonists. No more misleading statement could be made about
Newman's philosophy than to associate him with Platonism
of any kind, whether Pagan or Christian. Newman adopts
the sensationalist (Lockian) theory of knowledge. Ideas
are copies or modifications of the data presented by the
senses ; ' first principles are abstractions from facts, not
elementary truths prior to reasoning.' This is pure
nominalism, in its crudest form. It makes all arguments in
favour of the great truths of religion valueless ; for if there
are no universals, rational theism is impossible. It follows
that the famous scholastic ' proofs of God's existence ' have
for Newman no cogency whatever ; indeed it is difficult to
see how he can have escaped condemning the whole philosophy of St. Thomas Aquinas as a juggling with bloodless
concepts. Newman himself pleaded that he had no wish to
oppose the official dogmatics of his Church. But protesta-
tions are of no avail where the facts are so clear. ' The
natural theology of our schools,' says a writer in the *Tablet*,
quoted by Dr. Caldecott in his ' Philosophy of Religion,'
' is based frankly and wholly on the appeal to reason.'
This is notoriously true ; and what Newman thought of
reason we have already seen. His extreme disparagement
of the intellect seems to preclude what he calls ' real assent '
to the creeds and dogmas of Catholicism ; for these clearly

---

[1] *Grammar of Assent*, part i. c. 1 and 2.

consist of 'notional' propositions. But Newman would answer that the Church is a concrete fact, to which 'real assent' can be given; and the Church has guaranteed the truth of the notional propositions in question. But since reason is put out of court as a witness to truth, on what faculty, or on what evidence, does Newman rely? Feeling he distrusts; that side of mysticism, at any rate, finds no sympathy from him. Nor does he, like many Kantians and others, make the will supreme over the other faculties. Rather, as we have seen, he bases his reliance on the verdicts of the undivided personality, which he often calls conscience. This line of apologetic was at this very time being ably developed by Julius Hare. It is in itself an argument which has no necessary connexion with obscurantism. 'Personalism,' as it is technically called, reminds us that we do actually base our judgments on grounds which are not purely rational; that the intellect, in forming concepts, has to be content with an approximate resemblance to concrete reality; and that the will and feelings have their rights and claims which cannot be ignored in a philosophy of religion. But while it is compatible with a robust faith in the powers of the constructive intellect, personalism is beyond question a self-sufficient, independent, individualistic doctrine. When it is combined with a nominalist theory of knowledge, it naturally suggests that every man may and should live by the creed which bests suits his idiosyncrasies. Now there was much in Newman's temperament which made him turn in this direction. 'Lead, kindly Light' has been the favourite hymn of many an independent thinker, to whom the authority of the Church is less than nothing. But on another side Newman was all his life a fierce upholder of the principle of authority. His reason for accepting the dogmas of the Church, and for wishing to destroy heresiarchs like wild beasts, was certainly not that his basal personality testified to the truth and value of all ecclesiastical dogmas. He believed them 'by confiding in the testimony of others' —in other words, on the authority of the Catholic Church. If we push back the enquiry one step further, and ask on what grounds he chooses to prefer the authority of the Catholic Church to other authorities, such as natural science or philosophy, we are driven again to lay great stress on the almost political necessity which he felt that such a Divine society should exist. In accepting the authority of the Church, he accepted the authority of all that the Church teaches, in complete independence of human reason. But the Roman Church never professes to be independent of human reason. The official scholastic philosophy claims to be a demonstrative proof of theism.

Newman, then, was only half a Catholic. He accepted with all the fervour of a neophyte the principle of submission to Holy Church. But in place of the official intellectualist apologetic, which an Englishman may study to great advantage in the remarkably able series of manuals issued by the Jesuits of Stonyhurst, he substituted a philosophy of experience which is certainly not Catholic. The authority claimed by the Roman Church rests on one side upon revelation, on the other upon an elaborate structure of demonstrative reasoning, which the simple folk are allowed to ' take as read,' only because they cannot be expected to understand it, but which is declared to be of irresistible cogency to any properly instructed mind. To deny the validity of reasoning upon Divine things is to withdraw one of the supports on which Catholicism rests. Subjectivism, based on vital experience, mixes no better with this system than oil with water. Scholasticism prides itself on clearcut definitions, on irrefragable logic, on using words always in the same sense. For Newman, as for his disciples the Modernists, theological terms are only symbols for varying values, and he holds that the moment they are treated as having any fixed connotation, error begins. It is no wonder if learned Catholics thought that Newman did not play the game. Father Perrone, in spite of his friendship for the object of his criticism, declared that ' Newman miscet et confundit omnia.'

The accusation of scepticism, which was not unnaturally brought against him, was hotly resented by Newman, and with some justice. Of the intensity of his personal conviction there can be no doubt whatever. Indeed, it was just because his faith was in no danger that he cared so little

for any intellectual defence of it. He might have made
his own the lines of Wordsworth :

> ' Here then we rest ; not fearing for our creed
> The worst that human reasoning can achieve
> To unsettle or perplex it.'

Wordsworth too, it may be remembered, speaks of ' reason '
with hardly more respect than Newman himself as :

> ' The inferior faculty that moulds
> With her minute and speculative pains
> Opinion, ever changing.'

Robert Browning also, especially in his later years, uses
anti-intellectualist language equally uncompromising.
'Wholly distrust thy reason,' he says in ' La Saisiaz.'
Coleridge's distinction between 'understanding' and
' reason,' or Westcott's distinction between ' reason ' and
' reasoning,' might have saved these great writers from the
appearance, and perhaps more than the appearance, of
blaspheming against the highest and most divine faculty
of human nature. For the reason is something much
higher than logic-chopping ; it can provide, from its own
resources, a remedy for the intellectual error which is just
now miscalled intellectualism ; it is the activity of the whole
personality under the guidance of its highest part ; and
because it is a real unification of our disordered nature, it
can bring us into real contact with the higher world of Spirit.
Newman's scepticism was not doubtfulness about matters
of faith ; it was only a wholly unjustifiable contempt and
distrust for the unaided activity of the human mind. This
activity, as far as he could see, produced only various forms
of ' liberalism,' which he strangely enough regarded as a
kind of scepticism. Thus he retorted, with equal injustice,
the unjust charge brought against himself.

Newman has often been suspected or accused of quibbling
and intellectual dishonesty. Kingsley, whose healthy but
somewhat rough English morality and common sense were
revolted by Newman's whole attitude to life and conduct,
was unable to conceive how any educated man could believe
in winking Virgins and liquefying blood, and thought that

Newman must be dishonest. More recently Dr. Abbott
has accused him of being a *philomythus*. Judged by ordinary standards, Newman's criteria of belief do seem incompatible with intellectual honesty. Locke, whom Newman
resembles in his theory of knowledge, lays down a canon
which condemns absolutely the Cardinal's doctrine of assent.
' There is one unerring mark,' he says, ' by which a man
may know whether he is a lover of truth in earnest, namely,
the not entertaining any proposition with greater assurance
than the proofs it is built on will warrant.' Newman himself quotes this dictum, and argues against it that men do,
as a matter of fact, form their judgments in a very different
fashion. To most people, however, the fact that opinions
*are* so manufactured is no proof that they *ought* to be so.
To most people it seems plain that the practical necessity
of making unverified assumptions, and the habit of clinging
to them because we have made them, even after their falsity
has been exposed, is a satisfactory explanation of the prevalence of error, but not a reason for acquiescing in it. It
is useful, they hold, to point out how assumption has a
perilous tendency to pass for proof, not that we may con-
tentedly confuse assumption with proof, but that we may
be on our guard against doing so. But such is Newman's
dislike of ' reason ' that he rejoices to find that the majority
of mankind are, in fact, not guided by it. And then, having
made this discovery, he is quite ready to ' reason ' himself,
but not in the manner of an earnest seeker after truth.
Reason, for him, is a serviceable weapon of attack or defence, but he is like a man fighting with magic impenetrable
armour. He enjoys a bout of logical fence ; but it will
decide nothing for him : his ' certitude ' is independent
of it. It is easy to see that such an attitude must appear
profoundly dishonest to any man who accepts Locke's
maxim about truth-seeking. It is equally easy to see that
Newman would spurn the charge of dishonesty as hotly
as the charge of scepticism. His principles made it easy
for him to adopt the characteristic Catholic habit of ' believing ' anything that is pleasing to the religious imagination. His sermons are full of such phrases as ' Scripture
*seems* to show us ' ; ' why should we not believe . . .' ;

'who knows whether . . .,' and the like, all introducing some fantastic superstition. He deliberately accepts the insidious and deadly doctrine that 'no man is convinced of a thing who can endure the thought of its contradictory being true.' To which we may rejoin that, on the contrary, no man has a right to be convinced of anything until he has fairly faced the hypothesis of its contradictory being true. So long as Newman's method prevailed in Europe, every branch of practical knowledge was condemned to barrenness.

For what kind of knowledge is it which is acquired, not by the exercise of the discursive intellect, or by the evidence of our senses, but by the affirmations of our basal personality ? Surely the legitimate province of 'personalism' lies in the region of general ideas, or rather in the *Weltanschauung* as a whole. Our undivided personality protests against any philosophy which makes life irrational, or base, or incurably evil. It claims that those pictures of reality which are provided by the intellect, by the æsthetic sense, and by the moral sense, shall all have justice done to them in any attempted synthesis. It rejects materialism, metaphysical dualism, solipsism, and pessimism, on one or other of these grounds. Such a final interpretation of existence as any of these offers, leaves out some fundamental and essential factor of experience, and is therefore untenable. If no metaphysical scheme can be constructed which is at once comprehensive and inwardly consistent, personalism insists that we must acknowledge defeat for the time, rather than take refuge in a logical system which may be free from inner contradictions but which does not satisfy the whole man as a living and active spiritual being. This is a sound argument. But it is absurd to suppose that our personality, acting as an undivided whole, can decide whether the institutional Church, or one branch of it, is the Body of Christ and the receptacle of infallible revelation ; whether Christ was born at Bethlehem or Nazareth ; or whether Nestorius was a heretic. We have no magical sword for cutting these knots, and no miraculous guide to tell us that authority A is to be believed implicitly, while the possibility of authority B being right is not to be entertained even in thought.

Newman as usual supplies us with the best weapons against himself. It startles us to find, even in 1852, such a sentence as this : ' Revealed religion furnishes facts to other sciences, which those sciences, left to themselves, would never reach. Thus, in the science of history, the preservation of our race in Noah's ark is an historical fact, which history never would arrive at without revelation.' The transition from belief on the purely internal ground of personal assent to belief on the purely external ground of Church authority is certainly abrupt and hard to explain ; but Newman makes it habitually, without any consciousness of a *salto mortale.* In the ' Apologia ' he even says that the argument from personality is ' one form of the argument from authority.' The argument seems to be—' There is no third alternative besides Catholicism or Rationalism. But " personality " will not accept the dictation of reason ; therefore it must accept the authority of the Church.' It is a strange argument. All through his life he enormously exaggerated the moral and intellectual weight which should be attached to Church tradition. ' Securus judicat orbis terrarum ' were the words which rang in his ears at the supreme moment of his great decision. His ' orbis terrarum' was the Latin empire. And when even in those countries the authority of the Pope is rejected, he condemns modern civilisation as an aberration. This however is a complete abandonment of his own test. He first says ' The judgment of the great world is final ' ; and then ' If the world decides against Rome, so much the worse for the world.' After all, Newman had no right to complain if his opponents found his reasoning disingenuous. To make up our minds first, and to argue in favour of the decision afterwards, is in truth to make the reason a hewer of wood and drawer of water to the irrational part of our nature.

It is precisely his sympathy with Catholicism on the religious side, and his alienation from its intellectual method, which makes Newman's apologetic such a two-edged weapon. In attempting to defend Catholicism, he has gone far to explain it. To the historian, there is no great mystery about the growth and success of the Western Catholic Church. Christianity was already a syncretistic religion in the second century. Like the other forms of worship, with which it competed for the popular favour, it contained the necessary elements of mystery-cult, of ethical rule, of social brotherhood, and of personal devotion. But besides many genuine points of superiority, it had a decisive advantage over the religions of Isis and Mithra in the exclusiveness and intolerance which it derived from the Jewish tradition. When the failure of the last persecution forced the Empire to make a concordat with the Church, the transformation of the federated but autonomous Christian communities into a centralised theocratic despotism, claiming secular as well as spiritual sovereignty, was only a matter of time. It was inevitable, just as the principate of Augustus and the sultanate of Diocletian were inevitable ; but there is nothing specially divine or glorious about any of these phases of human evolution. The revolt of Northern Europe in the sixteenth century was equally inevitable ; and so is the alienation of enlightened minds from the Roman Church at the present day. Newman shows with great force and ingenuity that all the developments in the Roman system which Protestantism rejects as later accretions were natural and necessary. But this only means that the Catholic Church, in order to live, was compelled to adapt itself to the prevailing conditions of human culture in the countries where it desired to be supreme. The argument, so far as it goes, tells against rather than in favour of any special supernatural character belonging to that institution. And if the ' orbis terrarum,' which once gave its verdict in favour of Latin Catholicism, is now disposed to reverse its decision, how, on Newman's principle, can its right to do so be denied? The true reasons for the strength and vitality which the Roman Church still retains are not difficult to find. Its system possesses an inner consistency, which is dearly purchased by neglecting much that should enter into a large and true view of the world, but which guarantees to those who have once accepted it an untroubled calm and assurance very acceptable to those who have been tossed upon a sea of doubt. It surrounds itself with an impenetrable armour by persuading its adherents that all moral and intellectual scruples, in matters where Holy Church has pronounced its verdict, are suggestions of the Evil One, to be spurned like the prickings of sensuality. It has succeeded, by long experience, in providing satisfaction for nearly all the needs of the average man, and for all the needs of the average woman. In particular, the æsthetic tastes which, in Southern Europe at any rate, are closely connected with religious feeling, are fully catered for ; and those superstitions which the majority of mankind still love in their hearts, though they are somewhat ashamed of them, are allowed to luxuriate unchecked. Further, Catholicism encourages and blesses that *esprit de corps* which has produced the brightest triumphs of self-abnegation as well as the darkest crimes of cruel bigotry in human history. A Church which unites these advantages is in no danger of falling into insignificance, even if the best intellect and morality of the age are estranged from it. It may even have a great future as the nucleus of a conservative resistance to the social revolution. It is doubtful whether those who wish to preserve the traditions and civilisation of the past will be able to find anywhere, except in the Latin Church, an organisation sufficiently coherent and universal to provide a rallying ground for defence against the new barbarian invasion—proceeding this time not from the rude nations of the North, but from the crowded alleys of our great towns—which threatens to plunge us into a new Dark Age. The menace of the Red Peril will secure, for a long time to come, the survival of the Black.

But the Roman Catholicism which has a future is probably that of Manning, and not that of Newman. A Church which depends for its strength and prestige on the iron discipline of a centralised autocracy, and on the fanatical devotion of soldiers who know no duty except obedience, no cause except the interests of their society, can make no terms with the disintegrating nominalism, the uncertain subjectivism, of a mind like Newman's. It has been the strange fate of this great man, after driving a wedge deep into the Anglican Church, which at this day is threatened with disruption through the movement which he helped to originate, to have nearly succeeded in doing the same to the far more compact structure of Roman Catholicism.

The Modernist movement has from the first appealed to Newman as its founder, and has sought to protect itself under his authority. It is necessary to consider, as the last topic of this article, whether this affiliation can be allowed to be true. No one who has read any of Newman's works can doubt that he would have recoiled with horror from the destructive criticism of Loisy, the contempt for scholastic authority of Tyrrell, and the defiance hurled at the Papacy in the manifesto of the Italian Modernists. Newman's doctrine of Development was far removed from that of Bergson's ' L'Évolution Créatrice.' He defended the fact of development against the staticism of contemporary Anglicanism ; but his notion of development was more like the unrolling of a scroll than the growth of a tree or the expansion and change of a human character. ' Every Catholic holds,' he says, ' that the Christian dogmas were in the Church from the time of the Apostles ; that they were ever in their substance what they are now.' Compare this with the following words from the Italian manifesto : ' The supernatural life of Christ in the faithful and in the Church has been clothed in an historical form, which has given birth to what we might somewhat loosely call the Christ of legend. . . . Such a criticism does away with the possibility of finding in Christ's ministry even the embryonic form of the Church's later theological teaching.' ' A dogma,' says Le Roy, one of the ablest philosophers of the school, ' proclaims, above all, a prescription of practical order ; it is the formula of a rule of practical conduct. Why then should we not bring theory into harmony with practice ? '

These extracts mark a much later phase of the revolt against Catholic dogma and scholastic theology than can be found in Newman's writings. They are contemporary with the Pragmatism of James and Schiller, and the Activism of Bergson. So bold a defiance of tradition would have been impossible thirty years earlier. And yet, when Newman pours scorn upon human reason, and when he enthrones the ' conscience ' as the supreme arbiter of truth, is he not, in fact, preparing the way for these startling declarations, which imply a complete rupture with Catholic

authority ? Dogmas are indisputably ' notional' propositions ; that is to say, they belong to that class of truths
to which Newman ascribes only a very subordinate importance. We cannot, in his sense, ' assent ' to an historical
proposition as such, but only to the authority which has
ordered us to believe it. And is there any justification for
Newman's confidence that this authority may make apparent innovations, such as he admits to have been made
throughout the history of the Church, but no real changes ?
If he had been able to think out the implications of his
doctrine of development with the help of such arguments
as those of Bergson, would he not have seen that without
change and real innovation there can be no true evolution ?
Do not the fluidity and pragmatic character of dogma, so
much insisted on by Sabatier and Le Roy, follow from the
anti-intellectualist personalism which we have seen to be
the foundation of Newman's philosophy of religion ? The
Modernist might argue that he is only extending to the
history of the Church the doctrine of education by experience
which Newman found to be true in the life-history of the
individual. Life itself, with its experiences and its needs,
is the revealer of truth. We cannot anticipate the wisdom
of the future.

> ' I do not ask to see
> The distant scene ; one step enough for me.'

The kindly light leads a man on step by step ; it conducts
him from experience to experience, not without lapses
into error ; it reproves him if he desires to ' choose and see
his path.' If this is true in the history of the individual,
is it not probably also true in the history of the Church ?
And if it is true in the history of the Church, are not the
dogmatists wrong who have tried to legislate not only for
the present but the future, and to bind the Church for all
time to the formulations which appeared satisfactory to
themselves ? If Providence is leading the Church through
varied experiences in order to teach it greater wisdom, is
it not clear that we must not rashly preclude the possibility
of future revelation by stereotyping the results of some
earlier stage of experience ? Thus the empiricism of

Newman leads logically to consequences which he would have been among the first to reject.

Some rather shallow thinkers in this country have expressed their surprise and regret that the Vatican has refused to make any terms with Modernism. They have supposed that the fault lies with an ignorant and reactionary Pope. But there are many reasons why this dangerous and disintegrating tendency must be rigorously excluded from Roman Catholicism. In the first place, Modernism destroys the historical basis of Christianity, and converts the Incarnation and Atonement into myths like those of other dying and rising saviour-gods, which hardly pretend to be historical. But it was this foundation in history which helped largely to secure the triumph of Christianity over its rivals. In the place of the historical God-Man, Modernism gives us the history of the Church as an object of reverence. We are bidden to contemplate an institution of amazingly tough vitality but great adaptability, which in its determination to survive has not only changed colour like a chameleon but has from time to time put forth new organs and discovered new weapons of offence and defence. We ask for evidence that the Church has regenerated the world ; and we are shown how, by hook or by crook, it has succeeded in safeguarding its own interests. Ecclesiastical historians are ingenious and unscrupulous ; but it is impossible even for them to exhibit Church history as the record of a continuous intervention of the Spirit of Christ in human affairs. If any Spirit has presided over the councils of popes, cardinals, and inquisitors it is not that of the Founder of Christianity.

Further, the religious philosophy of Modernism is bad, much worse than the scholasticism which it derides. It is in essentials a revival of the sophistry of Protagoras. And if it were metaphysically more respectable than it is, it is so widely opposed to the whole system of Catholic apologetics, that if it were accepted, it would necessitate a complete reconstruction of Catholic dogma. Let any man read the Stonyhurst manuals, and say whether the radical empiricism of the Modernists could find a lodgment anywhere in such a system without disturbing the stability of the whole. Catholicism is one of the most compact structures in the world, and it rests on presuppositions which are far removed from those of Modernism. It is one thing to admit that dogmas in many cases have a pragmatic origin, and quite another to say that they may be invented or rejected with a pragmatic purpose. The healthy human intellect will never believe that the same proposition may be true for faith and untrue in fact ; but this is the Modernist contention.

Lastly, the subjectivism of Newman and the Modernists is fatal to that exclusiveness which is the corner-stone of Catholic policy. The analogy between the individual and the Church suggests that God may ' fulfil Himself in many ways, lest one good custom should corrupt the world.' As there are many individuals, each of whom is being guided separately by the ' kindly light,' so there may be many churches. The pragmatic proof of the truth of a religion, from the fact of its survival and successful working, does not justify the Roman claim to monopoly. The Protestant churches also display vitality, and their members seem to exhibit the fruits of the Spirit. The condemnations of Modernism published by the Vatican show that the Papal court is quite alive to this danger. To the outsider, indeed, it might seem a happy solution of a long controversy if the Roman Church would be content to claim the gifts of grace which are really hers, without denying the validity of the Orders and Sacraments of other bodies, and the genuineness of the Christian graces which they exhibit. It would then be admitted on all hands that some temperaments are more suited to Catholicism, others to Protestantism, and that the character of each man develops most satisfactorily under the discipline which suits his nature. But we must not expect any such concession from Rome ; and in truth such an admission would be the beginning of the end for Catholicism in its present form.

Our conclusion then is that although Newman was not a Modernist, but an exceedingly stiff conservative, he did introduce into the Roman Church a very dangerous and essentially alien habit of thought, which has since developed into Modernism. Perhaps Monsignor Talbot was not far wrong, from his own point of view, when he called him ' the most dangerous man in England.'  One side of his religion was based on principles which, when logically drawn out, must lead away from Catholicism in the direction of an individualistic religion of experience, and a substitution of history for dogma which makes all truth relative and all values fluid.   Newman's writings have always made genuine Catholics uneasy, though they hardly know why.  It is probable that here is the solution.

The character of Newman—for with this we must end— may seem to have been more admirable than lovable.  He was more apt to make disciples than friends.  Yet he was loved and honoured by men whose love is an honour, and he is admired by all who can appreciate a consistently unworldly life.  The Roman Church has been less unpopular in England since Newman received from it the highest honour which it can bestow.  Throughout his career he was a steadfast witness against tepid and insincere professions of religion, and against any compromise with the shifting currents of popular opinion.  All cultivated readers, who have formed their tastes on the masterpieces of good literature, are attracted, sometimes against their will, by the dignity and reserve of his style, qualities which belong to the man, and not only to the writer.  Like Goethe, he disdains the facile arts which make the commonplace reader laugh and weep.  ' Ach die zärtlichen Herzen ! ein Pfuscher vermag sie zu rühren ! '  Like Wordsworth, he might say ' To stir the blood I have no cunning art.'  There are no cheap effects in any of Newman's writings.  He is the most undemocratic of teachers.  Such men do what can be done to save a nation from itself, its natural enemy. They are not indifferent to fame, because they desire influence ; but they will do nothing to advertise themselves. The public must come to them ; they will not go to the public.  There have been other great men who have been as indifferent as Newman to the applause of the vulgar. But they have been generally either pure intellectualists or pure artists, in whom

> ' The intellectual power through words and things
> Went sounding on a dim and perilous way.'

Newman's ' confidence towards God ' was of a still nobler
kind. It rested on an unclouded faith in the Divine guidance, and on a very just estimate of the worthlessness of
contemporary praise and blame. There have been very
few men who have been able to combine so strong a faith
with a thorough distrust of both logic-chopping and
emotional excitement, and who, while denying themselves
these aids to conviction, have been able to say, calmly and
without petulance, that with them it is a very small thing
to be judged of man's judgment.

'What (he asks) can increase their peace who believe and
trust in the Son of God ? Shall we add a drop to the ocean, or
grains to the sand of the sea ? We pay indeed our superiors
full reverence, and with cheerfulness as unto the Lord ; and we
honour eminent talents as deserving admiration and reward ;
and the more readily act we thus, because these are little things
to pay.' [1]

Such unworldliness as this, in the well-chosen words of R. H.
Hutton, ' stands out in strange and almost majestic contrast to the eager turmoil of confused passions, hesitating
ideals, tentative virtues, and groping philanthropies,
amidst which it was lived.'

Another mark of greatness is unbroken consistency and
unity of aim in a long life. There are few parallels to the
neglect of his own literary reputation by Newman. Higher
interests, he thought, were at stake ; and so he had no
dream of building for himself ' a monument more durable
than brass,' and of claiming a pedestal among the great
writers of English prose and verse. He accepted long years
of literary barrenness ; he wrote historical essays for which
he had no special aptitude, and dogmatic disquisitions
which even his genius could not save from dulness ; he even
descended into mere journalism. The ' Apologia ' would
probably not have been written but for the accident of
Kingsley's attack. It has, no doubt, been said with truth
that Newman showed great dexterity in choosing opponents
with whom to cross swords—Kingsley, Pusey, Gladstone,

[1] *Parochial and Plain Sermons*, vii. 73.

and his old Anglican self. But this does not alter the fact that a man who must have been conscious of rare literary gifts made no attempt to immortalise himself by them. It was for the Church, and not for himself, that he wrote as well as lived.

That his life is for the most part a record of sadness and failure is no indication that he was not one of the great men of his time. Independence is no passport to success in a world where, as Swift said, climbing and crawling are performed in much the same attitude. And if we are right in our view that there was something in the composition of his mind which prevented him from being either a complete Catholic or a complete Protestant, this too is no obstacle to our recognition of his greatness. He has left an indelible mark upon two great religious bodies. He has stirred movements which still agitate the Church of England and the Church of Rome, and the end of which is not yet in sight. Anglo-Catholicism and Modernism are alien growths, perhaps, in the institutions where they have found a place ; but the man who beyond all others is responsible for grafting them upon the old stems is secure of his place in history.

# ST. PAUL

## (1914)

AMONG all the great men of antiquity there is none, with the exception of Cicero, whom we may know so intimately as Saul of Tarsus. The main facts of his career have been recorded by a contemporary, who was probably his friend and travelling companion. A collection of letters, addressed to the little religious communities which he founded, reveals the character of the writer no less than the nature of his work. Alone among the first preachers of Christianity, he stands before us as a living man. Οἷος πέπνυται, τοὶ δὲ σκιαὶ ἀΐσσουσι. We know very little in reality of Peter and James and John, of Apollos and Barnabas. And of our divine Master no biography can ever be written.

With St. Paul it is quite different. He is a saint without a luminous halo. His personal characteristics are too distinct and too human to make idealisation easy. For this reason he has never been the object of popular devotion. Shadowy figures like St. Joseph and St. Anne have been divinised and surrounded with picturesque legends ; but St. Paul has been spared the honour or the ignominy of being coaxed and wheeedled by the piety of paganised Christianity. No tender fairy-tales are attached to his cult ; he remains for us what he was in the flesh. It is even possible to feel an active dislike for him. Lagarde (' Deutsche Schriften,' p. 71) abuses him as a politician might vilify an opponent. ' It is monstrous ' (says he) ' that men of any historical training should attach any importance to this Paul. This outsider was

a Pharisee from top to toe even after he became a
Christian '—and much more to the same effect. Nietzsche
describes him as ' one of the most ambitious of men,
whose superstition was only equalled by his cunning. A
much tortured, much to be pitied man, an exceedingly
unpleasant person both to himself and to others. . . . He
had a great deal on his conscience. He alludes to enmity,
murder, sorcery, idolatry, impurity, drunkenness, and the
love of carousing.' Renan, who could never have made
himself ridiculous by such ebullitions as these, does not
disguise his repugnance for the ' ugly little Jew ' whose
character he can neither understand nor admire. These
outbursts of personal animosity, so strange in modern
critics dealing with a personage of ancient history, show
how vividly his figure stands out from the canvas. There
are very few historical characters who are alive enough
to be hated.

It is, however, only in our own day that the personal
characteristics of St. Paul have been intelligently studied ;
and the most valuable books about him are later than
the unbalanced tirades of Lagarde and Nietzsche, and the
carping estimate of Renan. In the nineteenth century, Paul
was obscured behind Paulinism. His letters were studied
as treatises on systematic theology. Elaborate theories
of atonement, justification, and grace were expounded on
his authority, as if he had been a religious philosopher
or theological professor like Origen and Thomas Aquinas.
The name of the apostle came to be associated with
angular and frigid disquisitions which were rapidly losing
their connexion with vital religion. It has been left for
the scholars of the present century to give us a picture of
St. Paul as he really was—a man much nearer to George
Fox or John Wesley than to Origen or Calvin ; the
greatest of missionaries and pioneers, and only incident-
ally a great theologian. The critical study of the New
Testament has opened our eyes to see this and many
other things. Much new light has also been thrown by
studies in the historical geography of Asia Minor, a work
in which British scholars have characteristically taken
a prominent part. The delightful books of Sir W. M.

Ramsay have now been supplemented by the equally attractive volume of another travelling scholar, Professor Deissmann. A third source of new information is the mass of inscriptions and papyri which have been discovered in the last twenty years. The social life of the middle and lower classes in the Levant, their religious beliefs and practices, and the language which they spoke, are now partially known to us, as they never were before. The human interest of the Pauline Epistles, and of the Acts, is largely increased by these accessions to knowledge.

The Epistles are real letters, not treatises by a theological professor, nor literary productions like the Epistles of Seneca. Each was written with reference to a definite situation; they are messages which would have been delivered orally had the Apostle been present. Several letters have certainly been lost; and St. Paul would probably not have cared much to preserve them. There is no evidence that he ever thought of adding to the Canon of Scripture by his correspondence. The author of Acts seems not to have read any of the letters. This view of the Epistles has rehabilitated some of them, which were regarded as spurious by the Tübingen school and their successors. The question which we now ask when the authenticity of an Epistle is doubted is, Do we find the same man? not, Do we find the same system? There is, properly speaking, no system in St. Paul's theology, and there is a singularly rapid development of thought. The 'Pastoral Epistles' are probably not genuine, though the defence of them is not quite a desperate undertaking. Of the rest, the weight of evidence is slightly against the Pauline authorship of Ephesians, the vocabulary of which differs considerably from that of the undoubted Epistles; and the short letter called 2 Thessalonians is open to some suspicion. The genuineness of Ephesians is not of great importance to the student of Pauline theology, unless the closely allied Epistle to the Colossians is also rejected; and there has been a remarkable return of confidence in the Pauline authorship of this letter. All the other Epistles seem to be firmly established.

The other source of information about St. Paul's life is the Acts of the Apostles, the value of which as a historical document is very variously estimated. The doubts refer mainly to the earlier chapters, before St. Paul appears on the scene. Sane criticism can hardly dispute that the 'we-passages,' in which the writer speaks of St. Paul and himself in the first person plural, are the work of an eye-witness, and that most of the important facts in the later chapters are from the same source. The difficult problem is concerned with the relation of this writer to the editor, who is responsible for the 'Petrine' part of the book. There is very much to be said in favour of the tradition that this editor, who also compiled the Third Gospel, was Lucas or Lucanus, the physician and friend of St. Paul. It does not necessarily follow that he was the fellow-traveller who in a few places speaks of himself in the first person. Luke (if we may decide the question for ourselves by giving him this name) must have been a man of very attractive character; full of kindness, loyalty, and Christian charity. He is the most feminine (not effeminate) writer in the New Testament, and shows a marked partiality for the tender aspects of Christianity. He is attracted by miracles, and by all that makes history picturesque and romantic. His social sympathies are so keen that his gospel furnishes the Christian socialist with nearly all his favourite texts. Above all, he is a Greek man of letters, dominated by the conventions of Greek historical composition. For the Greek, history was a work of art, written for edification, and not merely a bald record of facts. The Greek historian invented speeches for his principal characters; this was a conventional way of elucidating the situation for the benefit of his readers. Everyone knows how Thucydides, the most conscientious historian in antiquity, habitually uses this device, and how candidly he explains his method. We can hardly doubt that the author of Acts has used a similar freedom, though the report of the address to the elders of Ephesus reads like a summary of an actual speech. The narrative is coloured in places by the historian's love for the miraculous. Critics have also suspected an eirenical purpose in his treatment of the relations between St. Paul and the Jerusalem Church.

Saul of Tarsus was a Benjamite of pure Israelite descent, but also a Roman citizen by birth. His famous old Jewish name was Latinised or Graecised as Paulos (Σαῦλος means 'waddling,' and would have been a ridiculous name); he doubtless bore both names from boyhood. Tarsus is situated in the plain of Cilicia, and is now about ten miles from the sea. It is backed by a range of hills, on which the wealthier residents had villas, while the high glens of Taurus, nine or ten miles further inland, provided a summer residence for those who could afford it, and a fortified acropolis in time of war. The town on the plain must have been almost intolerable in the fierce Anatolian summer-heat. The harbour was a lake formed by the Cydnus, five or six miles below Tarsus; but light ships could sail up the river into the heart of the city. Thus Tarsus had the advantages of a maritime town, though far enough from the sea to be safe from pirates. The famous pass called the 'Cilician Gates' was traversed by a high-road through the gorge into Cappadocia. Ionian colonists came to Tarsus in very early times; and Ramsay is confident that Tarshish, 'the son of Javan,' in Gen. x. 4, is none other than Tarsus. The Greek settlers, of course, mixed with the natives, and the Oriental element gradually swamped the Hellenic. The coins of Tarsus show Greek figures and Aramaic lettering. The principal deity was Baal-Tarz, whose effigy appears on most of the coins. Under the successors of Alexander, Greek influence revived, but the administration continued to be of the Oriental type; and Tarsus never became a Greek city, until in the first half of the second century B.C. it proclaimed its own autonomy, and renamed itself Antioch-on-Cydnus. Great privileges were granted it by Antiochus Epiphanes, and it rapidly grew in wealth and importance. Besides the Greeks, there was a large colony of Jews, who always established themselves on the highways of the world's commerce. Since St. Paul was a ' citizen ' of Tarsus, i.e. a

member of one of the ' Tribes ' into which the citizens were
divided, it is probable (so Ramsay argues) that there was
a large ' Tribe ' of Jews at Tarsus ; for no Jew would have
been admitted into, or would have consented to join, a
Greek Tribe, with its pagan cult.

So matters stood when Cilicia became a Roman
Province in 104 B.C. The city fell into the hands of
the barbarian Tigranes twenty years later, but Gnaeus
Pompeius re-established the Roman power, and with it
the dominance of Hellenism, in 63. Augustus turned
Cilicia into a mere adjunct of Syria ; and the pride of
Tarsus received a check. Nevertheless, the Emperor
showed great favour to the Tarsians, who had sided with
Julius and himself in the civil wars. Tarsus was made a
' libera civitas,' with the right to live under its own laws.
The leading citizens were doubtless given the Roman
citizenship, or allowed to purchase it. Among these would
naturally be a number of Jews, for that nation loved
Julius Cæsar and detested Pompeius. But Hellenism
could not retain its hold on Tarsus. Dion Chrysostom,
who visited it at the beginning of the second century A.D.,
found it a thoroughly Oriental town, and notes that the
women were closely veiled in Eastern fashion. Possibly
this accounts for St. Paul's prejudice against unveiled
women in church. One Greek institution, however, survived and flourished—a university under municipal patronage. Strabo speaks with high admiration of the zeal for
learning displayed by the Tarsians, who formed the entire
audience at the professors' lectures, since no students
came from outside. This last fact shows, perhaps, that
the lecturers were not men of wide reputation ; indeed, it
is not likely that Tarsus was able to compete with Athens
and Alexandria in attracting famous teachers. The most
eminent Tarsians, such as Antipater the Stoic, went to
Europe and taught there. What distinguished Tarsus
was its love of learning, widely diffused in all classes of
the population.

St. Paul did not belong to the upper class. He was a
working artisan, a ' tent-maker,' who followed one of the
regular trades of the place. Perhaps, as Deissmann thinks,

the 'large letters' of Gal. vi. 11 imply that he wrote clumsily, like a working man and not like a scribe. The words indicate that he usually dictated his letters. The 'Acts of Paul and Thekla' describe him as short and bald, with a hook-nose and beetling brows; there is nothing improbable in this description. But he was far better educated than the modern artisan. Not that a single quotation from Menander (1 Cor. xv. 33) shows him to be a good Greek scholar; an Englishman may quote 'One touch of nature makes the whole world kin' without being a Shakespearean. But he was well educated because he was the son of a strict Jew. A child in such a home would learn by heart large pieces of the Old Testament, and, at the Synagogue school, all the *minutiæ* of the Jewish Law. The pupil was not allowed to write anything down; all was committed to the memory, which in consequence became extremely retentive. The perfect pupil 'lost not a drop from his teacher's cistern.' At the age of about fourteen the boy would be sent to Jerusalem, to study under one of the great Rabbis; in St. Paul's case it was Gamaliel. Under his tuition the young Pharisee would learn to be a 'strong Churchman.' The Rabbis viewed everything from an ecclesiastical standpoint. The interests of the Priesthood, the Altar, and the Temple overshadowed everything else. The Priestly Code, says Mr. Cohu, practically resolves itself into one idea: Everything in Israel belongs to God; all places, all times, all persons, and all property are His. But God accepts a part of His due; and, if this part is scrupulously paid, He will send His blessing upon the remainder. Besides the written law, the Pharisee had to take on himself the still heavier burden of the oral law, which was equally binding. It was a seminary education of the most rigorous kind. St Paul cannot reproach himself with any slackness during his novitiate. He threw himself into the system with characteristic ardour. Probably he meant to be a Jerusalem Rabbi himself, still practising his trade, as the Rabbis usually did. For he was unmarried; and every Jew except a Rabbi was expected to marry at or before the age of twenty-one.

He suffered from some obscure physical trouble, the nature of which we can only guess. It was probably epilepsy, a disease which is compatible with great powers of endurance and great mental energy, as is proved by the cases of Julius Cæsar and Napoleon. He was liable to mystical trances, in which some have found a confirmation of the supposition that he was epileptic. But these abnormal states were rare with him; in writing to the Galatians he has to go back fourteen years to the date when he was 'caught up into the third heaven.' The visions and voices which attended his active ministry prove nothing about his health. At that time anyone who underwent a psychical experience for which he could not account believed that he was possessed by a spirit, good or bad. It is significant that Tertullian, at the end of the second century, says that 'almost the majority of mankind derive their knowledge of God from visions.' The impression that St. Paul makes upon us is that of a man full of nervous energy and able to endure an exceptional amount of privation and hardship. A curious indication, which has not been noticed, is that, as he tells us himself, he five times received the maximum number of lashes from Jewish tribunals. These floggings in the Synagogues were very severe, the operator being required to lay on with his full strength. There is evidence that in most cases a much smaller number of strokes than the full thirty-nine was inflicted, so as not to endanger the life of the culprit. The other trials which he mentions— three Roman scourgings, one stoning, a day and night spent in battling with the waves after shipwreck, would have worn out any constitution not exceptionally tough.

We must bear in mind this terrible record of suffering if we wish to estimate fairly the character of the man. During his whole life after his conversion he was exposed not only to the hardships of travel, sometimes in half-civilised districts, but to 'all the cruelty of the fanaticism which rages like a consuming fire through the religious history of the East from the slaughter of Baal's priests to the slaughter of St. Stephen, and from the butcheries of

Jews at Alexandria under Caligula to the massacres of Christians at Adana, Tarsus, and Antioch in the year 1909 '—(Deissmann). It is one evil result of such furious bigotry that it kindles hatred and resentment in its victims, and tempts them to reprisals. St. Paul does speak bitterly of his opponents, though chiefly when he finds that they have injured his converts, as in the letter to the Galatians. Modern critics have exaggerated this element in a character which does not seem to have been fierce or implacable. He writes like a man engaged in a stern conflict against enemies who will give no quarter, and who shrink from no treachery. But the sharpest expression that can be laid to his charge is the impatient, perhaps half humorous wish that the Judaisers who want to circumcise the Galatians might be subjected to a severer operation themselves (Gal. v. 12). The dominant impression that he makes upon us is that he was cast in a heroic mould. He is serenely indifferent to criticism and calumny ; no power on earth can turn him from his purpose. He has made once for all a complete sacrifice of all earthly joys and all earthly ties ; he has broken (he, the devout Jewish Catholic) with his Church and braved her thunders ; he has faced the opprobrium of being called traitor, heretic, and apostate ; he has 'withstood to the face' the Palestinian apostles who were chosen by Jesus and held His commission ; he has set his face to achieve, almost single-handed, the conquest of the Roman Empire, a thing never dreamed of by the Jerusalem Church ; he is absolutely indifferent whether his mission will cost him his life, or only involve a continuation of almost intolerable hardship. It is this indomitable courage, complete self-sacrifice, and single-minded devotion to a magnificently audacious but not impracticable idea, which constitute the greatness of St. Paul's character. He was, with all this, a warm-hearted and affectionate man, as he proves abundantly by the tone of his letters. His personal religion was, in essence, a pure mysticism ; he worships a Christ whom he has experienced as a living presence in his soul. The mystic who is also a man of action, and a man of action because he is a mystic, wields a tremendous power over other men. He is like an invulnerable knight, fighting in magic armour.

It is an interesting and difficult question whether we should regard the intense moral dualism of the Epistle to the Romans as a confession that the writer has had an unusually severe personal battle with temptation. The moral struggle certainly assumes a more tragic aspect in these passages than in the experience of many saintly characters. We find something like it in Augustine, and again in Luther ; it may even be suggested that these great men have stamped upon the Christian tradition the idea of a harsher ' clash of yes and no ' than the normal experience of the moral life can justify. But it is not certain that the first person singular in such verses as ' O wretched man that I am ! who shall deliver me from this body of death ? ' is a personal confession at all. It may be for human nature generally that he is speaking, when he gives utterance to that consciousness of sin which was one of the most distinctive parts of the Christian religion from the first. It does not seem likely that a man of so lofty and heroic a character was ever seriously troubled with ignominious temptations. That he yielded to them, as Nietzsche and others have suggested, is in the highest degree improbable. Even if the self-reproaches were uttered in his own person, we have many other instances of saints who have blamed themselves passionately for what ordinary men would consider slight transgressions. Of all the Epistles, the Second to the Corinthians is the one which contains the most intimate self-revelations, and few can read it without loving as well as honouring its author.

We know nothing of the Apostle's residence at Jerusalem except the name of his teacher. But it was at this time that he became steeped in the Pharisaic doctrines which formed the framework in which his earlier Christian beliefs were set. It is now recognised that Pharisaism, far from being the antipodes of Christianity, was rather the quarter where the Gospel found its best recruits. The Pharisaic school contained the greater part of whatever faith, loyalty and piety re-

mained among the Jewish people; and its dogmatic
system passed almost entire into the earliest Christian
Church, with the momentous addition that Jesus was
the Messiah. A few words on the Pharisaic teaching
which St. Paul must have imbibed from Gamaliel are
indispensable even in an article which deals with Paul,
and not with Paulinism.

The distinctive feature of the Jewish religion is not,
as is often supposed, its monotheism. Hebrew religion
in its golden age was monolatry rather than monotheism; and when Jahveh became more strictly ' the only
God,' the cult of intermediate beings came in, and restored a quasi-polytheism. The distinctive feature in
Jewish faith is its historical and teleological character.
The God of the Jew is not natural law. If the idea of
necessary causation ever forced itself upon his mind, he
at once gave it the form of predestination. The whole
of history is an unfolding of the divine purpose; and so
history as a whole has for the Jew an importance which
it never had for a Greek thinker, nor for the Hellenised
Jew Philo. The Hebrew idea of God is dynamic and
ethical; it is therefore rooted in the idea of Time. The
Pharisaic school modified this prophetic teaching in
two ways. It became more spiritual; anthropomorphisms
were removed, and the transcendence of God above the
world was more strictly maintained. On the other hand,
the religious relationship became in their hands narrower
and more external. The notion of a covenant was defined
more rigorously; the Law was practically exalted above
God, so that the Rabbis even represent the Deity as
studying the Law. With this legalism went a spirit of
intense exclusiveness and narrow ecclesiasticism. As God
was raised above direct contact with men, the old animistic
belief in angels and demons, which had lasted on in
the popular mind by the side of the worship of Jahveh,
was extended in a new way. A celestial hierarchy was
invented, with names, and an infernal hierarchy too;
the malevolent ghosts of animism became fallen angels.
Satan, who in Job is the crown-prosecutor, one of God's
retinue, becomes God's adversary; and the angels, formerly

manifestations of God Himself, are now quite separated from Him. A supramundane physics or cosmology was evolved at the same time. Above Zion, the centre of the earth, rise seven heavens, in the highest of which the Deity has His throne. The underworld is now first divided into Paradise and Gehenna. The doctrine of the fall of man, through his participation in the representative guilt of his first parents, is Pharisaic ; as is the strange legend, which St. Paul seems to have believed (2 Cor. xi. 3), that the Serpent carnally seduced Eve, and so infected the race with spiritual poison. Justification, in Pharisaism as for St. Paul, means the verdict of acquittal. The bad receive in this life the reward for any small merits which they may possess ; the sins of the good must be atoned for ; but merits, as in Roman Catholicism, may be stored and transferred. Martyrdoms especially augment the spiritual bank-balance of the whole nation. There was no official Messianic doctrine, only a mass of vague fancies and beliefs, grouped round the central idea of the appearance on earth of a supernatural Being, who should establish a theocracy of some kind at Jerusalem. The righteous dead will be raised to take part in this kingdom. The course of the world is thus divided into two epochs— 'this age' and 'the age to come.' A catastrophe will end the former and inaugurate the latter. The promised deliverer is now waiting in heaven with God, until his hour comes ; and it will come very soon. All this St. Paul must have learned from Gamaliel. It formed the framework of his theology as a Christian for many years after his conversion, and was only partially thrown off, under the influence of mystical experience and of Greek ideas, during the period covered by the letters. The lore of good and bad spirits (the latter are 'the princes of this world' in 1 Cor. ii. 6, 8) pervades the Epistles more than modern readers are willing to admit. It is part of the heritage of the Pharisaic school.

It is very unlikely (in spite of Johannes Weiss) that St. Paul ever saw Jesus in the flesh. But he did come in contact with the little Christian community at Jerusalem. These disciples at first attempted to live as strict mem-

bers of the Jewish Church. They knew that the coming
Messiah was their crucified Master, but this belief
involved no rupture with Judaism. So at least they
thought themselves; the Sanhedrin saw more clearly
what the new movement meant. The crisis came when
numerous ' Hellenists ' attached themselves to the Church
—Jews of the Dispersion, from Syria, Egypt, and elsewhere. A threatened rupture between these and the
Palestinian Christians was averted by the appointment
of seven deacons or charity commissioners, among whom
Stephen soon became prominent by the dangerously
' liberal ' character of his teaching. Philo gives important testimony to the existence of a ' liberal ' school
among the Jews of the Dispersion, who, under pretext
of spiritualising the traditional law, left off keeping the
Sabbath and the great festivals, and even dispensed
with the rite of circumcision. Thus the admission of
Gentiles on very easy terms into the Church was no new
idea to the Palestinian Jews; it was known to them as
part of the shocking laxity which prevailed among their
brethren of the Dispersion. With Stephen, this kind of
liberalism seemed to have entered the group of ' disciples.'
He was accused of saying that Jesus was to destroy the
temple and change the customs of Moses. In his bold
defence he admitted that in his view the Law was valid
only for a limited period, which would expire so soon as
Jesus returned as Messiah. This was quite enough for
the Sanhedrin. They stoned Stephen, and compelled
the ' disciples ' to disperse and fly for their lives. Only
the Apostles, whose devotion to the Law was well known,
were allowed to remain. This last fact, briefly recorded
in Acts, is important as an indication that the persecution
was directed only against the liberalising Christians, and
that these were the great majority. Saul, it seems, had
no quarrel with the Twelve; his hatred and fanaticism
were aroused against a sect of Hellenist Jews who
openly proclaimed that the Law had been abrogated in
advance by their Master, who, as Saul observed with
horror, had incurred the curse of the Law by dying on a
gibbet. All the Pharisee in him was revolted; and he

led the savage heretic-hunt which followed the execution of Stephen.

What caused the sudden change which so astonished the survivors among his victims ? To suppose that nothing prepared for the vision near Damascus, that the apparition in the sky was a mere ' bolt from the blue,' is an impossible theory. The best explanation is furnished by a study of the Apostle's character, which we really know very well. The author of the Epistles was certainly not a man who could watch a young saint being battered to death by howling fanatics, and feel no emotion. Stephen's speech may have made him indignant ; his heroic death, the very ideal of a martyrdom, must have awakened very different feelings. An undercurrent of dissatisfaction, almost of disgust, at the arid and unspiritual seminary teaching of the Pharisees now surged up and came very near the surface. His bigotry sustained him as a persecutor for a few weeks more ; but how if he could himself see what the dying Stephen said that he saw ? Would not that be a welcome liberation ? The vision came in the desert, where men see visions and hear voices to this day. They were very common in the desert of Gobi when Marco Polo traversed it. ' The Spirit of Jesus,' as he came to call it, spoke to his heart, and the form of Jesus flashed before his eyes. Stephen had been right ; the Crucified was indeed the Lord from heaven. So Saul became a Christian ; and it was to the Christianity of Stephen, not to that of James the Lord's brother, that he was converted. The Pharisee in him was killed.

The travelling missionary was as familiar a figure in the Levant as the travelling lecturer on philosophy. The Greek language brought all nationalities together. The Hellenising of the East had gone on steadily since the conquests of Alexander ; and Greek was already as useful as Latin in many parts of the West. A century later, Marcus Aurelius wrote his Confessions in Greek ; and even in the middle of the third century, when the tide was beginning to turn in favour of Latin, Plotinus lectured in Greek at Rome. Christianity, within a few years after the Crucifixion, had allied itself definitely with the speech, and therefore inevitably with the spirit, of Hellenism. At no time since have travel and trade been so free between the West of Europe and the West of Asia. A Phrygian merchant (according to the inscription on his tomb) made seventy-two journeys to Rome in the course of his business-life. The decomposition of nationalities, and the destruction of civic exclusiveness, led naturally to the formation of voluntary associations of all kinds, from religious sects to trade unions; sometimes a single association combined these two functions. The Oriental religions appealed strongly to the unprivileged classes, among which genuine religious faith was growing, while the official cults of the Roman Empire were unsatisfying in themselves and associated with tyranny. The attempt of Augustus to resuscitate the old religion was artificial and unfruitful. The living movement was towards a syncretism of religious ideas and practices, all of which came from the Eastern provinces and beyond them. The prominent features in this new devotion were the removal of the supreme Godhead from the world to a transcendental sphere; contempt for the world and ascetic abnegation of 'the flesh'; a longing for healing and redemption, and a close identification of salvation with individual immortality; and, finally, trust in sacraments ('mysteries,' in Greek) as indispensable means of grace or redemption. This was the Paganism with which Christianity had to reckon, as well as with the official cult and its guardians. The established church it conquered and destroyed; the living syncretistic beliefs it cleansed, simplified, and disciplined, but only absorbed by becoming itself a syncretistic religion. But besides Christians and Pagans, there were the Jews, dispersed over the whole Empire. There were at least a million in Egypt, a country which St. Paul, for reasons unknown to us, left severely alone; there were still more in Syria, and perhaps five millions in the whole Empire. In spite of the fecundity of Jewish women, so much emphasised by Seeck in his history of the Downfall of the Ancient World, it is impossible that the Hebrew stock should have multiplied to this extent. There must have been a very large number of converts, who were admitted, sometimes without circumcision, on their profession of monotheism and acceptance of the Jewish moral code. The majority of these remained in the class technically called 'God-fearers,' who never took upon themselves the whole yoke of the Law. These half-Jews were the most promising field for Christian missionaries; and nothing exasperated the Jews more than to see St. Paul fishing so successfully in their waters. The spirit of propagandism almost disappeared from Judaism after the middle of the second century. Judaism shrank again into a purely Eastern religion, and renounced the dangerous compromise with Western ideas. The labours of St. Paul made an all-important parting of the ways. Their result was that Christianity became a European religion, while Judaism fell back upon its old traditions.

It is very unfortunate that we have no thoroughly trustworthy records of the Apostle's earlier mission preaching. The Epistles only cover a period of about ten years; and the rapid development of thought which can be traced during this short time prevents us from assuming that his earlier teaching closely resembled that which we find in the Letters. But if, during the earlier period, he devoted his attention mainly to those who were already under Jewish influence, we may be sure that he spoke much of the Messiahship of Jesus, and of His approaching return, these being the chief articles of faith in Judaic Christianity. This was, however, only the framework. What attracted converts was really the historical picture of the life of Jesus; his message of love and brotherhood, which they found realised in the little communities of believers; and the abolition of all external barriers between human beings, such as social position, race, and sex, which had undoubtedly been proclaimed by the Founder, and contained implicitly the promise of an universal religion. We can infer what the manner of his preaching was from the style of the letters, which were probably dictated like extempore addresses, without much preparation. He was no trained orator, and he thoroughly disdained the arts of the rhetorician. His Greek, though vigorous and effective, is

neither correct nor elegant. His eloquence is of the kind
which proceeds from intense conviction, and from a thorough
knowledge of Old Testament prophecy and psalmody—
no bad preparation for a religious teacher. If at times
he argued like a Rabbi, these frigid debates were as
acceptable to ancient Jews as they are to modern Scots-
men. And when he takes fire, as he deals with some
vital truth which he has lived as well as learned and
taught, he establishes his right to be called what he never
aimed at being—a writer of genius. Such passages as
1 Cor. xiii., Phil. ii., Rom. viii., rank among the finest
compositions in later Greek literature. Regarded merely
as a piece of poetical prose, 1 Cor. xiii. is finer than
anything that had been written in the Greek language
since the great Attic prose-writers. And if this was
dictated impromptu, similar outbursts of splendid eloquence were probably frequent in his mission-preaching.
Their effect must have been overwhelming, when reinforced by the flashing eye of the speaker, and by the
absolute sincerity which none could doubt who saw his
face and figure, furrowed by toil and scarred by torture.

In addressing the Gentiles, we may assume that
he followed the customary Jewish line of apologetic,
denouncing the folly of idolatry—an aid to worship which
is quite innocent and natural in some peoples, but which
the Jews never understood; that he spoke much of
judgment to come; and especially that he contrasted
the pure and affectionate social life of the Christian
brotherhood with the licentiousness, cruelty, injustice,
oppression, and mutual suspicion of Pagan society. This
argument probably struck home in very many ' Gentile '
hearts. The old civilisation, with all the brilliant qualities
which make many moderns regret its destruction, rested
on too narrow a base. The woman and the slave were
left out, the woman epecially by the Greeks, and the slave
by the Romans. Acute social inequalities always create
pride, brutality, and widespread sexual immorality. And
when the structure which maintained these inequalities
is itself tottering, the oppressed classes begin to feel
that they are unnecessary, and to hope for emancipation.

When St. Paul drew his lurid pictures of Pagan society steeped in unnatural abominations, without hope for the future, ' hateful and hating one another,' and then pointed to the little flock of Christians—among whom no one was allowed to be idle and no one to starve, and where family life was pure and mutual confidence full, frank and seldom abused—the woman and the slave, of whom Aristotle had spoken so contemptuously, flocked into his congregations, and began to organise themselves for that victory which Nietzsche thought so deplorable.

It is not necessary in this essay to traverse again the familiar field of St. Paul's missionary journeys. The first epoch, which embraces about fourteen years, had its scene in Syria and Cilicia, with the short tour in Cyprus and other parts of Asia Minor. The second period, which ends with the imprisonment in A.D. 58 or 59, is far more important. St. Paul crosses into Europe ; he works in Macedonia and Greece. Churches are founded in two of the great towns of the ancient world, Corinth and Ephesus. According to his letters, we must assume that he only once returned to Jerusalem from the great tour in the West, undertaken after the controversy with Peter ; and that the object of this visit was to deliver the money which he had promised to collect for the poor ' saints ' at Jerusalem. He intended after this to go to Rome, and thence to Spain—a scheme worthy of the restless genius of an Alexander. He saw Rome indeed, but as a prisoner. The rest of his life is lost in obscurity. The writer of the Acts does not say that the two years' imprisonment ended in his execution ; and if it was so, it is difficult to see why such a fact should be suppressed. If the charge against him was at last dismissed, because the accusers did not think it worth while to come to Rome to prosecute it, St. Luke's silence is more explicable. In any case, we may regard it as almost certain that St. Paul ended his life under a Roman axe during the reign of Nero.

' There is hardly any fact ' (says Harnack) ' which deserves to be turned over and pondered so much as this, that the religion of Jesus has never been able to root

itself in Jewish or even upon Semitic soil.' This extra-
ordinary result is the judgment of history upon the
life and work of St. Paul. Jewish Christianity rapidly
withered and died. According to Justin, who must have
known the facts, Jesus was rejected by the whole Jewish
nation 'with a few exceptions.' In Galilee especially,
few, if any, Christian Churches existed. There are other
examples, of which Buddhism is the most notable, of a
religion gaining its widest acceptance outside the borders
of the country which gave it birth. But history offers
no parallel to the complete vindication of St. Paul's policy
in carrying Christianity over into the Graeco-Roman
world, where alone, as the event proved, it could live.
This is a complete answer to those who maintain that
Christ made no break with Judaism. Such a statement is
only tenable if it is made in the sense of Harnack's words,
that 'what Gentile Christianity did was to carry out a
process which had in fact commenced long before in
Judaism itself, viz. the process by which the Jewish
religion was inwardly emancipated and turned into a
religion for the world.' But the true account would be
that Judaism, like other great ideas, had to ' die to live.'
It died in its old form, in giving birth to the religion of
civilised humanity, as the Greek nation perished in giving
birth to Hellenism, and the Roman in creating the
Mediterranean empire of the Caesars and the Catholic
Church of the Popes. The Jewish people were unable to
make so great a sacrifice of their national hopes. With
the matchless tenacity which characterises their race
they clung to their tribal God and their temporal and
local millennium. The disasters of A.D. 70 and of the
revolt under Hadrian destroyed a great part of the race,
and at last uprooted it from the soil of Palestine. But
conservatism, as usual, has had its partial justification.
Judaism has refused to acknowledge the religion of the
civilised world as her legitimate child ; but the nation
has refused also to surrender its life. There are no more
Greeks and Romans ; but the Jews we have always
with us.

St. Paul saw that the Gospel was a far greater and

more revolutionary scheme than the Galilean apostles
had dreamed of. In principle he committed himself from
the first to the complete emancipation of Christianity
from Judaism. But it was inevitable that he did not at
first realise all that he had undertaken. And, fortunately
for us, the most rapid evolution in his thought took place
during the ten years to which his extant letters belong.
It is exceedingly interesting to trace his gradual progress
away from Apocalyptic Messianism to a position very
near that of the Fourth Gospel. The evangelist whom
we call St. John is the best commentator on Paulinism.
This is one of the most important discoveries of recent
New Testament criticism.

In the earliest Epistles—those to the Thessalonians—
we have the naïve picture of Messiah coming on the
clouds, which, as we now know, was part of the
Pharisaic tradition. In the central group the Christology
is far more complex. Besides the Pharisaic Messiah, and
the records of the historical Jesus of Nazareth, we have
now to reckon with the Jewish-Alexandrian idea of the
generic, archetypal man, which is unintelligible without
reference to the Platonic philosophy. Philo is here a
great help towards understanding one of the most difficult parts of the Apostle's teaching. We have also, fully
developed, the mystical doctrine of the Spirit of Christ
immanent in the soul of the believer, a conception which
was the core of St. Paul's personal religion, and more than
anything else emancipated him from apocalyptic dreams
of the future. We have also a fourth conception, quite
distinct from the three which have been mentioned—that
of Christ as a cosmic principle, the instrument in creation
and the sustainer of all life in the universe. We must
again have recourse to Philo and his doctrine of the Logos,
to understand the genesis of this idea, and to the
Fourth Gospel to find it stated in clear philosophical form.
In this second period, these theories about the Person
of Christ are held concurrently, without any attempt
to reconcile or systematise them. The eschatology is
being seriously modified by the conception of a ' spiritual
body,' which is prepared for us so soon as our ' outward

man' decays in death. The resurrection of the flesh is explicitly denied (1 Cor. xv. 50); but a new and incorruptible 'clothing' will be given to the soul in the future state. Already the fundamental Pharisaic doctrine of the two ages—the present age and that which is to come —is in danger. St. Paul can now, like a true Greek, contrast the things that are seen, which are temporal, with the things that are not seen, which are eternal. The doctrine of the Spirit as a present possession of Christians brings down heaven to earth and exalts earth to heaven; the 'Parousia' is now only the end of the existing world-order, and has but little significance for the individual. These ideas have not displaced the earlier apocalyptic language; but it is easy to see that the one or the other must recede into the background, and that the Pharisaic tradition will be the one to fade.

The third group of Epistles—Philippians, Colossians, and Ephesians—are steeped in ideas which belong to Greek philosophy and the Greek mystery-religions. It would be impossible to translate them into any Eastern language. The Rabbinical disputes with the Jews about justification and election have disappeared; the danger ahead is now from theosophy and the barbarised Platonism which was afterwards matured in Gnosticism. The teaching is even more Christocentric than before; and the Catholic doctrine of the Church as the body of Christ is more prominent than individualistic mysticism. The cosmology is thoroughly Johannine, and only awaits the name of the Logos.

This receptiveness to new ideas is one of the most remarkable features in St. Paul's mind. Few indeed are the religious prophets and preachers whose convictions are still malleable after they have begun to govern the minds of others. St. Paul had already proved that he was a man who would 'follow the gleam,' even when it called him to a complete breach with his past. And the further development of his thought was made much easier by the fact that he was no systematic philosopher, but a great missionary who was willing to be all things to all

Q

men, while his own faith was unified by his strength of purpose, and by the steady glow of the light within.

It is difficult for us to realise the life of his little communities without importing into the picture features which belong to a later time. The organisation, such as it was, was democratic. The congregation as a whole exercised a censorship over the morals of its members, and penalties were inflicted 'by vote of the majority' (2 Cor. ii. 6). The family formed a group for religious purposes, and remained the recognised unit till the second century. In Ignatius and Hermas we find the campaign against family churches in full swing. The meetings were like those of modern revivalists, and sometimes became disorderly. But of the moral beauty which pervaded the whole life of the brotherhoods there can be no doubt. Many of the converts had formerly led disreputable lives; but these were the most likely to appreciate the gain of being no longer outlaws, but members of a true family. The heathen were amazed at the kind of people whom the Christians admitted and treated like brethren; but in the first century scandals do not seem to have been frequent. Women, who were probably always the majority, enjoyed a consideration unknown by them before. The extreme importance attached by the early Church to sexual purity made it possible for them to mix freely with Christian men; indeed, the strange and perilous practice of a 'brother' and a virgin sharing the same house seems to have already begun, if this is the meaning of the obscure passage in 1 Cor. vii. 36.

Chastity and indifference to death were the two qualities in Christians which made the greatest impression on their neighbours. Galen is especially interesting on the former topic. But we must add a third characteristic —the cheerfulness and happiness which marked the early Christian communities. 'Joy' as a moral quality is a Christian invention, as a study of the usage of χαρά in Greek will show. Even in Augustine's time the temper of the Christians, 'serena et non dissolute hilaris' was one of the things which attracted him to the Church. The secret of this happy social life was an intense

realisation of corporate unity among the members of the
confraternity, which they represented to themselves as
a ' mystery '—a mystical union between the Head and
members of a ' body.'  It is in this conception, and not
in ritual details, that we are justified in finding a real and
deep influence of the mystery-cults upon Christianity.
The Catholic conception of sacraments as bonds uniting
religious communities, and as channels of grace flowing
from a corporate treasury, was as certainly part of the
Greek mystery-religion as it was foreign to Judaism.
The mysteries had their bad side, as might be expected in
private and half-secret societies ; but their influence as a
whole was certainly good.  The three chief characteristics
of mystery-religion were, first, rites of purification, both
moral and ceremonial ; second, the promise of spiritual
communion with some deity, who through them enters
into his worshippers ; third, the hope of immortality,
which the Greeks often called ' deification,' and which
was secured to those who were initiated.

It is useless to deny that St. Paul regarded Christianity
as, at least on one side, a mystery-religion.  Why else
should he have used a number of technical terms which
his readers would recognise at once as belonging to the
mysteries ?  Why else should he repeatedly use the word
' mystery ' itself, applying it to doctrines distinctive of
Christianity, such as the resurrection with a ' spiritual
body,' the relation of the Jewish people to God, and,
above all, the mystical union between Christ and Christians ?
The great ' mystery ' is ' Christ in you, the hope of glory '
(Col. i. 27).  It was as a mystery-religion that Europe
accepted Christianity.  Just as the Jewish Christians
took with them the whole framework of apocalyptic
Messianism, and set the figure of Jesus within it, so
the Greeks took with them the whole scheme of the
mysteries, with their sacraments, their purifications and
fasts, their idea of a mystical brotherhood, and their
doctrine of ' salvation ' ($\sigma\omega\tau\eta\rho\iota\alpha$ is essentially a mystery
word) through membership in a divine society, wor-
shipping Christ as the patronal deity of their mysteries.

Historically, this type of Christianity was the origin

of Catholicism, both Western and Eastern ; though it is only recently that this character of the Pauline churches has been recognised. And students of the New Testament have not yet realised the importance of the fact that St. Paul, who was ready to fight to the death against the Judaising of Christianity, was willing to take the first step, and a long one, towards the Paganising of it. It does not appear that his personal religion was of this type. He speaks with contempt of some doctrines and practices of the Pagan mysteries, and will allow no *rapprochement* with what he regards as devil-worship. In this he remains a pure Hebrew. But he does not appear to see any danger in allowing his Hellenistic churches to assimilate the worship of Christ to the honours paid to the gods of the mysteries, and to set their whole religion in this framework, provided only that they have no part nor lot with those who sit at ' the table of demons '—the sacramental love-feasts of the heathen mysteries. The dangers which he does see, and against which he issues warnings, are, besides Judaism, antinomianism and disorder on the one hand, and dualistic asceticism on the other. He dislikes or mistrusts ' the speaking with tongues ' (γλωσσολαλία), which was the favourite exhibition of religious enthusiasm at Corinth. (On this subject Prof. Lake's excursus is the most instructive discussion that has yet appeared. The ' Testament of Job ' and the magical papyri show that gibberish uttered in a state of spiritual excitement was supposed to be the language of angels and spirits, understood by them and acting upon them as a charm.) He urges his converts to do all things ' decently and in order.' He is alarmed at signs of moral laxity on the part of self-styled ' spiritual persons '—a great danger in all times of ecstatic enthusiasm. He is also alive to the dangers connected with that kind of asceticism which is based on theories of the impurity of the body—the typical Oriental form of world-renunciation. But he does not appear to have foreseen the unethical and polytheistic developments of sacramental institutionalism. In this particular his Judaising opponents had a little more justification than he is willing to allow them.

There is something transitional about all St. Paul's teaching. We cannot take him out of his historical setting, as so many of his commentators in the nineteenth century tried to do. This is only another way of saying that he was, to use his own expression, a wise master-builder, not a detached thinker, an arm-chair philosopher. To the historian, there must always be something astounding in the magnitude of the task which he set himself, and in his enormous success. The future history of the civilised world for two thousand years, perhaps for all time, was determined by his missionary journeys and hurried writings. It is impossible to guess what would have become of Christianity if he had never lived; we cannot even be sure that the religion of Europe would be called by the name of Christ. This stupendous achievement seems to have been due to an almost unique practical insight into the essential factors of a very difficult and complex situation. We watch him, with breathless interest, steering the vessel which carried the Christian Church and its fortunes through a narrow channel full of sunken rocks and shoals. With unerring instinct he avoids them all, and brings the ship, not into smooth water, but into the open sea, out of that perilous strait. And so far was his masterly policy from mere opportunism, that his correspondence has been ' Holy Scripture ' for fifty generations of Christians, and there has been no religious revival within Christianity that has not been, on one side at least, a return to St. Paul. Protestants have always felt their affinity with this institutionalist, mystics with this disciplinarian. The reason, put shortly, is that St. Paul understood what most Christians never realise, namely, that the Gospel of Christ is not *a* religion, but religion itself, in its most universal and deepest significance.

# INSTITUTIONALISM AND MYSTICISM
## (1914)

IT happens sometimes that two opposite tendencies flourish together, deriving strength from a sense of the danger with which each is threatened by the popularity of the other. Where the antagonism is not absolute, each may gain by being compelled to recognise the strong points in the rival position. In a serious controversy the right is seldom or never all on one side ; and in the normal course of events both theories undergo some modification through the influence of their opponents, until a compromise, not always logically defensible, brings to an end the acute stage of the controversy. Such a tension of rival movements is very apparent in the religious thought of our day. The quickening of spiritual life in our generation has taken two forms, which appear to be, and to a large extent are, sharply opposed to each other. On the one side, there has been a great revival of mysticism. Mysticism means an immediate communion, real or supposed, between the human soul and the Soul of the World or the Divine Spirit. The hypothesis on which it rests is that there is a real affinity between the individual soul and the great immanent Spirit, who in Christian theology is identified with the Logos-Christ. He was the instrument in creation, and through the Incarnation and the gift of the Holy Spirit, in which the Incarnation is continued, has entered into the most intimate relation with the inner life of the believer. This revived belief in the inspiration of the individual has immensely strengthened the position of Christian apologists, who find their old fortifications no longer

tenable against the assaults of natural science and historical criticism.  It has given to faith a new independence,
and has vindicated for the spiritual life the right to stand
on its own feet and rest on its own evidence.  Spiritual
things, we now realise, are spiritually discerned.  The
enlightened soul can see the invisible, and live its true
life in the suprasensible sphere.  The primary evidence
for the truth of religion is religious experience, which
in persons of religious genius—those whom the Church
calls saints and prophets—includes a clear perception
of an eternal world of truth, beauty, and goodness, sur-
rounding us and penetrating us at every point.  It is the
unanimous testimony of these favoured spirits that the
obstacles in the way of realising this transcendental world
are purely subjective and to a large extent removable
by the appropriate training and discipline.  Nor is there
any serious discrepancy among them either as to the nature
of the vision which is the highest reward of human effort,
or as to the course of preparation which makes us able
to receive it.  The Christian mystic must begin with the
punctual and conscientious discharge of his duties to
society ;  he must next purify his desires from all worldly
and carnal lusts, for only the pure in heart can see God ;
and he may thus fit himself for ‘ illumination ’—the stage
in which the glory and beauty of the spiritual life, now
clearly discerned, are themselves the motive of action and
the incentive to contemplation ;  while the possibility of
a yet more immediate and ineffable vision of the Godhead is not denied, even in this life.  There is reason to
think that this conception of religion appeals more and
more strongly to the younger generation to-day.  It
brings an intense feeling of relief to many who have been
distressed by being told that religion is bound up with
certain events in antiquity, the historicity of which it is
in some cases difficult to establish ;  with a cosmology
which has been definitely disproved ;  and with a philosophy which they cannot make their own.  It allows
us what George Meredith calls ‘ the rapture of the forward view.’  It brings home to us the meaning of the
promise made by the Johannine Christ that there are many

things as yet hid from humanity which will in the future be revealed by the Spirit of Truth. It encourages us to hope that for each individual who is trying to live the right life the venture of faith will be progressively justified in experience. It breaks down the denominational barriers which divide men and women who worship the Father in spirit and in truth—barriers which become more senseless in each generation, since they no longer correspond even approximately with real differences of belief or of religious temperament. It makes the whole world kin by offering a pure religion which is substantially the same in all climates and in all ages—a religion too divine to be fettered by any man-made formulas, too nobly human to be readily acceptable to men in whom the ape and tiger are still alive, but which finds a congenial home in the purified spirit which is the 'throne of the Godhead.' Such is the type of faith which is astir among us. It makes no imposing show in Church conferences ; it does not fill our churches and chapels ; it has no organisation, no propaganda ; it is for the most part passively loyal, without much enthusiasm, to the institutions among which it finds itself. But in reality it has overleapt all barriers ; it knows its true spiritual kin ; and amid the strifes and perplexities of a sad and troublous time it can always recover its hope and confidence by ascending in heart and mind to the heaven which is closer to it than breathing, and nearer than hands and feet.

But on the other side we see a tendency, even more manifest if we look for external signs, to emphasise the institutional side of religion, that which prompts men and women to combine in sacred societies, to cherish enthusiastic loyalties for the Church of their early education or of their later choice, to find their chief satisfaction in acts of corporate worship, and to subordinate their individual tastes and beliefs to the common tradition and discipline of a historical body. It is now about eighty years since this tendency began to manifest itself as a new phenomenon in the Anglican Church. Since then, it has spread to other organisations. It has prompted a new degree of denominational loyalty in several Protestant bodies

on the Continent, in America, and in our own country;
and it has arrested the decline of the Roman Catholic
Church in countries where the outlook seemed least
hopeful from the ecclesiastical point of view. Such a
movement, so widespread and so powerful in its results, is
clearly a thing to be reckoned with by all who desire to
estimate rightly the signs of the times. It is a current
running in the opposite direction to the mystical tendency,
which regards unity as a spiritual, not a political ideal.
Fortunately, the theory of institutionalism has lately
been defended and expounded by several able writers
belonging to different denominations; so that we may
hope, by comparing their utterances, to understand the
attractions of the theory and its meaning for those who
so highly value it.

Aubrey Moore, writing in 1889, connected the Catholic
revival with the abandonment of atomism in natural
philosophy and of Baconian metaphysics. These were, he
thought, the counterpart of individualism in politics and
Calvinism in religion. The adherents of mid-Victorian
science and philosophy were bewildered by the phenomenon of 'men in the nineteenth century actually expressing a belief in a divine society and a supernatural
presence in our midst, a brotherhood in which men become
members of an organic whole by sharing in a common
life, a service of man which is the natural and spontaneous
outcome of the service of God.'[1]   In the view of this learned
and acute thinker, Catholicism, or institutionalism, is
destined to supplant Protestantism, as the organic theory
is destined to displace the atomic.

More recently Troeltsch, writing as a Protestant, has
emphasised the institutional side of religion in the most
uncompromising way.

'One of the clearest results of all religious history and religious
psychology is that the essence of all religion is not dogma and
idea, but cultus and communion, the living intercourse with
the Deity—an intercourse of the entire community, having its
vital roots in religion and deriving its ultimate power of thus

---

[1] Moore, *Science and the Faith*, Introduction.

uniting individuals, from its faith in God. . . . Whatever the future may bring us, we cannot expect a certainty and force of the knowledge of God and of His redemptive power to subsist without communion and cultus. And so long as a Christianity of any kind shall subsist at all, it will be united with a cultus, and with Christ holding a central position in the cultus.' [1]

From America, the last refuge of individualism, there has come a pronouncement not less drastic. Professor Royce, the author of the admirable metaphysical treatise entitled 'The World and the Individual,' has recently published a double series of Hibbert Lectures on 'The Problem of Christianity,' in which he affirms the institutionalist theory with a surprising absence of qualification. The whole book is dominated by one idea, advocated with a *naïveté* which would hardly have been possible to a theologian—the idea that churchmanship is the essential part of the Christian religion.

'The salvation of the individual man is determined by some sort of membership in a certain spiritual community—a religious community, and in its inmost nature a divine community, in whose life the Christian virtues are to reach their highest expression and the spirit of the Master is to obtain its earthly fulfilment. In other words, there is a certain universal and divine spiritual community. Membership in that community is necessary to the salvation of man. . . . Such a community exists, is needed, and is an indispensable means of salvation for the individual man, and is the fitting realm wherein alone the kingdom of heaven which the Master preached can find its expression, and wherein alone the Christian virtues can be effectively preached.' [2]

These statements, which in vigour and rigour would satisfy the most extreme curialist in the Society of Jesus, are not a little startling in an American philosopher, who, as far as the present writer knows, does not belong to any 'Catholic' Church. The thesis thus enunciated is the argument of the whole book, in which 'loyalty to the beloved com-

---

[1] Troeltsch, *Die Bedeutung der Geschichtlichkeit Jesu für den Glauben,* pp. 25 *sq.*
[2] Royce, *The Problem of Christianity,* vol. i. 39.

munity' is declared to be the characteristic Christian virtue. It is true that the satisfaction of Professor Royce's Catholic readers is destined to be damped in the second volume, where he forbids us to look for the ideal divine community in any existing Church, and expresses his conviction that great changes must come over the dogmatic teaching of Christianity. But for our purpose the significant fact is that throughout the book he insists that Christianity is essentially an institutional religion, the most completely institutional of all religions. For Professor Royce to be a Christian is to be a Churchman.

Our last witness shall be the learned Roman Catholic layman, Baron Friedrich von Hügel, the deepest thinker, perhaps, of all living theologians in this country. ' It is now ever increasingly clear to all deep impartial students that religion has ever primarily expressed and formed itself in cultus, in social organisation, social worship, intercourse between soul and soul and between soul and God ; and in symbols and sacraments, in contacts between spirit and matter.' He proceeds to discuss the strength and weakness of institutionalism in a perfectly candid spirit, but with too particular reference to the present conditions within the Roman Church to help us much in our more general survey. He mentions the drawbacks of an official philosophy, prescribed by authority ; ' only in 1835 did the Congregation of the Index withdraw heliocentric books from its list.' He emphasises the necessity of historical dogmas, but admits that orthodoxy cherishes, along with them, ' fact-like historical pictures ' which ' cannot be taken as directly, simply factual.' He vindicates the orthodoxy of religious toleration, and refuses to consign all non-Catholics to perdition, lamenting the tendency to identify absolutely the visible and invisible Church, which prevails among ' some of the (now dominant) Italian and German Jesuit Canonists.' Lastly, he boldly recommends the frank abandonment of the Papal claim to exercise temporal power in Italy. This is not so much a critique of institutionalism as the plea of a Liberal Catholic that the logic of institutionalism should not be allowed to override all other considerations.

The Baron is, indeed, himself a mystic, though also a strong believer in the necessity of institutional religion.

We have then a considerable body of very competent opinion, that a man cannot be a Christian unless he is a Churchman. To the mystic pure and simple, such a statement seems monstrous. Did not even Augustine say, ' I want to know God and my own soul ; these two things, and no third whatever ' ? What intermediary can there be, he will ask, between the soul and God ? What sacredness is there in an organisation ? Is it not a matter of common experience that the morality of an institution, a society, a state, is inferior to that of the individuals who compose it ? And is organised Catholicism an exception to this rule ? And yet we must admit the glamour of the idea of a divine society. It arouses that *esprit de corps* which is the strongest appeal that can be made to some noble minds. It calls for self-sacrifice and devoted labour in a cause which is higher than private interest. It demands discipline and co-operation, through which alone great things can be done on the field of history. It holds out a prospect of really influencing the course of events. And it there has been a historical Incarnation, it follows that God has actually intervened on the stage of history, and that it is His will to carry out some great and divine purpose in and by means of the course of history. With this object, as the Catholic believes, He established an institutional Church, pledged to the highest of all causes ; and what greater privilege can there be than to take part in this work, as a soldier in the army of God in His long campaign against the spiritual powers of evil ? The Christian institutionalist is the servant of a grand idea.

There are, however, a few questions which we are bound to ask him. First, is his idea of the Church Christian ? Did the Founder of Christianity contemplate or even implicitly sanction the establishment of a semi-political international society, such as the Catholic Church has actually been ? Orthodox Catholicism maintains that He did. Modernism admits that He did not, but adds that if He had known that the Messianic expectation was illusory, and that the existing world-order was to continue for thousands of years, He would certainly have wished that a Catholic Church should exist. And, argues the Modernist, if it is a good thing that a Catholic Church should exist, it is useless to quarrel with the conditions under which alone it can maintain its existence. The philosophical historian must admit that all the changes which the Catholic Church has undergone—its concessions to Pagan superstition, its secular power, its ruthless extirpation of rebels against its authority, its steadily growing centralisation and autocracy—were forced upon it in the struggle for existence. Those who wish that Church history had been different are wishing the impossible, or wishing that the Church had perished. But this argument is not valid as a defence of a divine institution. It is rather a merciless exposure of what happens, and must happen, to a great idea when it is enslaved by an institution of its own creation. The political organisation which has grown up round the idea ends by strangling it, and continues to fight for its own preservation by the methods which govern the policy of all other political organisations—force, fraud, and accommodation. There is nothing in the political history of Catholicism which suggests in the slightest degree that the spirit of Christ has been the guiding principle in its councils. Its methods have, on the contrary, been more cruel, more fraudulent, more unscrupulous, than those of most secular powers. If the Founder of Christianity had appeared again on earth during the so-called ages of faith, it is hardly possible to doubt that He would have been burnt alive or crucified again. What the Latin Church preserved was not the religion of Christ, which lived on by its inherent indestructibility, but parts of the Aristotelian and Platonic philosophies, distorted and petrified by scholasticism, a vast quantity of purely Pagan superstitions, and the *arcana imperii* of Roman Cæsarism. The normal end of Scholasticism is a mummified philosophy of authority, in which there are no problems to solve, but a great many dead pundits to consult. The normal end of a policy which exploits the superstitions of the peasant is a desperate warfare against education. The normal end of Roman

Imperialism is a sultanate like that of Diocletian. It is difficult to find a proof of infallible and supernatural wisdom in the evolution of which these are the last terms. We read with the utmost sympathy and admiration Baron von Hügel's loyal and reverent appeals to the authorities of his Church, that they may draw out the strong and beneficent powers of institutionalism, and avoid its insidious dangers. But it may be doubted whether such a policy is possible. The future of Roman Catholicism is, I fear, with the Ultramontanes. They, and not the Modernists, are in the line of development which Catholicism as an institution has consistently followed, and must continue to follow to the end. I can see no other fate in store for the *soma* of Catholicism ; the germ-cells of true Christianity live their own life within it, and are transmitted without taint to those who are born of the Spirit.

We must further ask the institutionalist what are his grounds for identifying the Church of God with the particular institution to which he belongs. On the institutionalist hypothesis, it might have been expected either that there would have been no divisions in Christendom, or that all seceding bodies would have shown such manifest inferiority in wisdom, morality, and sanctity, that the exclusive claims of the Great Church would have been ratified at the bar of history. This is, in fact, the claim which Roman Catholics make. But it can only be upheld by writing history in the spirit of an advocate, or by giving a preference, not in accordance with modern ethical views, to certain types of character which are produced by the monastic life of the Catholic 'religious.' It is increasingly difficult to find, in the lives of those who belong to any one denomination, proofs of marked superiority over other Christians. Of course, we know little of the real character of our neighbours as they appear in the eyes of God ; but in considering a theory which lays so much stress on history as Catholic institutionalism does, we are bound to make use of such evidence as we have. And the evidence does not support the theory that we cannot be Christians unless we are Catholics. Nor does it even countenance the view that we cannot be Christians unless we are enthusiastic members of *some* religious corporation. Professor Royce seems to have been carried away by the idea which prompted him to write his book ; but a little thought about the characters of his acquaintances might have given him pause.

The mechanical theory of devolution which assumes so much importance in some fashionable Anglican teaching about the Church need not detain us long. The logical choice must ultimately be between the great international Catholic Church and what Auguste Sabatier called the religion of the Spirit. The religion of all Protestants, when it is not secularised, as it too often is, belongs to this latter type, even when they lay most stress on the idea of brotherhood and corporate action. For with them institutions are never much more than associations for mutual help and edification. The Protestant always hopes to be saved *qua* Christian, not *qua* Churchman.

A third question which must be asked is whether institutionalism in practice makes for unity among Christians, or for division. Too often the chief visible sign of the ' corporate idea ' of which so much is said, is the rigidity of the spikes which it erects round its own particular fold. The obstacles to acts of reunion (which in no way carry with them the necessity of formal amalgamation) are raised almost exclusively by stiff institutionalists. The much-discussed Kikuyu case has brought this home to everybody. But for these uncompromising Churchmen, Christians of all denominations would be glad enough to meet together at the Lord's table on special occasions like the service which gave rise to this controversy. Anglicans are well aware that the differences of opinion within their body are far greater than those which separate some of them from Protestant Nonconformity, and others of them from Rome. Allegiance to this or that denomination is generally an accident of early surroundings. To make these external classifications into barriers which cannot be crossed is either an absurdity or a confession that a Church is a political aggregate. A Roman Monsignor explained, *à propos* of the Kikuyu service, that no Roman Catholic could ever communicate

in a Protestant church, because in so doing he would
be guilty of an act of apostasy, and would be no longer a
Roman Catholic. The attitude is consistent with the
Roman claim to universal jurisdiction ; for any other
body it would be absurd. The stiff institutionalist is
debarred by his theory from fraternising with many who
should be his friends, while he is bound to others with whom
he has no sympathy. His theory is once more found to
conflict with the facts.

Lastly, we must ask whether institutionalism is really
a spiritual and moral force. Of the advantages of *esprit
de corps* I have spoken already. No one can doubt that
unity is strength, or that Catholicism has an immense
advantage over its rivals in the efficiency of its organisation. But is not this advantage dearly purchased ?
Party loyalty is notoriously unscrupulous. The idealised
institution becomes itself the object of worship, and it
is entirely forgotten that a Christian Church ought to
have no ' interests ' except the highest welfare of humanity.
The substitution of military for civil ethics has worked
disastrously on the conduct of Churchmen. Theoretically
it is admitted by Roman casuists that an immoral order
ought not to be obeyed ; but it is not for a layman to
pronounce immoral any order received from a priest ;
if the order is really immoral, ' obedience ' exonerates
him who executes it ; in all other cases disobedience is
a deadly sin. The result of this submission of private
judgment is that the voice of conscience is often stifled,
and unscrupulous policies are carried through by Churchmen, which secular public opinion would have condemned
decisively and rejected. The persecution of Dreyfus is a
recent and strong instance. If all France had been Catholic,
the victim of this shocking injustice would certainly have
died in prison. It is extremely doubtful whether the
presence of a highly organised Church is conducive to moral
and social reform in a country. The temptation to play a
political game seems to be always too strong. In Ireland,
the priesthood has probably helped to maintain a comparatively high standard of sexual morality, but it cannot
be said that the Irish Catholic population is in other re-

spects a model of civilisation and good citizenship. In education especially the influence of ecclesiasticism has been almost uniformly pernicious, so that it seems impossible for any country where the children are left under priestly influence to rise above a certain rather low level of civilisation.

The strongest claim of institutionalism to our respect is probably the beneficial restraint which it exercises upon many persons who need moral and intellectual guidance. It is the fashion to disparage the scholastic theology, and it has certainly suffered by being congealed, like everything else that Rome touches, into a hard system ; but it is immeasurably superior to the theosophies and fancy religions which run riot in the superficially cultivated classes of Protestant countries. The undisciplined mystic, in his reliance on the inner light, may fall into various kinds of *Schwärmerei* and superstition. In some cases he may even lose his sanity for want of a wise restraining influence. It is not an accident that America, where institutionalism is weakest, is the happy hunting-ground of religious quacks and cranks. Individualists are too prone to undervalue the steadying influence of ancient and consecrated tradition, which is kept up mainly by ecclesiastical institutions. These probably prevent many rash experiments from being tried, especially in the field of morals. Even writers like Dr. Frazer insist on the immense services which consecrated tradition still renders to humanity. These claims may be admitted ; but they come very far short of the glorification of institutionalism which we found in the authors quoted a few pages back.

The institutionalist, however, may reply that he by no means admits the validity of Sabatier's antithesis between religions of authority and the religion of the Spirit. His own religion, he believes, is quite as spiritual as that of the Protestant individualist. He may quote the fine saying of a medieval mystic that he who can see the inward in the outward is more spiritual than he who can only see the inward in the inward. We may, indeed, be thankful that we have not to choose between two mutually exclusive types of religion. The Quaker, whom we may take as the type of anti-institutional mysticism,

R

has a brotherhood to which he is proud to belong, and for which he feels loyalty and affection. And Catholicism has been rich in contemplative saints who have lived in the light of the Divine presence. The question raised in this essay is rather of the relative importance of these two elements in the religious life, than of choosing one and rejecting the other. I will conclude by saying that our preference of one of these types to the other will be largely determined by our attitude towards history. I am glad to see that Professor Bosanquet, in his fine Gifford Lectures, has the courage to expose the limitations of the ' historical method,' now so popular. He protests against Professor Ward's dictum that ' the actual is wholly historical,' as a view little better than naïve realism. History, he says, is a hybrid form of experience, incapable of any considerable degree of being or trueness. It is a fragmentary diorama of finite life-processes seen from the outside, and very imperfectly known. It consists largely of assigning parts in some great world-experience to particular actors—a highly speculative enterprise. To set these contingent and dubious constructions above the operations of pure thought and pure insight is indeed a return to the philosophy of the man in the street. ' Social morality, art, philosophy, and religion take us far beyond the spatio-temporal externality of history ; these are concrete and necessary living worlds, and in them the finite mind begins to experience something of what individuality must ultimately mean.' Our inquiry has thus led us to the threshold of one of the fundamental problems of philosophy—the value and reality of time. For the institutionalist, happenings in time have a meaning and importance far greater than the mystic is willing to allow to them. Like most other great philosophical problems, this question is largely one of temperament. Christianity has found room for both types. I believe, however, that the aberrations or exaggerations of institutionalism have been, and are, more dangerous, and further removed from the spirit of Christianity than those of mysticism, and that we must look to the latter type, rather than to the former, to give life to the next religious revival.

# THE INDICTMENT AGAINST CHRISTIANITY
## (1917)

No thinking man can deny that this war has grievously stained the reputation of Europe. Even if the verdict of history confirms the opinion that the conspiracy which threw the torch into the powder-magazine was laid by a few persons in one or two countries, and that the unparalleled outrages which have accompanied the conflict were ordered by a small coterie of brutal officers, we cannot forget that these crimes have been committed by the responsible representatives of a civilised European power, and that the nation which they represent has shown no qualms of conscience. That such a calamity, the permanent results of which include a holocaust of European wealth and credit, accumulated during a century of unprecedented industry and ingenuity, the loss of innumerable lives, and the destruction of all the old and honourable conventions which have hitherto regulated the intercourse of civilised nations with each other, in war as well as in peace, should have been possible, is justly felt to be a reproach to the whole continent, and especially to the nations which have taken the lead in its civilisation and culture. The ancient races of Asia, which have never admitted the moral superiority of the West, are keenly interested spectators of our suicidal frenzy. A Japanese is reported to have said, ' We have only to wait a little longer, till Europe has completed her *hara kiri.*' This is, indeed, what any intelligent observer must think about the present struggle. Just as the feudal barons of England destroyed each other and brought the feudal system to an end in the Wars of the Roses, so the great industrial nations are rending to pieces the whole fabric of modern industrialism, which can never be reconstructed. Mr. Norman Angell was perfectly right in his argument that a European war would be ruinous to both sides. The material objects at stake, such as the control of the Turkish Empire and the African continent, are not worth more than an insignificant fraction of the war-bill. We are witnessing the suicide of a social order, and our descendants will marvel at our madness, as we marvel at the senseless wars of the past.

There has, it is plain, been something fundamentally wrong with European civilisation, and the disease appears to be a moral one. With this conviction it is natural that men should turn upon the official custodians of religion and morality, and ask them whether they have been unfaithful to their trust, or whether it is not rather proved that the faith which they profess is itself bankrupt and incapable of exerting any salutary influence upon human character and action. Christianity stands arraigned at the bar of public opinion. But it is not without significance that the indictment should now be urged with a vehemence which we do not find in the records of former convulsions. It was not generally felt to be a scandal to Christianity that England was at war for 69 years out of the 120 which preceded the battle of Waterloo. Either our generation expected more from Christianity, or it was far more shocked by the sudden outbreak of this fierce war than our ancestors were by the almost chronic condition of desultory campaigning to which they were accustomed. The latter is probably the true reason. The belief in progress, which at the beginning of the industrial revolution was an article of faith, had become a tacitly accepted presupposition of all serious thought ; and even those who were dubious about the moral improvement of mankind in other directions, seldom denied that we were more humane and peaceable than our forefathers. The disillusion has struck our self-complacency in its most vital spot. Nothing in our own experience had prepared us for the hideous savagery and vandalism of German warfare, the first accounts of which we received with blank amazement and incredulity. Then, when disbelief was no longer possible, there awoke within us a sense of fear for our homes and women and children— a feeling to which modern civilised man had long been a stranger. We had not supposed that the non-combatant population of any European country would ever again be exposed to the horrors of savage warfare. This, much more than the war itself, has made thousands feel that the house of civilisation is built upon the sand, and that Christianity has failed to subdue the most barbarous instincts of human nature. Christians cannot regret that the flagrant contradiction between the principles of their creed and the scenes that have been enacted during the last three years is fully recognised. But the often repeated statement that 'Christianity has failed' needs more examination than it usually receives from those who utter it.

History acquaints us with two kinds of religion, which, though they are not entirely separate from each other, differ very widely in their effects upon conduct and morality. The *religio* which Lucretius hated, and from which he strangely hoped that the atomistic materialism of Epicurus had finally delivered mankind, has its roots in the sombre and confused superstitions of the savage. Fear, as Statius and Petronius tell us, created the gods of this religion. These deities are mysterious and capricious powers, who exact vengeance for the transgression of arbitrary laws which they have not revealed, and who must be propitiated by public sacrifice, lest some collective punishment fall on the tribe, blighting its crops and smiting its herds with murrain, or giving it over into the hand of its enemies. This religion makes very little attempt to correct the current standard of values. Its rewards are wealth and prosperity ; its punishments are calamity in this world and perhaps torture in the next. It is not, however, incapable of moralisation. The wrath of heaven may visit not the innocent violation of some *tabu*, but cruelty and injustice. In the historical books of the Old

Testament, though Uzzah is stricken dead for touching the ark, and the subjects of King David afflicted with pestilence because their ruler took a census of his people, Jehovah is above all things a righteous God, who punishes bloodshed, adultery, and social oppression. So in Greece the Furies pursue the homicide and the perjurer, till the name of his family is clean put out. Herodotus tells us how the family of Glaucus was extinguished because he consulted the oracle of Delphi about an act of embezzlement which he was meditating.

International law was protected by the same fear of divine vengeance. The murder of heralds must by all means be expiated. When the Romans repudiate their 'scrap of paper' with the Samnites, they deliver up to the enemy the officers who signed it, though (with characteristic 'slimness') not the army which the mountaineers had captured and liberated under the agreement. To destroy the temples in an enemy's country was an act of wanton impiety; Herodotus cannot understand the religious intolerance which led the Persians to burn the shrines of Greek gods. Thus religion had a restraining influence in war throughout antiquity, and in the Middle Ages. The Pope, who was believed to hold the keys of future bliss and torment, was frequently, though by no means always, obeyed by the turbulent feudal lords, and often enforced the sanctity of a contract by the threat or the imposition of excommunication and interdict. In order to make these penalties more terrible, the torments of those who died under the displeasure of the Church were painted in the most vivid colours. But in the official and popular Christian eschatology, as in the terrestrial theodicy of the Old Testament, there is little or no moral idealism. The joys or pains of the future life are made to depend, in part at least, on the observance or violation of the moral law, but they are themselves of a kind which the natural man would desire or dread. They are an enhanced, because a deferred, retribution of the same kind which in more primitive religions promises earthly prosperity to the righteous, and earthly calamities to the wicked. Values, positive and negative, are taken nearly as they stand in the estimation of the average man.

But there is another religious tradition, which in Greece was almost separated from the official and national cults, and among the Hebrews was often in opposition to them. The Hebrew prophets certainly proclaimed that 'the history of the world is the judgment of the world,' and often assumed, too crudely as it seems to us, that national calamities are a proof of national transgression ; but the whole course of development in prophecy was towards an autonomous morality based on a spiritual valuation of life. Its quarrel with sacerdotalism was mainly directed against the unethical *tabu*-morality of the priesthood ; the revolt was grounded in a lofty moral idealism, which found expression in a half-symbolic vision of a coming state in which might and right should coincide. The apocalyptic prophecies of post-exilic Judaism, which were not based, like some political predictions of the earlier prophets, on a statesmanlike view of the international situation, but on hopes of supernatural intervention, had their roots in visions of a new and better world-order. This aspiration, which had to disentangle itself by degrees from the patriotic dreams of a stubborn and unfortunate race, was projected into the near future, and was mixed with less worthy political ambitions which had a different origin. The prophet always foreshortens his revelation, and generally blends the city of God with a vision of his own country transfigured. We see him doing this even to-day, in his Utopian dreams of social reconstruction.

And so it has always been. We remember Condorcet foretelling a reign of truth and peace just before he was compelled to flee from the storm of calumny to die in a damp cell at Bourg la Reine ; and Kant hailing the approach of a peaceful international republic while Napoleon was preparing to drown Europe in blood. Apocalyptism is a compromise between the religion of rewards and punishments and the religion of spiritual deliverance. It calls a new world into existence to redress the balance of the old ; but its discontent with the old is mainly the result of a moral and spiritual valuation of life. Greek philosophy has really much in common with Hebrew prophecy, though the Greek envisaged his ideal world as the eternal background of reality, and not under the form of history. In its maturest form, it is a transvaluation of all values in accordance with an absolute ideal standard—that of the Good, the True, and the Beautiful. This idealism appears in a still more drastic form in the religions of Asia, which preach deliverance by demonetising at a stroke all the world's currency. Spiritual values are alone accepted; man wins peace and freedom by renouncing in advance all of which fortune may deprive him.

We are apt to assume, in deference to our theories of human progress, that the evolution of religion is normally from a lower to a higher type. It would, indeed, be absurd to question that the religion of a civilised people is usually more spiritual and more rational than that of barbarians. But none the less, the history of religions is generally a history of decline. In Judaism the prophets came before the Scribes and the Pharisees. Brahmanism and Buddhism were both degraded by superstitions and unethical rites. Christianity, which began as a republication of the purest prophetic teaching, has suffered the same fate. In each case, when the revelation has lost its freshness, and the enthusiasm which it evoked has begun to cool, a reversion to older habits of thought and customs takes place; and sometimes it may be said that the old religion has really conquered the new.

Christianity, as taught by its Founder, is based on a transvaluation of values even more complete than that of Stoicism and the later Platonism, because, while it regards the objects of ordinary ambition as a positive hindrance to the higher life, it accepts and gives value to those pains of sympathy which Greek thought dreaded, as detracting from the calm enjoyment of the philosophic life. This acceptance of the world's suffering, from which every other spiritual religion and philosophy promise a way of escape, is perhaps the most distinctive feature of Christian ethics. In practice, it thus achieves a more complete conquest of evil than any other system; and by bringing sorrow and sympathy into the Divine life, it not only presents the character and nature of the Deity in a new light, but opens out a new ideal of moral perfection. This is not the place for a discussion of the main characteristics of the Gospel of Christ, and they are familiar to us all. But, since we are now considering the charge of failure brought against Christianity in connexion with the present world-war, it seems necessary to emphasise two points which are not always remembered.

The first is that there is no evidence that the historical Christ ever intended to found a new institutional religion. He neither attempted to make a schism in the Jewish Church nor to substitute a new system for it. He placed Himself deliberately in the prophetic line, only claiming to sum up the series in Himself. The whole manner of His life and teaching was prophetic. The differences which undoubtedly may be found between His style and that of the older prophets do not remove Him from the company in which He clearly wished to stand. He treated the institutional religion of His people with the independence and indifference of the prophet and mystic; and the hierarchy, which, like other hierarchies, had a sure instinct in discerning a dangerous enemy, was not slow to declare war to the knife against Him. Such, He reminded His enemies, was the treatment which all the prophets had met with from the class to which those enemies belonged. This, then, is the first fact to remember. Institutional Christianity may be a legitimate and necessary historical development from the original Gospel, but it is something alien to the Gospel itself. The first disciples believed that they had the Master's authority for expecting the end of the existing world-order in their own lifetime. They believed that He had come forward with the cry of 'Hora novissima!' Whether they misunderstood Him or not, they clearly could not have held this opinion if they had received instructions for the constitution of a Church.

The second point on which it is necessary to insist is that Christ never expected, or taught His disciples to expect, that His teaching would meet with wide acceptance, or exercise political influence. 'The world' —organised human society—was the enemy and was to continue the enemy. His message, He foresaw, would be scorned and rejected by the majority ; and those who preached it were to expect persecution. This warning is repeated so often in the Gospels that it would be superfluous to give quotations. He made it quite plain that the big battalions are never likely to be gathered before the narrow gate. He declared that only false prophets are well spoken of by the majority. When we consider the revolutionary character of the Christian idealism, its indifference to nearly all that passes for 'religion' with the vulgar, and its reversal of all current valuations, it is plain that it is never likely to be a popular creed. As surely as the presence of high spiritual instincts in the human mind guarantees its indestructibility, so surely the deeply-rooted prejudices which keep the majority on a lower level must prevent the Gospel of Christ from dominating mundane politics or social life.

Moreover, the actual extent of its influence cannot be estimated. The inwardness and individualism of its teaching make its apparent effectiveness smaller than its real power, which works secretly and unobserved. The vices which Christ regarded with abhorrence are perversions of character—hypocrisy, hard-heartedness, and worldliness or secularity ; and who can say what degree of success the Gospel has achieved in combating these ? The method of Christianity is alien to all externalism and machinery ; it does not lend itself to those accommodations and compromises without which nothing can be done in politics. As Harnack says, the Gospel is not one of social improvement, but of spiritual redemption. Its influence upon social and political life is indirect and obscure, operating through a subtle modification of current valuations, and curbing the competitive and acquisitive instincts, which nearly correspond with what Christ called 'Mammon' and St. Paul 'the flesh.' Christianity is a spiritual dynamic, which has very little to do directly with the mechanism of social life.

It is, therefore, certain that when we speak of Christianity as a factor in human life, we must not identify it with the opinions or actions of the multitudes who are nominally Christians. We must not even identify it, without qualification, with the types of character exhibited by those who try to frame their lives in accordance with its precepts. For these types are very largely determined by the ideals which belong to the stage through which the life of the race is passing; and these differ so widely in different ages and countries that the historian of religion might well despair if he was compelled to regard them all as typical manifestations of the same idea. There are times when the disciple of Christ seems to turn his back upon society; he is occupied solely with the relation of the individual soul to God. These are periods when the opportunities for social service are much restricted by a faulty structure of the body politic; periods when secular civilisation is so brutal, or so servile, that the religious life can only be led in seclusion from it. At another time the typical Christian seems to be the active and valiant soldier of a militant corporation. At another, again, he is a philanthropist, who devotes his life to the redress of some great wrong, such as slavery, or the promotion of a more righteous system of production and distribution. In all these types we can trace the operation of the genius of Christianity, but they are partial manifestations of it, with much alien admixture. The spirit of the age, as well as the spirit of Christ, has moulded the various types of Christian piety.

If there has ever been a time when organised Christianity was a concrete embodiment of the pure principles of the Gospel, we must look for it in the era of the persecutions, when the Church had already gained coherence and discipline and a corporate self-consciousness, and was still preserved from the corrupting influence of secularity by the danger which attended the profession of an illicit creed. A vivid picture of the Christian communities at this period has been given by Dobschütz, whose learning and impartiality are unimpeachable. The Church at this time demanded from its followers an unreserved confession, even when this meant death. It was a brotherhood within which there was no privileged class. Men and women, the free and the slave, had an equal share in it. It abolished the fundamental Greek distinction of civilised and barbarian. It looked with contempt on none. Its great organisation was spread by purely voluntary means, till it gained a firm footing throughout the Empire and beyond it. To a large extent it was an association for mutual aid. Wherever anyone was in need, help was at hand. The tangible advantages of belonging to such a guild were so great that the Church had to enforce labour on all who could work, as a condition of sharing in the benefits of membership. Social distinctions, such as those of rich and poor, master and slave, were not abolished, but they had lost their sting, because genuine affection, loyalty and sympathy neutralised these inequalities. Great importance was laid on truth, integrity in buinesss, and sexual purity. A complete rupture with pagan standards of morality was insisted on from new members. The human body must be kept holy, as the temple of God. Revenge was forbidden, and injustice was endured with meekness and pardon. This is no imaginary picture. In that brief golden age of the Church, such were indeed the characteristics of the Christian society. In the opinion of Dobschütz the moral condition of the Church in the second century was much higher than among St. Paul's converts in the first. The paucity of references to sins of the flesh, and to fraud, is to be accounted for by the actual rarity of such offences. For a short time, then, the artificial selection effected by the persecutions kept the Church pure ; and from the happy pictures which we can reconstruct of this period we can judge what a really Christian society would be like.

The history of institutional Catholicism must be approached from a different side. Troeltsch argues with much cogency that the Catholic Church must be regarded rather as the last creative achievement of classical antiquity than as the beginning of the Middle Ages. Its growth belongs mainly to the political history of

Europe ; the strictly religious element in it is quite subordinate. There is, as Modernist critics have seen, a real break between the Palestinian Gospel and the elaborate mystery-religion, with its graded hierarchy, its Roman organisation, its Hellenistic speculative theology, which achieved the conquest of the Empire in the fourth century. The Church, as Loisy says, determined to survive and to conquer, and adapted itself to the demands of the time. It has travelled far from the simple teaching of the earthly Christ ; though we may, if we choose, hold that His spirit continued to direct the growing and changing institution which, as a matter of history, had its source in the Galilean ministry. In truth, however, the extremely efficient organisation of the Roman Church began in self-defence and was continued for conquest. It is one of the strongest of all human institutions, so that it was said before the war that it is one of the ' three invincibles,' the other two being the German Army and the Standard Oil Trust.

But our admiration for the subtle and tenacious power of this corporation must not blind us to its essentially political character. Its policy has been always directed to self-preservation and aggrandisement ; it is an *imperium in imperio*, which has only checked fanatical nationalism by the competing influence of a still more fanatical partisanship. In the present war, the problem before the Pope's councillors was whether the friendship of the Central Powers or that of the Entente was best worth cultivating ; and the unshaken loyalty of Austria to the Church, together with a natural preference for German methods of governing as compared with democracy, turned the scale against us. In Ireland, in Canada and in Spain the Catholic priests have been formidable enemies of our cause. As for the other Churches, they have not the same power of arbitrating in national quarrels. The Russian Church has never been independent of the secular government ; and the Anglican and Lutheran Churches can hardly be expected to be impartial when the vital interests of England or Germany are at stake. Lovers of peace have not much to hope for from organised religion. National Christianity, as Mr. Bernard Shaw says, will only be possible when we have a nation of Christs.

The downfall of the medieval European system, though in truth it was a theory rather than a fact, has removed some of the restraints upon war. The determining principle of the medieval political theory was the conception of a ' lex Dei,' which included the ' lex Mosis,' the ' lex Christi,' and the ' lex ecclesiæ,' but which also, as ' lex naturæ,' comprised the law, science, and ethics of antiquity. These laws were super-national, and no nation dared explicitly to repudiate them. They formed the basis of a real system of international law, resting, like everything else in the Middle Ages, on supposed divine authority.

This theory, with its sanctions, was shattered at the Renaissance ; and the Machiavellian doctrine of the absolute State, accepted by Bacon and put into practice by Frederick the Great, has prevailed ever since, though not without frequent protests. The rise of nationalities, each with an intense self-consciousness, has facilitated the adoption of a theory too grossly immoral to have found favour except in the peculiar circumstances of modern civilisation. The emergence of nationalities was often connected with a legitimate struggle for freedom ; and at such times *esprit de corps* seems to be almost the sum of morality, the substitute for all other virtues. Loyalty is one of the most attractive of moral qualities, and it necessarily inhibits criticism of its own objects, which has the appearance of treason. But, unless the aims of the corporate body which claims our absolute allegiance are right and reasonable, loyalty may be, and often has been, the parent of hideous crimes, and a social evil of the first magnitude. The perversion of *esprit de corps* does incalculable harm in every direction, destroying all sense of honour and justice, of chivalry and generosity, of sympathy and humanity. It involves a complete repudiation of Christianity, which breaks down all barriers by ignoring them, and insists on love and justice towards all mankind without distinction. The worship of the State has during the last half-century been sedulously and artificially fostered in Germany, until it has produced a kind of moral insanity. Even philosophical historians like Troeltsch seem unable to see the monstrosity of a political doctrine which has caused his country to be justly regarded as the enemy of the whole human race. Eucken, writing some years before the war, in a rather gingerly manner deprecates *Politismus* as a national danger ; but he does not dare to grasp the nettle firmly. It is possible that this deification of the State in Germany may be in part due to an unsatisfied instinct of worship. In Roman Catholic countries, where there must be a divided allegiance, patriotism never, perhaps, assumes such sinister and fanatical forms.

But we shall not understand the attraction which this naked immoralism in international affairs exercises over the minds of many who are not otherwise ignoble, if we do not remember that the repudiation of the Christian ethical standard has been equally thorough in commercial competition. The German officer believes himself to have chosen a morally nobler profession than that of the business-man ; he serves (he thinks) a larger cause, and he is content with much less personal reward. Socialist assailants of our industrial system, much as they dislike war, would probably agree with him. It is not necessary to condemn all competition. The desire to excel others is not reprehensible, when the rivalry is in rendering useful social service. But it cannot be denied that the present condition of industry is such that a heavy premium is offered to mere cupidity ; that the fraternal social life which Christianity enjoins is often literally impossible, except at the cost of economic suicide ; and that in a competitive system a business man is, by the very force of circumstances, a warrior, though war is an enemy of love and destructive of Christian society. When the object of bargaining is to give as little and gain as much as possible, the Christian standard of values has been rejected as completely as it was by Machiavelli himself. The competition between two parties to a bargain is often a competition in unserviceableness. Money is very frequently made by creating a local and temporary monopoly, which enables

the vendor to squeeze the purchaser. In all such transactions one man's gain is another man's loss. This state of
things, the evils of which are almost universally recognised
and deplored, marks the end of the glorification of productive industry which was one result of the Reformation.

Hardly anything distinguishes modern from medieval
ethics more sharply than the emphasis laid by Protestant
morality on the duty of making and producing something
tangible. Theoretically the Protestant may hold that
'doing ends in death,' and he may sing these words on
Sunday ; but his whole life on week days is occupied in
strenuous 'doing.' We find in Calvinism and Quakerism
the genuinely religious basis of the modern business life,
which, however, has degenerated sadly, now that the largest
fortunes are made by dealing in money rather than in commodities. In the books of Samuel Smiles, and in Clough's
poem beginning ' Hope ever more and believe, O Man,' we
find the Gospel of productive work preached with fervour.
It is out of favour now in England ; but in America we
still see quaint attempts to make business a religion, as in
the Middle Ages religion was a business. In these circles,
it is productive activity as such to which value is attached,
without much enquiry as to the utility of the product. The
result has been an immense accumulation of the apparatus
of life, without any corresponding elevation in moral standards. The mischiefs wrought by modern commercialism
are largely the fruit of the purely irrational production
which it encourages. There are, says Professor Santayana,
Nibelungen who toil underground over a gold which they
will never use, and in their obsession with production be-
grudge themselves all inclinations to recreation, to merri-
ment, to fancy. Visible signs of such unreason appear in
the relentless and hideous aspect which life puts on ; for
those instruments which emancipate themselves from their
uses soon become hateful. 'A barbaric civilisation, built on
blind impulse and ambition, should fear to awaken a deeper
detestation than could ever be aroused by those more
beautiful tyrannies, chivalrous or religious, against which
past revolutions have been directed.' We cannot, indeed,
be surprised that this ideal of productive work as a means

of grace, precious for its own sake, has no attraction for the masses, and that independent thinkers like Edward Carpenter should write books on ' Civilisation, its Cause and Cure.'

This Puritan ideal is not so much unchristian as narrow and unintelligent ; but the money-making life has of late become more and more frankly predatory and anti-social. The great trusts, and the arts of the company-promoter, can hardly be said to perform any social service ; they exist to levy tribute on the public. We may say therefore that, though war between the leading nations of the world had become a strange idea and a far-off memory, we had by no means risen above the principles and practices of war in our internal life. The immunity from militarism hitherto enjoyed by Britain and the United States was a fortunate accident, not a proof of higher morality. Our fleet protected both ourselves and the Americans from the necessity of maintaining a conscript army ; but we had drifted into a condition in which civil war seemed not to be far off, and in which violence and lawlessness were increasing. By a strange inconsistency, many who on moral or religious grounds condemned wars between nations were found to condone or justify acts of war against the State, organised by discontented factions of its citizens. Revolutionary strikes, prepared long in advance by forced levies of money which were candidly called war-funds, had as their avowed aim the paralysis of the industries of the country and the reduction of the population to distress by withholding the necessaries of life. These acts of civil war, and disgraceful outbreaks of criminal anarchism, were justified by persons who professed a conscientious objection to defending their homes and families against a foreign invader. This state of mind proves how little essential connexion there is between democracy and peace. It discloses a confusion of ideas even greater than the antithesis between industrialism and militarism in the writings of Herbert Spencer. On this latter fallacy it is enough to quote the words of Admiral Mahan : ' As far as the advocacy of peace rests on material motives like economy and prosperity, it is the service of Mammon ; and the bottom of the platform will drop out

s

when Mammon thinks that war will pay better.' This is
notoriously what has happened in Germany. A short war,
with huge indemnities, seemed to German financiers a
promising speculation. If such were the rotten foundations upon which anti-militarism in this country was
based, the Churches cannot be blamed for giving the peace-
movement a rather lukewarm support.

In Germany there was no internal anarchy, such as
prevailed in England ; there was also no illusion about
the imminence of war. Our politicians ought to have read
the signs of the times better ; but they were too intent on
feeling the pulse of the electorate at home to attend to
disturbing and unwelcome symptoms abroad. The causes
of the war are not difficult to determine. War has long
been a national industry of Germany, and the idea of it
evoked no moral repugnance. The military virtues were
extolled ; the military profession enjoyed an astonishing
social prestige ; the learned class proclaimed the biological
necessity of international conflicts. The army believed
itself to be invincible, and it had begun to control the policy
of the country ; where these two conditions exist, no diplo-
macy can avert war. Professionalism always has a selfish
and anti-social element in its code, and the professionalism
of the soldier is always prone to override the rights and
disdain the scruples of civilians.

The dominant classes in Germany also found that their
power was being undermined by the growing industriali-
sation. The steady increase in the social-democratic vote
was a portent not to be disregarded. A letter from a
German officer to a friend in Roumania, which found its
way into the newspapers, tells a great deal of truth in a
few words. ' You cannot conceive,' he wrote, ' what difficulty we had in persuading our Emperor that it was necessary to let loose this war. But it has been done ; and I
hope that for a long time to come we shall hear no more
in Germany of pacifism, internationalism, democracy, and
similar pestilent doctrines.' Sir Charles Walston, in his
thoughtful book ' Aristodemocracy,' lays great stress on
this. ' It appeared to me,' he says, ' ever since 1905, that
in the immediate future it was all a question as to whether

the labour-men, the practical pacifists, would arrive at the
realisation of their power before the militarists had forced
a war upon us, or whether the military powers would anticipate this result, and within the next few years force a war
upon the world.' To the influence of the military was added
the cupidity of the commercial and financial class. The
law of diminishing returns was driving capital further and
further afield ; and large profits, it was hoped, might be
made by the exploitation of backward countries and the
reduction of their inhabitants to serfdom. To a predatory
and parasitic class war seems only a logical extension of the
principles upon which it habitually acts ; and for this reason
privileged orders seldom feel much moral compunction
about a war-policy. Lastly, among the causes of the war
must be reckoned one which has received far too little attention from social and political philosophers—the tenacious
and half-unconscious memories of a race. Injustice comes
home to roost, sometimes after an astonishingly long in-
terval. The disaffection of Catholic Ireland would be quite
unintelligible without the massacres of the sixteenth century
and the unjust trade-legislation of the seventeenth and
eighteenth. The bitterness of the working class in England
has its roots in the earlier period of the industrial revolution
(about 1760–1832), when the labourer, with his wife and
children, was treated as the ' cannon-fodder ' of industry.
Similarly, the seeds of Prussian brutality and aggressiveness
were sown at Jena and in the raiding of Prussia for recruits
before the Moscow expedition. If such were the causes of
the great world-war, how little can be hoped from courts of
international arbitration !

These considerations have, perhaps, made it clear that
the main causes of international conflicts are what the
Epistle of St. James declares them to be—' the lusts that
war in your members,' the pugnacious and acquisitive instincts which pervade our social life in times of peace, and
not least in those nations which pride themsleves on having
advanced beyond the militant stage. There are some who
accept this state of things as natural and necessary, and
who blame Christianity for carrying on a futile campaign

against human nature. This is a very different indictment from that which condemns Christianity for tolerating a preventible evil ; and it is, in our opinion, even less justified. The argument that, because war has always existed, it must always continue to exist, is justly ridiculed by Mr. Norman Angell. ' It is commonly asserted that old habits of thought can never be shaken ; that, as men have been, so they will be. That, of course, is why we now eat our enemies, enslave their children, examine witnesses with the thumbscrew, and burn those who do not attend the same church.'

The long history of war as a racial habit explains why a ruinous and insane anachronism shows such tenacity ; for the conditions which established the habit among primitive tribes demonstrably no longer exist. It is probably true, as William James says, that ' militarist writers without exception regard war as a biological or sociological necessity ' ; lawyers might say the same about litigation. But ' laws of nature ' are not efficient causes, and it is open to any óne to prove that they are not laws, if he can break them with impunity. It would be the height of pessimistic fatalism to hold that men must always go on doing that which they hate, and which brings them to misery and ruin. Man is not bound for ever by habits contracted during his racial nonage ; his moral, rational, and spiritual instincts are as natural as his physical appetites ; and against them, as St. Paul says, ' there is no law.' Huxley's Romanes Lecture gave an unfortunate support to the mischievous notion that the ' cosmic process ' is the enemy of morality. The truth seems to be that Nature presents to us not a categorical imperative, but a choice. Do we prefer to pay our way in the world, or to be parasites ? War, with very few exceptions, is a mode of parasitism. Its object is to exploit the labour of other nations, to make them pay tribute, or to plunder them openly, as the Germans have plundered the cities of Belgium. War is a parasitic industry ; and Christianity forbids parasitism. Nature has her own penalties for the lower animals which make this choice, and they strike with equal severity ' the peoples that delight in war.' The bellicose nations have nearly all perished.

There remains, however, a class of wars which escapes this condemnation ; and about them difficult moral problems may be raised. We can hardly deny to a growing and civilised nation the right to expand at the expense of barbarous hunters and nomads. No one would suggest that the Americans ought to give back their country to the Indians, or that Australia should be abandoned to the aborigines. But were the Anglo-Saxons justified in expropriating the Britons, and the Spaniards the Aztecs ? There is room for differences of opinion in these cases ; and a very serious problem may arise in the future, as to whether the European races are morally justified in using armed force to restrict Asiatic competition. As a general principle, we must condemn the expropriation of any nation which is in effective occupation of the soil. The popular estimate of superior and inferior races is thoroughly unchristian and unscientific, as is the prejudice against a dark skin. The opinion that a nation which is increasing in population has a right to expel the inhabitants of another country to make room for its own emigrants is surely untenable. If it justifies war at all, it sanctions a war of extermination, which would attain its objects most completely by massacring girls and young women. The pressure of population is a real cause of war ; but the moral is, not that war is right, but that a nation must cut its coat according to its cloth, and limit its numbers.

Unless we justify wars of extermination, war has no biological sanction, and Christianity is not flying in the face of nature by condemning it. On the contrary, by condemning every form of parasitism, it indicates the true path of evolution. It is equally right in rejecting the purely economic valuation of human goods. The ' economic man ' does not exist in nature ; he is a fictitious creature who is responsible for a great deal of social injustice. Some modern economists, like Mr. Hobson, would substitute for the old monetary standards of production and distribution an attempt to estimate the ' human costs ' of labour. Creative work involving ingenuity and artistic qualities is not ' costly ' at all, unless the hours of labour, or the nervous strain, exceed the powers of the worker. More monotonous

work is not costly to the worker if the day's labour is fairly
short, or if some variety can be introduced.   The human
cost is greatly increased if the worker thinks that his labour
is useless, or that it will only benefit those who do not
deserve the enjoyment of its fruits.   Work which only
produces frivolous luxuries is and ought to be unwelcome
to the producer, even if he is well paid.   It must also be
emphasised that worry and anxiety take the heart out of
a man more than anything else.   Security of employment
greatly reduces the 'human cost' of labour.   These considerations are comparatively new in political economy.
They change it from a highly abstract science into a study
of the conditions of human welfare as affected by social
organisation.   The change is a victory for the ideas of
Ruskin and Morris, though not necessarily for the practical
remedies for social maladjustments which they propounded.
It brings political economy into close relations with ethics
and religion, and should induce economists to consider
carefully the contribution which Christianity makes to the
solution of the whole problem.   For Christianity has its
remedy to propose, and it is a solution of the problem of
war, not less than of industrial evils.

Christianity gives the world a new and characteristic
standard of values.   It diminishes greatly the values which
can accrue from competition, and enhances immeasurably
the non-competitive values.   'A man's life consisteth not
in the abundance of the things which he possesseth.'   'Is
not the life more than meat, and the body than raiment ? '
' The Kingdom of God is not meat and drink, but righteousness and peace and joy in the Holy Ghost.'   Passages like
these are found in every part of the New Testament.   This
Christian idealism has a direct bearing on the doctrine of
' human costs.'   Work is irksome, not only when it is
excessive or ill-paid, but when the worker is lazy, selfish,
envious or discontented.   There is one thing which can
make almost any work welcome.   If it is done from love or
unselfish affection, the human cost is almost *nil*, because
it is not counted or consciously felt.   This is no exaggeration
when it is applied to the devoted labour of the mother and
the nurse, or to that of the evangelist conscious of a divine

vocation. But in all useful work the keen desire to render social service, or to do God's will, diminishes to an incalculable extent the ' human cost ' of labour. This principle introduces a deep cleavage between the Christian remedy and that of political socialism, which fosters discontent and indignation as a lever for social amelioration. Men are made unhappy in order that they may be urged to claim a larger share of the world's wealth. Christianity considers that, measured by human costs, the remedy is worse than the disease. The adoption of a truer standard of value would tear up the lust of accumulation by the roots, and would thus effect a real cure. It would also stop the grudging and deliberately bad work which at present seriously diminishes the national wealth.

The Christian cure is the only real cure. It is the fashion to assume that militarism and cupidity are vices of the privileged classes, and that democracies may be trusted neither to plunder the minority at home nor to seek foreign adventures by unjust wars. There is not the slightest reason to accept either of these views. Political power is always abused ; an unrepresented class is always plundered. Nor are democracies pacific, except by accident. At present they do not wish to see the capital which they regard as their prospective prey dissipated in war ; and for this reason their influence in our time will probably be on the side of peace. But, as soon as the competition of cheap Asiatic labour becomes acute, we may expect to see the democracies bellicose and the employing class pacific. This is not guess-work ; we already see how the democracies of California and Australia behave towards immigrants from Asia. Readers of Anatole France will remember his description of the economic wars decreed by the Senate of the great republic, at the end of ' L'Île des Pingouins.' It would, indeed, be difficult to prove that the expansion of the United States has differed much, in methods and morals, from that of the European monarchies ; and the methods of trade-unions are the methods of pitiless belligerency. Democracy and socialism are broken reeds for the lover of peace to lean upon.

In conclusion, our answer to the indictment against

Christianity is that institutional religion does not represent the Gospel of Christ, but the opinions of a mass of nominal Christians. It cannot be expected to do much more than look after its own interests and reflect the moral ideas of its supporters. The real Gospel, if it were accepted, would pull up by the roots not only militarism but its analogue in civil life, the desire to exploit other people for private gain. But it is not accepted. We have seen that the Founder of Christianity had no illusions as to the reception which His message of redemption would meet with. The ' Prince of this World ' is not Christ, but the Devil. Nevertheless, He did speak of the ' whole lump ' being gradually leavened, and we shall not exceed the limits of a reasonable and justifiable optimism if we hope that the accumulated experience of humanity, and perhaps a real though very slow modification for the better of human nature itself, may at last eliminate the wickedest and most insane of our maleficent institutions. The human race has probably hundreds of thousands of years to live, whereas our so-called civilisation cannot be traced back for more than a few thousand years. The time when ' nation shall not lift up sword against nation, neither shall they learn war any more,' will probably come at last, though no one can predict what the conditions will be which will make such a change possible.

The signs are not very favourable at present for internationalism. The great nations, bankrupt and honeycombed with social unrest, will be obliged after the war to organise themselves as units, with governments strong enough to put down revolutions, and directed by men of the highest mercantile ability, whose main function will be to increase productiveness and stop waste. We may even see Germany mobilised as one gigantic trust for capturing markets and regulating prices. A combination so formidable would compel other nations, and our own certainly among the number, to adopt a similar organisation. This would, of course, mean a complete victory for bureaucratic state-socialism, and the defeat of democracy and trade-union syndicalism. Such a change, which few would just now welcome, will occur if no other form of state is able to survive ; and this is what we may live to see. But there is no finality about any experiments in government. A period of internationalism may follow the intense national-ism which historical critics foresee for the twentieth century. Or perhaps the international labour-organisations may be too strong for the centralising forces. It is just possible that Labour, by a concerted movement during the violent reaction against militarism which will probably follow the war, will forbid any further military or naval prepara-tions to be made.

Whatever forms reconstruction may take, Christianity will have its part to play in making the new Europe. It will be able to point to the terrible vindication of its doctrines in the misery and ruin which have overtaken a world which has rejected its valuations and scorned its precepts. It is not Christianity which has been judged and condemned at the bar of civilisation ; it is civilisation which has de-stroyed itself because it has honoured Christ with its lips, while its heart has been far from Him. But a spiritual religion can win a victory only within its own sphere. It can promise no Deuteronomic catalogue of blessings and cursings to those who obey or disobey its principles. Social happiness and peace would certainly follow a whole-hearted acceptance of Christian principles ; but they would not certainly bring wealth or empire. ' Philosophy,' said Hegel, ' will bake no man's bread ' ; and it is only in a spiritual sense that the meek-spirited can expect to possess the earth. Nevertheless, it is a mistake to suppose that a Christian nation would be unable to hold its own in the struggle for existence. A nation in which every citizen endeavoured to pay his way and to help his neighbour would be in no danger of servitude or extinction. The mills of God grind slowly, but the future does not belong to lawless violence. In the long run, the wisdom that is from above will be justified in her children.

# SURVIVAL AND IMMORTALITY

## (1917)

THE recrudescence of superstition in England was plain to all observers many years before the war ; it was perhaps most noticeable among the half-educated rich. Several causes contributed to this phenomenon. The craving for the supernatural, a very ancient and deeply rooted thought-habit, had been suppressed and driven underground by the arrogant dominance of a materialistic philosophy, and by the absorption of society in the pursuit of gain and pleasure. Modern miracles were laughed out of court. But materialism has supernaturalism for its nemesis. An abstract science, erecting itself into a false philosophy, leaves half our nature unsatisfied, and becomes morally bankrupt before its intellectual errors are exposed. Supernaturalism is the refuge of the materialist who wishes to make room for ideal values without abandoning the presuppositions of materialism. By dovetailing acts of God into the order of nature, he materialises the spiritual, but brings the Divine will into the world of experience, from which it had been expelled, and produces a rough scheme of providential government, by which he can live.

The revolt against scientific materialism was made much easier by the disintegration of the mechanical theory itself. Biology found itself cramped by the categories of inorganic science, and claimed its autonomy. The result was a fatal breach in the defences of materialism, for biology is being driven to accept final causes, and would be glad to adopt some theory of vitalism, if it could do so without falling back into the old error of a mysterious ' vital force.'

Biological truth, it is plain, cannot be reduced to the purely quantitative categories of mathematics and physics. Then psychology aspired to be a philosophy of real existence, and attacked both absolutism and materialism. The pretensions of psychology rehabilitated subjectivism and founded pragmatism, till reactionary theology took heart of grace and defended crude supernaturalism, with the whole apparatus of sacerdotal magic, as the 'Gospel for human needs.' All protection against the grossest superstitions was thus swept away. With no fixed standard of reference to distinguish fact from fiction, it was possible to argue that 'whatever suits souls is true.'

In this atmosphere many old habits of thought reasserted themselves. While we enjoyed peace and prosperity, the credulity of the public found its chief outlet in various systems of faith-healing and in the time-honoured pretensions of priest-craft. But the devastation which the war has brought into countless loving families has turned the current of superstition strongly towards necromancy. The 'will to believe,' no longer inhibited and suspected as a reason for doubt, has been allowed to create its own logic. A few highly educated men, who have long been playing with occultism and gratifying their intellectual curiosity by exploring the dark places of perverted mysticism, have been swept off their feet by it, and their authority, as 'men of science,' has dispelled the hesitation of many more to accept what they dearly wished to believe. The longing of the bereaved has created for itself a spurious and dreary satisfaction.

One cause of this strange movement cannot be emphasised too strongly. It proves that the Christian hope of immortality burns very dimly among us. Those who study the utterances of our religious guides must admit that it is so. References to the future life had, before the war, become rare even in the pulpit. The topic was mainly reserved for letters of condolence, and was then handled gingerly, as if it would not bear much pressure. Working-class audiences and congregations listened eagerly to the wildest promises of an earthly utopia the day after tomorrow, but cooled down at once when they were reminded that 'if in this life only we have hope in Christ, we are of all men most miserable.' Accordingly, the clerical demagogue showed more interest in the unemployed than in the unconverted., Christianity, which began as a revolutionary idealism, had sunk into heralding materialistic revolution. Such teachers have no message of hope and comfort for those who have lost their dearest. And they have, in fact, been deserted. Their secularised Christianity was received with half-contemptuous approval by trade unions, but far deeper hopes, fears, and longings have now been stirred, which concern all men and women alike, and on the answers to which the whole value of existence is now seen to depend. Christianity can answer them, but not the Churches through the mouths of their accredited representatives. And so, instead of 'the blessed hope of everlasting life,' the bereaved have been driven to this pathetic and miserable substitute, the barbaric belief in ghosts and dæmons, which was old before Christianity was young. And what a starveling hope it is that necromancy offers us! An existence as poor and unsubstantial as that of Homer's Hades, which the shade of Achilles would have been glad to exchange for serfdom to the poorest farmer, and with no guarantee of permanence, even if the power of comforting or terrifying surviving relations is supposed to persist for a few years. Such a prospect would add a new terror to death ; and none would desire it for himself. It is plainly the dream of an aching heart, which cannot bear to be left alone.

But, it will be said, there is scientific evidence for survival. This claim is now made. Cases are reported, with much parade of scientific language and method, and those who reject the stories with contemptuous incredulity are accused of mere prejudice. Nevertheless, I cannot help being convinced that if communications between the dead and the living were part of the nature of things, they would have been established long ago beyond cavil. For there are few things which men have wished more eagerly to believe. It is no doubt just possible that among the vibrations of the fundamental ingredients of our world—those attenuated forms of matter which are said to be not even 'material,' there may be some which act as vehicles for psychical interchange.  If such psychic waves exist, the discovery is wholly in favour of materialism.  It would tend to rehabilitate those notions of spirit as the most rarefied form of matter—an ultra-gaseous condition of it—which Stoicism and the Christian Stoic Tertullian postulated.  The meaning of ' God is Spirit ' could not be understood till this insidious residue of materialism had been got rid of.  It is a retrograde theory which we are asked to re-examine and perhaps accept.  The moment we are asked to accept ' scientific evidence ' for spiritual truth, the alleged spiritual truth becomes for us neither spiritual nor true.  It is degraded into an event in the phenomenal world, and when so degraded it cannot be substantiated.  Psychical research is trying to prove that eternal values are temporal facts, which they can never be.

The case for necromancy is no better if we leave ' scientific proof ' alone, and appeal to the relativist metaphysics of the psychological school.  Intercourse with the dead is, we are told, a real psychical experience, and we need not worry ourselves with the question whether it has any ' objective truth.'  But we cannot allow psychology to have the last word in determining the truth or falsehood of religious or spiritual experience.  The extravagant claims of this science to take the place of philosophy must be abated.

Psychology is the science which describes mental states, as physical science describes the behaviour of matter in motion.  Both are abstract sciences.  Physical science treats nature as the totality of things conceived of as independent of any subject ; psychology treats inner experience as independent of any object.  Both are outside any idea of value, though it is needless to say that the votaries of both sciences trespass habitually, and often unconsciously. Both are dualisms with one side ignored or suppressed. When psychology meddles with ontological problems— when, for instance, it denies the existence of an Absolute, or says that reality cannot be known—it is taking too much upon itself, and has fallen into the same error as the materialism of the last century.  On such questions as the immortality of the soul it must remain silent.

Faith in human immortality stands or falls with the belief in *absolute values*. The interest of consciousness, as Professor Pringle-Pattison has said in his admirable Gifford Lectures, lies in the ideal values of which it is the bearer, not in its mere existence as a more refined kind of fact. Idealism is most satisfactorily defined as the interpretation of the world according to a scale of value, or, in Plato's phrase, by the Idea of the Good. The highest values in this scale are absolute, eternal, and super-individual, and lower values are assigned their place in virtue of their correspondence to or participation in these absolute values. I agree with Münsterberg that the conditional and subjective values of the pragmatist have no meaning unless we have acknowledged beforehand the independent value of truth. If the proof of the merely individual significance of truth has itself only individual importance, it cannot claim any general meaning. If, on the other hand, it demands to be taken as generally valid, the possibility of a general truth is acknowledged from the start. If this one exception is granted, the whole illusory universe of relativism is overthrown. To deny any thought which is more than relative is to deprive even scepticism itself of the presuppositions on which it rests. The logical sceptic has no *ego* to doubt with. ' Every doubt of absolute values destroys itself. As thought it contradicts itself ; as doubt it denies itself ; as belief it despairs of itself.' It is not necessary or desirable to follow Münsterberg in identifying valuation with will. He talks of the will judging ; but the will cannot judge. In contemplating existence we use our will to fix our attention, and then try conscientiously to prevent it from influencing the verdict. But this illegitimate use of the word ' will ' does not impair the force of the argument for absolute values.

Now, valuation arranges experience in a different manner from natural science. The attributes of reality, in our world of values, are Goodness, Truth, and Beauty. And we assert that we have as good reason to claim objective reality for these Ideas as for anything in the world revealed to our senses. ' All claims on man's behalf,' says Professor Pringle-Pattison, ' must be based on the objectivity of the values revealed in his experience, and brokenly realised there. Man does not make values any more than he makes reality.' Our contention is that the world of values, which forms the content of idealistic thought and aspiration, is the real world; and in this world we find our own immortality.

But there could be no greater error than to leave the two worlds, or the two 'judgments,' that of existence and that of value, contrasted with each other, or treated as unrelated in our experience. A value-judgment which is not also a judgment of existence is in the air; it is the baseless fabric of a vision. Existence is itself a value, and an ingredient in every valuation; that which has no existence has no value. And, on the other side, it is a delusion to suppose that any science can dispense with valuation. Even mathematics admits that there is a right and a wrong way of solving a problem, though by confining itself to quantitative measurements it can assert no more than a hypothetical reality for its world. It is quite certain that we can think of no existing world without valuation.

'The ultimate identity of existence and value is the venture of faith to which mysticism and speculative idealism are committed.'[1] It is indeed the presupposition of all philosophy and all religion; without this faith there can, properly speaking, be no belief in God. But the difference between naturalism and idealism may, I think, be better stated otherwise than by emphasising the contrast between existence and value, which it is impossible for either side to maintain. Naturalism seeks to interpret the world by investigation of origins; idealism by investigation of ends. The one finds the explanation of evolution in that from which it started, the other in that to which it tends. The one explains the higher by the lower; the other the lower by the higher. This is a plain issue; either the world shows a teleology or it does not. If it does, the philosophy based on the inorganic sciences is wrong. And the attempt to explain the higher by the lower becomes mischievous or

---

[1] Quoted by Professor Pringle-Pattison from an article by me in the *Times* Literary Supplement.

impossible when we pass from one *order* to another. In speaking of different ' orders,' we do not commit ourselves to any sudden breaks or leaps in evolution. The organic may be linked to the inorganic, soul to the lower forms of life, spirit to soul. But whether the ' scale of perfection ' is a ladder or an inclined plane, new categories are necessary as we ascend it. And unless we admit an inner teleology as a determining factor in growth, many facts even in physiology are hard to explain.

If the basis of our faith in the world-order is the conviction that the Ideas of the Good, the True, and the Beautiful are fully real and fully operative, we must try to form some clear notion of what these Ideas mean, and how they are related to each other. The goal of Truth, as an absolute value, is unity, which in the outer world means harmony, in the intercourse of spirit with spirit, love ; and in the inner world, peace or happiness. The goal of Goodness as an absolute value is the realisation of the ought-to-be in victorious moral effort. Beauty is the self-recognition of creative Spirit in its own works ; it is the expression of Nature's own deepest character. Beauty gives neither information nor advice ; but it satisfies a part of our nature which is not less Divine than that which pays homage to Truth and Goodness.

Now, these absolute values are supra-temporal. If the soul were in time, no value could arise ; for time is always hurling its own products into nothingness, and the present is an unextended point, dividing an unreal past from an unreal future. The soul is not in time ; time is rather in the soul. Values are eternal and indestructible. When Plotinus says that ' nothing that really *is* can ever perish ' (ἀπολεῖται οὐδὲν τῶν ὄντων), and when Höffding says that ' no value perishes out of the world,' they are saying the same thing. In so far as we can identify ourselves in thought and mind with the absolute values, we are sure of our immortality.

But it will be said that in the first place this promise of immortality carries with it no guarantee of survival in time, and in the second place that it offers us, at last, only an impersonal immortality. Let us take these two

objections in turn, though they are in reality closely
connected.

We must not regard time as an external, inhuman, unconscious process. Time is the frame of soul-life ; outside
this it has no existence. The entire cosmic process is the
life-frame of the universal Soul, the Divine Logos. With
this life we are vitally connected, however brief and unimportant the span and the task of an individual career may
seem to us. If my particular life-meaning passes out of
activity, it will be because the larger life, to which I belong,
no longer needs that form of expression. My death, like
my birth, will have a teleological justification, to which my
supra-temporal self will consent. When a good man's work
in this world is done, when he is able to say, without
forgetting his many failures, ' I have finished the work
that Thou gavest me to do,' surely his last word will be,
' Lord, now lettest Thou Thy servant depart in peace ' ;
not, ' Grant that I may flit for a while over my former home,
and hear what is happening to my country and my family.'
We may leave it to our misguided necromancers to describe
the adventures of the disembodied ghost—

> ' Quo cursu deserta petiverit, et quibus ante
> Infelix sua tecta supervolitaverit alis.'

The most respectable motive which leads men to desire a continuance of active participation in the affairs of time is that
which Tennyson expresses in the often-quoted line, ' Give
her the wages of going on, and not to die.' We may feel
that we have it in us to do more for God and our fellow-men
than we shall be able to accomplish in this life, even if it be
prolonged to old age. Is not this a desire which we may
prefer as a claim ? And in any case, it is admitted that
time is the form of the will. Are we to have no more will
after death ? Further, is our probation over when we die ?
What is to be the fate of that large majority who, so far as
we can see, are equally undeserving of heaven and of hell ?
To these questions no answer is possible, because we are
confronted with a blank wall of ignorance. We do not
know whether there will be any future probation. We

T

do not know whether Robert Browning's expectation of 'other tasks in other lives, God willing,' will be fulfilled.

> 'And I shall thereupon
> Take rest, ere I be gone
> Once more on my adventure brave and new.'

The question here raised is whether there is such a thing as reincarnation. This belief, so widely held at all times by eminent thinkers, and sanctioned by some of the higher religions, cannot be dismissed as obsolete or impossible. But if it is put in the form, ' Will the same self live again on earth under different conditions ? ' it may be that no answer can be given, not only because we do not know, but because the question itself is meaningless. The psycho-physical organism which was born at a certain date and which will die on another date is compacted of idiosyncrasies, inherited and acquired, which seem to be inseparable from its history as born of certain parents and living under certain conditions. It is not easy to say what part of such an organism could be said to maintain its identity, if it were housed in another body and set down in another time and place, when all recollection of a previous state has been (as we must admit) cut off. The only continuity, it seems to me, would be that of the racial self, if there is such a thing, or of the directing intelligence and will of the higher Power which sends human beings into the world to perform their allotted tasks.

The second objection, which, as I have said, is closely connected with the first, is that idealism offers us a merely impersonal immortality. But what is personality ? The notion of a world of spiritual atoms, ' solida pollentia simplicitate,' as Lucretius says, seems to be attractive to some minds. There are thinkers of repute who even picture the Deity as the constitutional President of a collegium of souls. This kind of pluralism is of course fundamentally incompatible with the presuppositions of my paper. The idea of the ' self ' seems to me to be an arbitrary fixation of our average state of mind, a half-way house which belongs to no order of real existence. The conception of an abstract ego seems to involve three assumptions, none of which is

true. The first is that there is a sharp line separating subject from object and from other subjects. The second is
that the subject, thus sundered from the object, remains
identical through time. The third is that this indiscerptible
entity is in some mysterious way both myself and my
property. In opposition to the first, I maintain that the
foci of consciousness flow freely into each other even on
the psychical plane, while in the eternal world there are
probably no barriers at all. In opposition to the second,
it is certain that the empirical self is by no means identical
throughout, and that the spiritual life, in which we may
be said to attain real personality for the first time, is only
' ours ' potentially. In opposition to the third, I repeat
that the question whether it is ' my ' soul that will live in
the eternal world seems to have no meaning at all. In
philosophy as in religion, we had better follow the advice
of the Theologia Germanica and banish, as far as possible,
the words ' me and mine ' from our vocabulary. For personality is not something given to start with. It does not
belong to the world of claims and counter-claims in which
we chiefly live. We must be willing to lose our soul on this
level of experience, before we can find it unto life eternal.
Personality is a teleological fact ; it is here in the making,
elsewhere in fact and power. So in the case of our friends.
The man whom we love is not the changing psycho-physical
organism ; it is the Christ in him that we love, the perfect
man who is struggling into existence in his life and growth.
If we ask what a man is, the answer may be either,
' He is what he loves,' or ' He is what he is worth.' The
two are not very different. Thus I cannot agree with
Keyserling, who in criticising this type of thought
(with which, none the less, he has great sympathy)
says that ' mysticism, whether it likes it or not, ends
in an impersonal immortality.' For impersonality is a
purely negative conception, like timelessness. What is
negated in ' timelessness ' is not the reality of the present,
but the unreality of the past and future. So the ' impersonality ' which is here (not without warrant from the
mystics themselves) said to belong to eternal life is really
the liberation of the idea of personality. Personality is

allowed to expand as far as it can, and only so can it come into its own. When Keyserling adds, 'The instinct of immortality really affirms that the individual is not ultimate,' I entirely agree with him.

The question, however, is not whether in heaven the circumference of the soul's life is indefinitely enlarged, but whether the centre remains. These centres are centres of consciousness; and consciousness apparently belongs to the world of will. It comes into existence when the will has some work to do. It is not conterminous with life; there is a life which is below consciousness, and there may be a life above consciousness, or what we mean by consciousness. We must remind ourselves that we are using a spatial metaphor when we speak of a centre of consciousness, and a temporal one when we ask about a continuing state of consciousness; and space and time do not belong to the eternal world. The question therefore needs to be transformed before any answer can be given to it. Spiritual life, we are justified in saying, must have a richness of content; it is, potentially at least, all embracing. But this enhancement of life is exhibited not only in extension but in intensity. Eternal life is no diffusion or dilution of personality, but its consummation. It seems certain that in such a state of existence individuality must be maintained. If every life in this world represents an unique purpose in the Divine mind, and if the end or meaning of soul-life, though striven for in time, has both its source and its achievement in eternity, this, the value and reality of the individual life, must remain as a distinct fact in the spiritual world.

We are sometimes inclined to think, with a natural regret, that the conditions of life in the eternal world are so utterly unlike those of the world which we know, that we must either leave our mental picture of that life in the barest outline, or fill it in with the colours which we know on earth, but which, as we are well aware, cannot portray truly the life of blessed spirits. To some extent this is true; and whereas a bare and colourless sketch of the richest of all facts is as far from the truth as possible, we may allow ourselves to fill in the picture as best we can, if we remember the risks which we run in doing so. There are, it seems to me, two chief risks in allowing our imagination to create images of the bliss of heaven. One is that the eternal world, thus drawn and painted with the forms and colours of earth, takes substance in our minds as a second physical world, either supposed to exist somewhere in space, or expected to come into existence somewhen in time. This is the heaven of popular religion ; and being a geographical or historical expression, it is open to attacks which cannot be met. Hence in the minds of many persons the whole fact of human immortality seems to belong to dreamland. The other danger is that, since a geographical and historical heaven is found to have no actuality, the hope of eternal life, with all that the spiritual world contains, should be relegated to the sphere of the 'ideal.' This seems to be the position of Höffding, and is quite clearly the view of thinkers like Santayana. They accept the dualism of value and existence, and place the highest hopes of humanity in a world which has value only and no existence. This seems to me to be offering mankind a stone for bread. Martineau's protest against this philosophy is surely justified :

'Amid all the sickly talk about "ideals," it is well to remember that as long as they are a mere self-painting of the yearning spirit, they have no more solidity than floating air-bubbles, gay in the sunshine and broken by the passing wind. You do not so much as touch the threshold of religion, so long as you are detained by the phantoms of your thought; the very gate of entrance to religion, the moment of its new birth, is the discovery that your gleaming ideal is the everlasting real.'[1]

But though our knowledge of the eternal world is much less than we could desire, it is much greater than many thinkers allow. We are by no means shut off from realisation and possession of the eternal values while we live here. We are not confined to local and temporal experience. We know what Truth and Beauty mean, not only for ourselves but for all souls throughout the universe, and for God Himself. Above all, we know what Love means. Now

[1] *Study of Religion*, vol. i. 12.

Love, which is the realisation in experience of spiritual existence, has an unique value as a hierophant of the highest mysteries. And Love guarantees personality, for it needs what has been called *otherness*. In all love there must be a subject and an object, and a bond between them which transcends without annulling their separateness. What this means for personal immortality has been seen by many great minds. As an example I will quote from Plotinus' picture of life in the spiritual world. This writer is certainly not inclined to overestimate the claims of separate individuality, and he is under no obligation to make his doctrine conform to the dogmas of any creed.

'Spirits yonder see themselves in others. For there all things are transparent, and there is nothing dark or resisting, but everyone is manifest to everyone internally, and all things are manifest; for light is manifest to light. For everyone has all things in himself and sees all things in another, so that all things are everywhere and all is all and each is all, and infinite the glory.'[1]

This eternal world is about us and within us while we live here. 'Heaven is nearer to our souls than the earth is to our bodies.' The world which we ordinarily think of as real is an arbitrary selection from experience, corresponding roughly to the average reaction of life upon the average man. Some values, such as existence, persistence, and rationality, are assumed to be 'real'; others are relegated to the 'ideal.' Under the influence of natural science, special emphasis is laid on those values with which that science is engaged. But our world changes with us. It rises as we rise, and falls as we fall. It puts on immortality as we do. 'Such as men themselves are, such will God appear to them to be.'[2] Spinoza rightly says that all true knowledge takes place *sub specie æternitatis*. For the πνευματικὸς the whole of life is spiritual, and, as Eucken says, he recognises the whole of the spiritual life as his own life-being. He learns, as Plotinus declares in a profound sentence, that 'all things that are Yonder are also Here below.'

---

[1] *Ennead*, v. 8, 4.
[2] From John Smith, the Cambridge Platonist.

Is it then the conclusion of the whole matter that eternal life is merely the true reading of temporal life ? Is earth, when seen with purged vision, not merely the shadow of heaven, but heaven itself ? If we could fuse past, present, and future into a *totum simul*, an ' Eternal Now,' would that be eternity ? This I do not believe. A full understanding of the values of our life in time would indeed give us a good *picture* of the eternal world ; but that world itself, the abode of God and of blessed spirits, is a state higher and purer than can be fully expressed in the order of nature. The *perpetuity* of natural laws as they operate through endless ages is only a Platonic ' image ' of eternity. That all values are perpetual is true ; but they are something more than perpetual : they are eternal. These laws are the creative forces which shape our lives from within ; but all the creatures, as St. Augustine says in a well-known passage, declare their inferiority to their Creator. ' We are lower than He, for He made us.' Scholastic theologians interposed an intermediary which they called *ævum* between time and eternity. *Ævum* is perpetuity, which they rightly distinguished from true eternity. Christianity is philosophically right in insisting that our true home, our *patria*, is ' not here.' Nor is it in any place : it is with God, ' whose centre is everywhere and His circumference nowhere.' There remaineth a rest for the people of God, when their warfare on earth is accomplished.

A Christian must feel that the absence of any clear revelation about a *future* state is an indication that we are not meant to make it a principal subject of our thoughts. On the other hand, the more we think about the eternal values the happier we shall be. As Spinoza says, ' Love directed towards the eternal and infinite fills the mind with pure joy, and is free from all sadness. Wherefore it is greatly to be desired, and sought after with our whole might.' But he also says, and I think wisely, that there are few subjects on which the ' free ' man will ponder less often, than on death. The end of life is as right and natural as its beginning ; we must not rebel against the common lot, either for ourselves or for our friends. We are to live in the present though not for the present. The two lines of Goethe which

Lewis Nettleship was so fond of quoting convey a valuable lesson :

> ' Nur wo du bist, sei alles, immer kindlich :
> So bist du alles, bist unüberwindlich.'

' Death does not count,' as Nettleship used to say ; and he met his own fate on the Alps with a cheerfulness which showed that he believed it. The craving for mere survival, no matter under what conditions, is natural to some persons, and those who have it not must not claim any superiority over those who shudder at the idea of resigning this ' pleasing, anxious being.' Some brave and loyal men, like Samuel Johnson, have feared death all their lives long ; while others, even when fortune smiles upon them, ' have a desire to depart and to be with Christ, which is far better.' But the longing for survival, and the anxious search for evidence which may satisfy it, have undoubtedly the effect of binding us to earth and earthly conditions ; they come between us and faith in true immortality. They cannot restore to us what death takes away. They cannot lay the spectre which made Claudio a craven.

> ' Ay, but to die and go we know not where ;
> To lie in cold obstruction and to rot ;
> This sensible warm motion to become
> A kneaded clod ; and the delighted spirit
> To bathe in fiery floods, or to reside
> In thrilling regions of thick-ribbed ice ;
> To be imprisoned in the viewless winds,
> And blown with restless violence round about
> The pendent world ; or to be worse than worst
> Of those that lawless and uncertain thoughts
> Imagine howling ! 'tis too horrible !
> The weariest and most loathéd earthly life
> That age, ache, penury, and imprisonment
> Can lay on nature, is a paradise
> To what we fear of death.'

We know now, if we did not know it three years ago, that the average man can face death, and does face it in the majority of cases, with a serenity which would be incomprehensible if he did not know in his heart of hearts that it does not matter much.  He may have no articulated faith in immortality, but, like Spinoza, he has 'felt and experienced that he is eternal.'  Perhaps he only says to himself, ' Who dies if England lives ? '  But the England that lives is his own larger self, the life that is more his own life than the beating of his heart, which a bullet may still for ever.  And if the exaltation of noble patriotism can ' abolish death, and bring life and immortality to light ' for almost any unthinking lad from our factories and hedge-rows, should not religion be able to do as much for us all ?  And may it not be that some touch of heroic self-abnegation is necessary before we can have a soul which death cannot touch ?  When Christ said that those who are willing to lose their souls shall save them, is not this what He meant ?  We must accustom ourselves to breathe the air of the eternal values, if we desire to live for ever.  And a strong faith is not curious about details.  ' Beloved, now are we sons of God ; and it doth not yet appear what we shall be.  But we know that when He is made manifest we shall be like Him, for we shall see Him as He is.'

THE END

Printed by SPOTTISWOODE, BALLANTYNE & Co. LTD
Colchester, London & Eton, England